Tripoli

Tripoli
A History

John Wright

Signal

Signal Books
Oxford

First published in 2015 by
Signal Books Limited
36 Minster Road
Oxford OX4 1LY
www.signalbooks.co.uk

ISBN 978-1-909930-19-3 Paper

Cover Design: Tora Kelly
Production: Tora Kelly
Cover Images: © John Warburton-Lee Photography/Alamy
Printed in India
Images: p.i Luycken/Wikimedia Commons p.xiii Bryn Jones/Wikimedia
Commons; p.9 courtesy Esso; p.11 Marzolono/Shutterstock; p.18 Martin Beek/
Wikimedia Commons; p.22 Bibliothèque Nationale de France/Wikimedia
Commons; p.40 Wikimedia Commons; p.45 Library of Congress, Washington
DC; p.53 Wikimedia Commons; p.61 Wikimedia Commons; p.71 private
collection; p.76 private collection; p.78 Library of Congress, Washington DC;
p.84 courtesy John Wright; p.90 courtesy John Wright; p.97 NARA/Wikimedia
Commons; p.108 private collection; p.116 David Holt/Wikimedia Commons;
p.129 Jill Dougherty/Wikimedia Commons; p.133 Project Gutenberg; p.152
courtesy Esso; p.161 courtesy John Wright; p.162 courtesy John Wright; p.163
courtesy John Wright; p.170 Abdul-Jawad Elhusuni/Wikimedia Commons;
p.176 private collection; p.189 Abdul-Jawad Elhusuni/Wikimedia Commons;
p.190 Abdul-Jawad Elhusuni/Wikimedia Commons; p.194 Abdul-Jawad
Elhusuni/Wikimedia Commons; p.205 NH53/Wikimedia Commons; p.209
courtesy Esso; p.211 DSpace@Cambridge

Contents

Author's Preface

This is usually the place where authors disclaim, or apologize for, what they see as the defects of their work. I only wish to out on record that I have written many books, articles, academic papers, radio scripts and other material on Libya in general and Tripoli in particular over the past fifty years. Inevitably, in writing this latest book I have drawn on, plagiarized, modified, amplified, compressed, criticized and corrected my own previous work, or otherwise drawn inspiration from it. The following chapters therefore include passages, nuggets of information, facts, opinions, or even quotations from others, that may seem vaguely familiar to some of my earlier readers. But I trust that I have kneaded, mixed and blended them in such a way that they now seem to be fresh and essential ingredients of my story, rather than mere repetitions and retrievals from an old hack's past output.

Note on Transliteration

Transliteration of Arabic into Roman script is a notoriously vexed exercise, subject always to the criticisms and corrections of those who claim to know better. In his Preface to the 1935 Cape edition of *The Seven Pillars of Wisdom*, T. E. Lawrence explained that "only three vowels are recognized in Arabic, and some of the consonants have no equivalent in English". He chose to ignore what he called the existing "systems of transliteration" and to follow "the old fashion of writing the best phonetic approximation according to ordinary English spelling". So far so good, for most of the Arabic-speaking world.

But there are special difficulties in the case of Libya. It is the only Arabic-speaking country ever subject to *Italian* rules of transliteration (drawn up in 1915 by the great Arabist, C. A. Nallino). The trouble is that by the 1950s this unique and at least consistent standard was being undermined by all-pervading Anglo-American usage. So to avoid confusion I have in this book expressed most place and proper names according to this newer and more widespread practice, while still keeping a few such familiar Italian spellings as Tagiura and Gefara. And where I discuss such buildings as Tripoli's Uaddan Hotel the Teatro Miramare or such urban features as Piazza Castello and Lungomare Volpi, built or laid out by Italian architects and town planners in the colonial era, I have kept the original names, disregarding later mutations. Such apparent inconsistencies are surely an unavoidable outcome of historical and cultural processes. After all, most of the world still knows the subject of this book as Tripoli, and not by the name its own people have long used, Tarablus al-Gharb (as it appears in "standard" transliteration).

Introduction

Tripoli—how lightly those three syllables slip off the tongue! Like many historical places, it has the long common experiences of survival, invasion and revolution, bombardment and destruction, plague, poverty and prosperity, rebuilding and expansion, anarchy, oppression and freedom, expulsions and immigrations. Then it has its own special marks and memories of Arab rule and European intervention, Ottoman imperialism, the fantasies of Fascism, the delusions of a "popular authority", the joyous overthrow of old tyrants and the popular acclaim of likely new ones.

Yet this has always appeared as an unprepossessing place, hardly seeming to deserve such alluring titles as "The Gateway to Africa", "The Magic Gate of the Sahara" or "The Bride of the Sea". This town has never had the historical and intellectual cachet of Egyptian Alexandria, the urbanity of Tunis, the commanding presence of Algiers or the splendours and fascination of the great "imperial" cities of Morocco. To outsiders and new arrivals, it usually seemed insignificant, the least of the Barbary capitals and, until the Italians set to work on it early in the twentieth century, small, poor and dilapidated. But appearances may deceive, and it is important for other reasons. During the Italo-Turkish war of 1911-12 (or Italo-*Libyan* war as our political correctors now insist) Winston Churchill called this "the noble possession of Tripoli". In doing so he, at least, appreciated that it then still was, as it had been for the past thousand years at least, a prize well worth taking. And so it has been in the century since Churchill duly recognized its noble significance. For this small and seemingly insignificant port, which up to the twentieth century never counted more than 20-30,000 inhabitants, has often attracted the attention of the latest expanding Great Power ambitious to take, hold and exploit a strategic and/or trading base on the long southern, African, shore of the Central Mediterranean.

The earliest known founders of the future city were the Phoenicians, sailing merchant-adventurers from the Levant who some 2,500 years ago first understood the potential of this rare natural harbour on the surprisingly inhospitable coast of North Africa. Tripoli was the settlement of Ui'at and together with other Phoenician trading posts at the anchorages at Sabratha to the west and Leptis to the east, it was a precarious foothold between Sahara and Mediterranean on the edge of the vast, forbidding and unknown African continent. It is still not wholly clear why the business-like Phoenicians settled at three separate places along a single 120-mile stretch of the North African coast between the Greater and Lesser Syrtes. But it is likely they sought trade in more attractive and marketable "luxury" goods than the raw produce of local farming and herding on meagre, pre-desert land, or the slaves readily available elsewhere in the Mediterranean.

Tripoli later became Roman Oea, noted mainly as an exporter of the produce of improved and wider local agriculture. Northern Tripolitania was not so much an imperial granary as a source of the low-grade olive oil used in the public and private baths, and burned in the lamps, of Rome and its empire. Then, in more difficult times during the rule of the Germanic Vandal invaders and the Byzantine imperial re-conquest (fifth-sixth centuries) Christian Tripoli emerged as the sole survivor of the original trio of trading ports. The collective name Tripolis was thus transferred to this one remaining port itself. It was also, by extension, given to the vast province of Tripolitania, and indeed for many centuries up to the twentieth, to all the land now known as Libya (itself the original Greek name for North Africa west of Egypt).

To the Muslim Arabs the city they conquered was, as it still is, Tarablus al-Gharb, Tripoli of the West, as distinct from the Levantine port. By the time the Arabs invaded North Africa in the seventh century, native Berber merchants had already mastered the sophisticated new enterprise of the Saharan trading caravan, relying on camels originally acclimatized from western Asia. With the additional stimulus of Islam, they then opened up the Sahara and the lands beyond it to regular commercial contact with the Mediterranean world. As the largest Mediterranean trade counter nearest to the Great Desert, the "White City", as the medieval Arab traveller Al-Tigiani called it, gained from this economic and social revolution, prospering on regular trans-Saharan trade with inner Africa, seaborne trade with southern Europe and its islands, and the overland or maritime trade and pilgrim traffic to Egypt and the Levant. Its obvious wealth gained from the import of black slaves and gold from inner Africa, and its position as a strategic sally-port on the central Mediterranean narrows, made it a choice prey for a succession of militant European powers: the

Sicilian Normans in the twelfth century; freebooting Genoese in the fourteenth; and expansionist, imperial Spain (which called it "one of the two eyes of Christendom") and then the Knights of Malta early in the sixteenth. But in 1551 this stronghold fell to Ottoman Turkey whose expanding naval power was only checked at Malta in 1565 and then at Lepanto in 1571. Tripoli thereafter became a semi-independent Ottoman regency, notorious for over two centuries as one of the Barbary "nests of corsairs", its swift galleys preying on Christian merchant shipping and on the coasts and islands of southern Europe.

In the seventeenth century the greater European naval powers—France, England, Holland and Venice—began accrediting consuls to this still nominally Ottoman regency to protect their Mediterranean commercial and shipping interests; but they would also assert their rights with outraged naval assaults on the port when diplomacy failed. When the effectively independent Karamanli regime came to power in 1711, the corsair menace gradually weakened, and after the Napoleonic wars Tripoli's trans-Saharan trade in black slaves became almost the sole means of economic and political survival in an otherwise impoverished environment. Soon after Ottoman Turkey replaced the Karamanli regime with its own direct rule in 1835, Britain largely abandoned earlier attempts to make Tripoli its exclusive gateway into unknown and unexploited inner Africa. For the next 75 years, as Saharan trade declined, the town languished as a neglected outpost of the waning Ottoman Empire, and a place of banishment for its political exiles. It was a survivor from earlier times, its unspoiled Islamic character and its impoverished public face little changed until the early twentieth century. With little in its outward appearance reflecting its former wealth as an emporium trading with three continents, it was generally considered an unpromising colonial possession by most of the European powers busy dividing the more inviting parts of Africa between themselves.

But in 1911 Italy suddenly seized this strategic prize from the Turks, believing it was coming as "a fruitlessly-invited and long-expected friend" of the native Libyans. So the town took on another new role on the Italian "Fourth Shore" of the Mediterranean, fulfilling modern Rome's imperial hopes and aspirations, the *Bel Suol d'Amore* that was to confirm newly-united Italy's emergence as a Great Power alongside Great Britain, France, Imperial Germany, Austria and Russia. In 1911-12 this also became the first active theatre of the new mechanized warfare of the twentieth century, with Italian motor transport, radio and, most spectacularly, aeroplanes and airships, all making their first battle trials against Turkish and Libyan irregular forces around or over the city and its oasis. The easy occupation of this bridgehead (even if "pacification" of all Libya was to take another twenty years) led to the expansion and development of what was soon an Italian Mediterranean city, becoming under Fascism a suitable and prestigious setting for the regime's mass public ceremonial.

The Second World War brought occupation by British forces in January 1943, an event then considered as significant to the Allies' fortunes as the contemporary German surrender to the Red Army at Stalingrad. There followed a period of austerity under a "care and maintenance" British Military Administration, and the migration of many Jews to Israel and Italians back to Italy. Independence came in 1951 within a destitute Libyan federal kingdom dominated by Sanussi interests from the distant eastern province of Cyrenaica, under which Tripoli (still with the appearance and services of an Italian provincial town) shared with Benghazi the role of joint federal capital.

The discovery and exploitation of oil in Libya in the 1950s and 1960s brought problems of distributing and spending the new, unearned national wealth to best economic and social effect. With British and American military bases nearby, an active international oil industry with many satellite services, mass internal migration, and still with large and active Italian, Jewish and Maltese resident communities, Tripoli became a cosmopolitan, multicultural boom town. It doubled in size in a few years, its spreading concrete suburbs housing the new expatriate colonies, and its tin and cardboard shanty towns the rural migrants.

This prize fell to the rising forces of militant Arab nationalism in 1969, when young Captain Muammar Gaddafi replaced the Sanussi monarchy with a Libyan Arab Republic and proclaimed the popular revolution he had been planning for years. He restored Tripoli as sole capital of a "state of the masses", although it had no room for such unwanted minorities as Tripoli's Italians and Jews. Over the next 42 years the city became a focus of the Gaddafi cult, reflecting in all its political, economic and social fortunes the vagaries of his personal and eccentric rule. While Tripoli was bombed by the exasperated Reagan administration in 1986, after Gaddafi's international rehabilitation in 2003-04 its people turned out to welcome Western and other foreign notables visiting the leader in his Bedouin tent within his fortified urban compound. And the same people duly took to the streets to rejoice in the tyrant's overthrow and squalid death in 2011, almost a century to the day since the invading Italian fleet had bombarded the city in order to "liberate" it from Turkish oppression. That city is now one hundred times larger in both population (estimated at over two million) and in extent than it then was.

This "noble possession of Tripoli" has indeed had many varied meanings to its invaders and rulers over the centuries. So it has had to travellers who have been there for many different reasons and under many varying circumstances. Some passed through medieval Tripoli as Muslim sages and pilgrims, while making a long journey (a *rihla*) of spiritual,

Modern Tripoli, seen from the Corinthia Hotel

geographical or social enlightenment; other arrivals were visiting foreign merchants; or they were Christian slaves or captives, eventually ransomed or otherwise freed, who recorded their experiences; others again were the resident consuls representing the diplomatic and mercantile interests of the greater European maritime powers in this small but pestiferous Barbary corsair state. Then, from the early nineteenth century, came a succession of British and other European explorers, to whom Tripoli, with its Saharan hinterland, seemed the natural gateway to unknown inner Africa. From about 1880 until 1911 other inquiring travellers arrived with a more specific mission: Italian scientists, businessmen and journalists assessing the colonial potential of this last Turkish North African possession. Contemporary with them were moneyed, leisured European or American tourists intrigued by the town as a curiosity, a physical and social survivor from earlier times, which they described in travel books usually well illustrated with their own good photographs and bad artwork. While Italy's invasion of 1911 inspired the national poet, Gabriele D'Annunzio, to new heights of nationalist fervour—"peace shines out in Latin Tripoli"—the newly-landed Italian soldiers and sailors, and the world's first fighting airmen, made in their letters home rather more sober assessments of the local military and political situation. If Italian and Fascist Tripoli was more admired than derided by foreign visitors in the 1920s and 1930s, so the post-1943 British military administration, and the city as joint capital of the independent Libyan Kingdom in the 1950s and 1960s, also attracted a largely sympathetic response from outsiders. But as the citadel-capital of the Gaddafi regime, from 1969 to 2011, Tripoli again enjoyed as unsavoury an international reputation as ever it had done when it had been a base of the dreaded Barbary corsairs over several earlier centuries.

All these foreign opinion-makers have over the centuries left many accounts of their personal experiences of the town and its oasis. They will be quoted in the following chapters to add further contemporary colour to the ever-evolving story of this intriguing place which still seems partly to deserve its century-old title of "Tripoli, the Jewel of Africa".

Chapter One
The Setting

Previous to entering the Bay of Tripoli, a few miles from the land, the country is rendered picturesque by various tints of beautiful verdure: no object whatever seems to interrupt the evenness of the soil, which is of a light colour, almost white, and interspersed with long avenues of trees, for such is the appearance of the numerous palms planted in regular rows and kept in the finest order. Miss Tully (1783)

Tripoli, like other successful historical cities, has been set down in the right place. While it lies off to one side of the notional space where the three Old World continents come together, it is on that extended frontier where the fringes of the Sahara meet the waves of the Mediterranean. This trading port, often also a fortress, an arsenal and a capital city, thus shares the complex horizons of the central and eastern Mediterranean with southern Europe and its islands; with the Aegean Sea, Crete and Cyprus; and with Asiatic Anatolia and the Levant. As also a Saharan caravanserai, a trading oasis, it used to traffic in one direction with fecund Egypt, in another with its closer neighbours of the Maghreb (north-west Africa) and, most importantly, across the Great Desert. Its roads lead through the Sahara to the Sudan (in its widest, Arabic geographical sense of those lands of black peoples just south of the desert), and so on into the heartlands of tropical Africa, itself the most isolated of the three Old World continents.

Thus Tripoli stands on the very edges of two great natural wildernesses, the open "liquid plains of the sea" and the desert spaces: both are quite large enough to have seemed, in the past, as almost separate worlds in themselves. These are contrasting environments, but they have in common the Sahara's similarity to the sea as a largely featureless and dangerous space, not easily travelled. Its coasts are defined as the areas where the desert merges into the more fertile lands at its edges—the Sahel (coast in Arabic); its oases and mountain blocks are its islands; and its trading caravans traditionally navigated its chartless wastes by following the same clusters of stars that guided mariners across the open ocean.

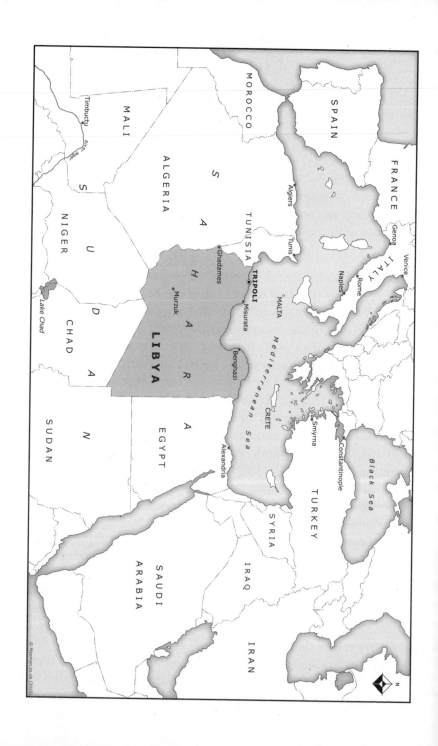

The Setting

Few places on earth are more desolate than the Sahara. When this largest of the hot deserts took on its present form some 4,000-5,000 years ago, it became a formidable obstacle to human contact. It cut off "black" inner Africa from its "white" Mediterranean neighbours to the north, as it isolated the North African coastlands—the "Island of the Maghreb", the Arabs were to call it—from the mass of the continent to the south. Yet this is not a closed frontier. There are ways across the Sahara, long, difficult, dangerous, but not impossible, that have long served as selective filters to human contact. They have allowed small parties of dedicated traders, travelling scholars and men of religion, as well as predatory raiders, to carry goods, ideas, influences and warfare into and across the desert, to the wide, populous lands of Sudanic Africa.

The Sahara is difficult because it can be both very hot, yet at times cold enough for frost. It lacks water, rain and vegetation, and any moisture is sucked up by strong eroding winds. While Saharan "weather" changes little from day to day, there is a distinct "summer": a hot season with high sun from May to September; "winter" is a relatively cooler season, often with chilling winds and freezing nights and dawns. The desert's few and isolated inhabitants, suspicious of outsiders, share the often harsh and hostile character of its many different landscapes. But, above all, the Sahara is difficult because it is vast, even continental, in scale. It stretches almost without a break from the Atlantic Ocean in the west to the Red Sea in the east, and from the southernmost point of the Mediterranean at El Agheila on the Gulf of Sirte to Lake Chad, or to the River Niger near Timbuctu—an area rather larger than the continental United States. Tripoli is almost as far from Lake Chad as it is from London, and further from the Atlantic coast of Mauritania than it is from the north of Scotland.

Saharan Africa has not always been a desert, for the climate has fluctuated markedly over the past 20,000 years. A long, dry spell was followed by a wet phase of perhaps 10,000 years; at its peak, Lake Chad became an inland sea as large as today's Caspian, receiving an estimated sixteen times its present inflow. Northern Africa then probably offered many centres of amenity to its various peoples, both "white" and "black" pastoralists. Although today's main north-south racial divides were perhaps then already apparent, there was likely to have been mutual cultural assimilation when a widespread Neolithic pastoral culture flourished over what is now the largest of hot deserts. It is a culture still attested by the litter of stone artefacts and the many rock art sites scattered across the Sahara.

Because of its location, northern Africa is always prone to desertification. Starting some 4,000 years ago, the Sahara's relatively rapid desiccation hardened existing geographical divisions between the desert and the lands to the north and particularly the south of it, separating peoples and cultures. With the ever-deeper drought, much of the desert became uninhabitable, and in places almost impassable, forcing the black Saharans into the shrinking oases, or southwards to the more attractive lands of the Sahel. But the ancestors of the black (but not Negro) Tebu have survived in the Tibesti massif, and in its piedmont deserts of the central Sahara between Chad and Libya. The white Libyan Berbers who remained in the desert adapted to its deepening aridity by becoming nomads as their sole economic and social option, moving with flocks and herds to exploit thin seasonal pastures.

Travellers have habitually crossed the desert from North Africa to the Sudan for one particular reason that justified the time, the costs and dangers of a journey of weary months over appalling country: profitable trade, mostly in staple goods that became exotic luxuries by the time they reached the far side of the desert. Such business is likely to have developed through contacts nomads made during their seasonal migrations and predatory visits to oases and desert edge communities, where they would claim their yearly "right" to a large share of harvests and other output. Regular markets and yearly fairs grew up where different peoples came together. Trading middlemen started supplying goods and services to transhumant nomads, oasis-dwellers or settled communities within or on either side of the desert. They had mainly to meet the simple demands of primitive subsistence economies that themselves produced few goods worth trading over long distance. Contacts were also limited by unsuitable transport animals: donkeys and bullocks are not adapted to long desert journeys. But the introduction of the Asiatic horse into Africa shortly after 1000 BC lengthened the scope of raiding forays and trading enterprise by nomads who need always to widen their thin margins of survival by such activities.

North Africa and the Sahara have, with few exceptions, never been prime sources of raw materials or manufactured trade goods. Rather, the ports of the Mediterranean coast and the trading oases of the northern

Sahara have always been entrepôts, forwarding goods between three main markets: to the north, Mediterranean Europe and its islands; to the east, Egypt and the Levant; and Black Africa to the south. Such intercontinental trade began, on a very limited scale, with the emergence of the Mediterranean mercantile empires about 3,000 years ago.

The series of substantial peninsulas defining the northern Mediterranean shores—Iberia, Italy, the Balkans, Anatolia—and their many small and few large islands, contrast with the long, mainly low and less interesting African coast, with its sparse offshore islands and, apart from the everlasting Nile, its lack of permanent outflowing rivers. With an overall length of about 2,300 miles (Gibraltar-Beirut) and greatest widths of up to 1,000 miles, the Mediterranean (with the Black Sea as an annex reaching into the Eurasian land mass) would be a continent, were it all land. It is quite large and varied enough to seem to the human (and especially the Greek) imagination to be peopled with freaks and monsters, with enchantresses and giants, with sinister and potentially disastrous natural and mythological challenges. Its long open courses between island and island, and island and mainland were always daunting to early navigators who would never willingly sail at night, in winter or out of sight of land.

Tripoli sits on the central basin of the Mediterranean's three. It is thus an important strategic sally-port on the central narrows between the Maltese archipelago (just over 200 miles to the north); the mid-channel islands of Pantelleria and Lampedusa; the south-west coast of Sicily; and the coastlands of Tunisia and Tripolitania. As a maritime trading centre serving three continents, it is well sited to send out merchant shipping to Tunisia to the west; to Egypt and the Levant to the east; northwards to Malta, Sicily and Italy; or north-eastwards to the large island of Crete and the cluster of Aegean archipelagos, as well as western Anatolia and the Bosporus. The islands were important because in the past they provided small, vulnerable sailing ships with stretches of relatively smooth, sheltered water. They were also necessary landfalls where repairs could be made, crews rested, fresh supplies of food and water taken on board, and perhaps some profitable business done.

Of course sailing the Mediterranean was often hazardous, for this is not always the benign, azure sea of popular imagination. Before steam ships arrived about 1840, most Mediterranean voyages were made in the

supposed "safe" sailing season from April to October; only a foolhard
master, or one under great commercial or other pressures, would take
the risk of sailing during the winter when the "stress of weather" wa
often too great. But at any time of the year, wind, currents and weathe
could be unfavourable for small sailing craft making voyages eastward
or north-eastwards from Tripoli. The prevailing north-east or north-wes
winds made navigation difficult in both directions along the exposed
North African coasts. Ships sailing north-east from Tripoli, to Crete and
the Aegean, had to stand well out to sea soon after leaving port, since
otherwise they risked being swept by prevailing winds and currents into
the Gulf of Sirte, with its submerged, uncharted reefs and shoals. Even
those who survived shipwreck on the notoriously exposed and desolate
coast risked death from thirst or starvation at that barren juncture of the
Sahara and Mediterranean. Or they were likely to be robbed, killed or
enslaved by predatory local tribesmen, who from the Middle Ages on
made a speciality of stripping even poor passing pilgrims of their few
possessions.

But such hazards did not detract from the commercial and strategic
value of Tripoli as a port on the tideless middle sea. This is one of the
very few natural harbours along the whole of the surprisingly exposed
inhospitable coasts of North Africa, and much better than the open
roadstead at ancient Sabratha, to the west, or the little estuary at Lepti
Magna, to the east. At Tripoli a small triangular peninsula, dominated
by a small hillock and readily defended from the landward approach
juts northwards from the coast, ending in a chain of low, rocky islets
prolonged to the north-east as a half-submerged reef. This protecting reef
encloses a crescent-shaped lagoon, well over a mile across, and further
enclosed by a secondary, eastern reef. With various hazardous shoals and
shallows, water depths inside this natural harbour range from nine to
24 feet. Although this safe haven is protected from the north-westerly
winds, a stormy north-easter can still drive ashore craft supposedly riding
safely at anchor. Another cluster of rocky islets to the north-west of the
main Tripoli peninsula provides a secondary and more exposed harbour
useful only to the small merchant ships of earlier times or, at best, to small
modern fishing boats.

In ancient times this no doubt seemed a welcome and easily defended
haven for adventurous prospecting mariners exploring an unknown

dangerous coast. But, until the Italians set to serious work on it early in the twentieth century, this port's low-lying reefs made difficulties and dangers for helmsmen steering ships into or out of it, particularly in bad weather. Ships often had to heave to offshore for days at a time, waiting for safer conditions, before attempting to navigate the narrow, unmarked channel between the rocks.

Climate and Commerce

The climate of Tripoli, broadly described as "Mediterranean", comes under the contrasting and alternating influences of the sea and the desert. Thus the summer heat from the Sahara is usually tempered by daily sea breezes which bring relief in the hottest months (May-September), with their temperatures of up to 30°C by day, yet with rather cool nights. But the benign sea influence is defeated by the dreaded Sirocco or *Ghibli*—a blast of hot, dust-laden air from the Sahara that can blow for up three enervating days, hide the midday sun and scatter fine dust even inside tightly-shuttered rooms. A *Ghibli* may occur at any time of year, but is more likely in April, May and June and in late summer. Local gardeners believe that the date palm produces its best fruit only after it has endured a full-blown *Ghibli* at least once in the season; while in Fezzan, the deep Sahara, a prolonged *Ghibli* is said to cause pregnancies in camels without any male intervention.

More rain falls in the year over the town and its oasis than in any other part of western Libya—an annual average of about 15 inches (compared with the London average of 26 inches). But most of this falls between November and February (December is the wettest month), with little or no rain between late March and October. These rains are thus enough to carry the groves and gardens of the oasis through to early summer, when green growth can be maintained until the autumn through the twice-daily labour of irrigation from an abundant underlying water table. Up to the twentieth century this supply seemed inexhaustible, despite the large number of shallow wells it supplied. For Tripoli, like the rest of Libya, has no permanent open rivers or even streams (the Wadi Megenin, on the west of the oasis, flows to the sea only briefly, if sometimes heavily, after winter rains), nor even any permanent lakes or ponds. The town and its surroundings have therefore always relied on wells yielding water more or less saline, depending on how close they are to the sea, and on domestic tanks and cisterns to store winter rainwater collected from the flat roof of buildings.

Tripoli's oasis—and especially the favoured area east of the town wall known as the *Menscia*—is clearly a natural centre for human activity with a fairly easy and healthy climate. There is underground water, light soil and natural vegetation which, with basic care, cultivation and irrigation could in the past reasonably support an urban and oasis population of at least 50,000. Such assets were greatly enhanced by the adjacent natural harbour. Without the human exploitation of the oasis, the harbour in itself would have had no great value; without the harbour, the oasis might never have become an extensive market garden supplying a trading port. This combination of fortunate factors helps to explain Tripoli's long and mostly successful survival while its nearer coastal neighbours, the ports of Sabratha and Leptis, were after some centuries of achievement eventually abandoned and deserted.

Tripoli has more exploitable natural advantages than the purely local ones, enabling it in due course to emerge as a place of trade serving the three Old World continents. The Mediterranean penetrates deepest into the Sahara—and thus comes closest to central Africa—at the southernmost point of the Gulf of Sirte at El Agheila. But there are no good harbours, indeed any natural harbours, or means of settled livelihood, on that long exposed and barren coast. Its hinterland, moreover, is dominated by the Libyan Desert, the world's largest true desert, and a serious obstacle to overland travel. But the northernmost Tripolitanian coastlands, although further from the deep Sahara, offer better ways of crossing it, since no fewer than three roads into the interior start there: and Tripoli has usually had access to all three of them.

The first leads across the Sahara to the south-west, to the lands of the Niger Bend where West Africa's largest river swings northward in a loop to meet the desert. The first stage of this road exploits the phenomenon of the small oasis of Ghadames, some 250 miles south-west of Tripoli, or about two weeks of caravan travel. Situated "like an island in the ocean", this small, solitary oasis owes its very existence to an abundant spring whose waters are sparingly shared and channelled throughout the town and its gardens. Ghadames has been a trading centre for at least 2,500 years. Its traders (some of them settled as family agents in distant markets

A traditional shallow well in the Tripoli oasis, worked by human and animal power. The picture dates from the early 1960s.

across northern and Sudanic Africa) were the essential middlemen exploiting fluctuations of supply and demand within and on both sides of the Sahara. Managing the meagre resources of a business environment sub-continental in scale, and with the negotiated, essential "protection" of desert predators, they always traded in goods with a high value-to-weight ratio, well able to withstand the length, delays, mishandling, heat, dust and costs of desert travel. By this process they transformed common staples or raw produce bought cheaply on one side of the desert into exotic luxuries, to be sold as such, by the time they finally reached the other side.

Tripolitania's two other main roads across the middle desert served the oases of the province of Fezzan. These oases are rare habitable locales strung along a series of roughly parallel east-west depressions with abundant water close to the surface. They are nearly in mid-Sahara, about one-third of the way down the easiest route from Tripoli to Lake Chad. They are also at about the middle of the long, diagonal north-east/south-west route between the lower Nile valley and the Niger Bend. As a crossroads of the central Sahara, and a natural corridor for travel (and historical migration) across the desert, the Fezzanese oases have always been an essential resting place for travellers. They could also be a terminus in their own right, where trading caravans broke up and dispersed. Besides offering fresh supplies, animals, equipment and guides for onward travel, the main Fezzanese oases also held regular markets and fairs on this important trading frontier between "white" and "black" northern Africa. These gatherings might last for weeks or even months, prolonging the slow processes of moneyless chaffering, exchange and barter. Travellers hoping to continue their journeys across the Sahara from Fezzan might have to wait for many weeks, even for months, while traders, with their animals, supplies, and goods and trade slaves bound for the intended destination, slowly came together as a fresh caravan.

Travellers from Tripoli to Fezzan had a choice of two roads. The main one, and one of the oldest and regularly-used ways across the Sahara, avoided the difficult "bad lands" of southern Tripolitania by making a broad sweep to the south-east after leaving the Mediterranean coastlands. It crossed the series of large *wadis* (water-courses, usually dry) emptying into the Gulf of Sirte, passing then through the Giofra oases and over the Gebel Soda, finally leading down to the trading oases of the central Fezzan. By Saharan standards, this route offered relatively easy and secure

A mid-nineteenth-century view of Murzuk, capital and chief slave market of the mid-Saharan province of Fezzan.

travelling for large, cumbersome and slow trading caravans, which might take six weeks or more on the journey. But travellers between Tripoli and Fezzan who valued speed over ease and security had the choice of a third Saharan road. Leading more or less due south from the coast, this crossed the wild, inhospitable and stony plateau of the Hammada al-Hamra, shortening the journey to Fezzan in terms of distance by perhaps a third compared with the longer, easier road further east. Clearly this faster route was suitable only for light caravans unencumbered by heavy loads of trade goods, or (from the early Middle Ages onwards) by gangs of black slaves being driven on foot from the African interior to the Mediterranean coast.

From Fezzan, the main road to Lake Chad passed between the Tibesti and Ajjer uplands, with their hostile landscapes and inhabitants. It then followed the long oasis chain of Kawar southwards, finally to reach the flat lands leading to Lake Chad—a total distance from the Mediterranean of about 1,500 miles, or many months of caravan travel, not including long halts. This route may also be regarded as a natural corridor allowing, even encouraging, the historic migration of peoples into and across the Sahara.

The Fezzan itself seems to have emerged (in a very limited way) as a crossroads of northern African trade and communications in the first millennium BC, largely through the agency of the Garamantes. This Berber people may have founded the Sahara's first recognizable state, based on long-distance horse-borne business with both sides of the great desert. Their main centre was at Germa in the Wadi Agial; but half a dozen different Fezzanese market oases were to predominate at different times over the centuries.

Tripoli owed its historical fortune to its role as the Mediterranean terminus of this so-called Garamantian road, as well as the road from Ghadames; and the predominance of these roads was in turn ensured by having as their Mediterranean outlet such a well-placed port as Tripoli. So the port and the roads, through good times and even the bad ones, together served as perhaps the surest and most regular arteries of two-way trade and communications between one side of the central Sahara and the other, providing inner, Sudanic Africa with long, difficult but essential links to the outside world. Other main routes across the eastern and western Sahara had differing fortunes, their usefulness and importance varying greatly over the centuries with changing political, economic, social, environmental and other conditions on both sides of the desert, and sometimes within it as well.

The Sirtica, the desert lands between the settlements of northern Tripolitania and Cyrenaica, where the Sahara meets the Mediterranean, has always been a barrier to human contact. Until Fascist Italy built the great *Litoranea*, the coast road linking the two provinces of the Libyan colony, it was easier and safer to travel from Tripoli to Benghazi by sea rather than overland. Yet with the rise of Islam in the seventh century, and its obligation on the faithful to make the pilgrimage to Mecca at least once in a lifetime, large pilgrim caravans from north-west Africa (the Maghreb), and later the western Sudan as well, began to beat a yearly path to Tripoli. From the early Middle Ages, the city thus took on a further role as an important place of rest and repair, and also a market for overland east-west trade. There pilgrims readied themselves to face the natural hazards and the robber-bands of the "abomination of desolation" of the Sirtica on their way to Cyrenaica, Egypt and, eventually, the Holy Cities of the Hijaz.

The Phoenicians, adventurous sea traders from the Lebanese coast, seem to have arrived in North Africa in very small numbers nearly 3,000 years ago, founding what were to become the first identifiable trading towns (*emporia*). The lands west of Egypt were then largely inhabited by a series of Berber pastoral tribes (later described in some detail by the Greek geographer-historian Herodotus of the fifth century BC). The origins of the Berbers are obscure, but their languages suggest a West Asian origin, and it is likely that after arriving in North Africa they had overrun and replaced older, aboriginal peoples. Attractive human habitats such as the small Tripoli peninsula and its attached oasis may well have had a settled, agricultural population, perhaps living in a few scattered villages, one of them quite likely to have been on the site of the future Tripoli. But the main economic activity would have been animal herding along the coast and across the Gefara plain, up to the escarpment which marks the beginning of the Gebel Nefusah, the uplands of north-west Tripolitania with their own moderately productive, rain-fed agriculture.

After founding Carthage and other trading posts in Tunisia, the Phoenicans later (at least 2,500 years ago) saw the commercial possibilities of three trading sites on the coast of northern Tripolitania: at Sabratha, at Leptis (Lpqy) and at Tripoli (Ui'at). Tripoli thus became one of the earliest towns of North Africa, if not of all Africa, and one of the oldest to be continuously inhabited down to the present day. On this score it is older certainly than Fez or Marrakesh, Algiers or Tunis, Alexandria or Cairo. For at least the last 2,500 years it has been a forum of human activity, a fortress and an intercontinental trading centre.

Chapter Two
The "White City"

A most wealthy and powerful city with vast markets... Ibn Haukal

The Phoenicians, trading mariners from the Levant, seem first to have arrived in North Africa on their way to somewhere else. Their early voyages westwards, along the full length of the Mediterranean, were driven partly by profitable trade in rare metals from Spain. Daring sailors though the Phoenicians were, like all others in antiquity, they would never willingly sail out of sight of land, or at night, or in winter. Thus as they first cautiously felt their way along the barren and inhospitable coasts of North Africa, they needed to find a series of havens where every night, or at the threat of bad weather, they could anchor close inshore, or beach their ships. They soon discovered the very few secure anchorages and natural harbours on this long, desolate and dangerous coast, and especially those with drinking water and perhaps some fresh supplies. Temporary settlements might be made at such places when ships needed repair, or were caught away from home at the onset of winter.

So the Phoenicians were the earliest known people to settle, if only seasonally at first, on the future site of Tripoli, with its little peninsula, its natural harbour, its fresh water and its fertile oasis. Then ships on routine trading voyages between the two ends of the Mediterranean might begin calling regularly as such settlements became established as permanent victualling stations. Carthage, near modern Tunis, was traditionally founded in 814 BC, but the sparse archaeological evidence suggests that the settlements of northern Tripolitania came into existence much later: Lpqy (Leptis) in the mid or late seventh century, Sabratha at the end of the sixth and Ui'at (Tripoli) in the fifth century. There is some speculation that the Phoenicians founded these three settlements as trading ports to forestall attempts by Greeks from Cyrenaica to do so. But it is not clear why three separate and possibly rival markets, served by similar sources and supplying similar outlets, were needed within one, 120-mile stretch of the Tripolitanian coast.

The "White City"

As maritime traders and outsiders, the newcomers were unlikely to have penetrated the Sahara and its existing commercial systems. Those would have been, as they always were, the monopoly of the desert peoples, and most notably the Garamantes of the central Fezzan who controlled the main trade outlets between inner Africa and the Mediterranean. But it is not clear what business the Phoenicians found and exploited on, or through, the Tripolitanian coastlands. They are likely to have sought more attractive and widely marketable "luxury" goods than the local, low-grade agricultural and pastoral products, or the slaves readily available elsewhere in the Mediterranean world. Trans-Saharan trade was not only handicapped by the "tyranny of distance" of a vast desert, but also by the natural poverty, and thus the limited purchasing or bartering power, of communities on the coast, in the Sahara itself and in the lands of inner Africa beyond it. Gold was a possible trans-Saharan import (although its main sources were far off, in western Africa); North African ivory was another. But a regular trade across the desert in black slaves from inner Africa did not develop until a thousand years later, in the early Middle Ages.

Phoenician civilization was an offshoot of the older civilizations of the Near and Middle East, overlaid with a mercantile sophistication acquired through contact with many other lands, peoples and cultures. These traders thus brought the international, Mediterranean civilization of the first millennium BC to the coastlands of North Africa; and their language, religion, culture, agriculture and technology increasingly influenced the local Berber tribespeople. The Phoenicians are credited with introducing such Asiatic plants as the olive, the vine, the peach and the fig into North Africa, the olive being particularly well suited to the climate and the light, sandy soils. If a great city such as Carthage had an enormous civilizing impact on northern Tunisia, even the local influence of a small settlement such as Tripoli must have been considerable. Very early on, this town's basic, historical character was established as a distinct, exotic, urban milieu, ruled, managed and populated by a moving and cosmopolitan mix of outsiders and locals. It was a diverse, evolving place, a cultural intrusion, always separate from, but still an influence on, the largely unchanging, pastoral or nomadic Berber (or later Arab-Berber) tribal environment beyond the seaside oasis. It was a character, and a distinction, that were to persist, to a greater or lesser degree, until the twentieth century, if not the twenty-first.

Tripoli: A History

Tripoli and its two neighbouring settlements grew and quietly prospered as their original Phoenician domination was replaced by the closer authority of Carthage itself. Prosperity depended on wider and better agriculture, but was hampered always by the difficult local environment vulnerable to periodic drought and locust invasions. And most of the import and re-export exchange by sea and the desert was still on a petty scale, compared with the later trade of Roman Tripolitania, and the richer and more exotic trading monopolies enjoyed by medieval Tripoli. Then the long crisis of the Carthaginian wars with expansionist Rome; the rise of North Africa's native, if short-lived, Numidian kingdom; the final destruction of Carthage in 146 BC; and Rome's increasing local involvements, eventually brought coastal Tripolitania into the Roman Empire in the middle of the first century BC. Some three centuries of *Pax Romana* followed, an interlude mostly of peace, combined with a local prosperity and civic confidence that was to be reflected in the prodigious late-Roman imprint on this hitherto largely disregarded, unimportant province, and particularly on its trio of seaports. Oea (Tripoli) and its two neighbouring ports were then largely populated by a mix of local Berber and Phoenician stock: Libyphoenician in type, language and culture; and there was not necessarily much immigration by Roman (Italian) or other colonists. But there were probably small urban and rural communities of Jews, who had first migrated into Cyrenaica in the sixth century BC and who had later moved into and made converts in Tripolitania as well.

Even more than under the Phoenicians and the Carthaginians, Roman Tripolitania prospered as an important agricultural province. The climate at that time seems to have been barely more favourable than it is now: the difference was the careful conservation and use of the limited seasonal rainfall and underground water supplies during the Roman centuries. This was not necessarily due to the influence or enterprise of foreign colonists. More likely, it was the work of indigenous Libyphoenician farmers who continued their own traditional and proven conservation methods, while taking advantage of settled local conditions greatly to extend the cultivated area, and produce on a commercial scale. Within the common trade zone of the empire, they were able to supply the flourishing demand for produce from across the Mediterranean, which the Romans called *Mare Nostrum*—Our Sea—and which they had at last freed from piracy.

Dry farming was extended deep into the pre-desert interior, especially where normally dry but seasonally flooded river beds (*wadis*) offered better growing conditions. Roman Tripolitania was not a granary of empire (rainfall was too limited for large-scale cereals cultivation), but rather a prime producer and exporter of low-grade olive oil. This oil was used not so much in the kitchens of the empire as in its bath houses; by makers of soaps, perfumes and medicines; and burned in its dim, smelly lamps. The very scale of this oil industry is attested by the large numbers of Roman-era olive presses still standing across the hill country of Tripolitania. They are identified by their massive stone uprights and lintels, and by their channelled, oil-collecting stone slabs (structures which one over-imaginative, late-nineteenth century antiquarian took to be megalithic pagan sacrificial sites). Olive oil was exported in large clay amphorae carefully stowed in the holds of small sailing ships; the "empties" were presumably regularly returned. There was other important agricultural output (particularly barley and grapes), as well as market-gardening, and stock raising (particularly sheep and goats) on the Gefara Plain inland from Oea, but all subject to wide seasonal variations. The Asiatic camel was probably introduced from western Asia and acclimatized early in the Christian era.

Of course, the three ports of Roman Tripolitania prospered from this abundant commercial agriculture, both as its export outlets, and as the residential and commercial bases of local and foreign dealers, entrepreneurs and absentee landlords. The archaeological evidence of the Roman-era prosperity of Oea (Tripoli) is scanty because it is largely inaccessible under the still living, built up Old City. But the survival of a monument as costly and prestigious as the second-century Arch of Marcus Aurelius, and the excavated remains of large, luxurious villas in the suburban oasis as far to the east as Tagiura, and along the coast west of the city, suggest that while in the early Roman era Oea was politically and economically the least of the three neighbouring and rival markets, by the fourth century it may well have overtaken Sabratha in importance, and was perhaps beginning even to rival the provincial capital, Leptis Magna. It largely owed such developments, and its eventual sole survival, to its better natural harbour, its more secure position, its productive oasis, and eventually to its defensive walls.

Again, it has to be assumed, if not convincingly proved, that Roman Oea and its neighbours exported North African wild animals (including

Roman mosaic, Castle Museum, Tripoli.

not yet extinct elephants and lions) for the Roman circuses, and prospered also on trans-Saharan trade. But it can be argued that there was no regular traffic across the desert before the rise of the camel-mounted Berber nomad in the early Christian era, and probably not until after the arrival of the camel-mounted Muslim Arabs in the seventh century. There is no convincing list of goods that might have been regularly traded through the Sahara to generate the profits to reward merchants for the hardships, risks and dangers of a year-long round trip. There is no firm evidence that gold dust, animal skins, ivory, drugs and ingredients for perfume-making, and black slaves—the staples of inner Africa's medieval northbound trade—were carried across the Sahara from time to time in the Classical era and re-exported through Roman Oea and its two rival ports. As for African slaves (the basis of Tripoli's medieval and later Saharan trade), there were few blacks, either slave or free, outside Africa in the ancient world; and anyway they were surplus to requirements (except, perhaps as exotic household ornaments) in the slave societies of the Mediterranean. Yet there are arguments for an active Saharan trade through the agency of the Garamantes of Fezzan. They were perhaps a confederation of Berber tribes, credited with exploiting the so-called Garamantian road from Carthaginian and Roman Oea and Leptis to Lake Chad. They may have controlled a trading system linking inner Africa through the Tripolitanian ports to the commercial networks of the Mediterranean world; but again the evidence is scanty and uncertain.

Christianity seems to have arrived in second-century Oea through local Jews' contacts with communities of Jewish converts in Cyrenaica and Rome. By the third century there was a Bishop of Oea (he attended the Council of Carthage in 256). In the fourth century, after Christianity became the official religion of the empire, the Donatist schism started the divide within the North African Church. This schism, particularly in Tripolitania, eventually took the form of a popular, often violent and destructive Berber revolt against Roman secular and ecclesiastical authority. Oea and Leptis were represented by Donatist bishops at the Council of Carthage where in 411 St. Augustine had both of them, and their followers, condemned as heretics.

Roman North Africa's golden age was by then near its end. Military security that had protected the settled lands from the nomadic and semi-nomadic peoples of the Sahara for the best part of four centuries was failing in the face of the increasingly bold incursions of desert tribesmen. In the mid-fourth century such invaders did huge economic damage to the undefended countryside of Tripolitania; only Oea and the other cities were saved by their new defensive walls; and such protection could not save Leptis and Sabratha from the collapse of their agricultural infrastructure, the local economy and then civil life by the end of the century. In the following century North Africa was overrun by the Vandals, a Germanic people who had earlier invaded Roman Spain. Established in the coastal cities of Tripolitania, they demolished the city walls of Leptis and Sabratha, but left those of Oea standing. Thus still protected, apparently still intact and socially and economically active, Christian Tripoli from then on emerged as the sole survivor of the original trio of towns, and eventually took on the name all three had shared for centuries past. But it survived in a narrower, culturally and materially impoverished and more troubled world. The pre-desert and desert trading hinterland was now dominated by Berber tribes whose recent mastery of the camel as a mount for raiding warriors, and its exploitation as a long-distance commercial carrier, had given them much greater mobility within the Sahara itself and on its northern fringes. And in the meantime, the formerly secure Roman Mediterranean was again beset by the pirates who made all sea borne trade and contact hazardous for the next 1,500 years.

The Byzantines reconquered Tripolitania and ousted its Vandal ruler in the year 533, but over the next century they were unable to restore the security and prosperity of Roman times, for the tribes had become too independent to submit readily to the new and alien rulers on the coast. By the end of the sixth century, Tripolitania had largely reverted to its old, pre-Roman nomadic pastoralism. Leptis and Sabratha were by then little more than small fortified naval dockyards, ghost towns with perhaps a few hundred squatters living among the magnificent ruins. Tripoli was the only port of some slight commercial or strategic significance between Carthage and Alexandria, and even its trade across both the Sahara and the Mediterranean was languishing in the cold economic climate.

The Muslim Arabs

Of all the many peoples who have invaded and occupied North Africa over the past 3,000 years, the Muslim Arabs have had, and still have, the greatest and most lasting influence on those lands and their native Berber peoples. The original Muslim Arab conquests of the seventh century separated North Africa from the long influence of European, and latterly Christian, civilization. The former *Mare Nostrum* of the Roman Mediterranean became a hostile frontier between Afro-Asian Islam to the east and south and European Christendom to the north and west. Tripoli found itself occupying an exposed position on the front line of a permanent zone of confrontation between two rival and apparently incompatible civilizations. Yet just as the natural hostility of the desert environment could be overcome to Tripoli's advantage by the enticement of profitable trans-Saharan trade, so it was soon found that trans-Mediterranean religious or ideological barriers could also in practice be breached during the early Middle Ages and after by simple, two-way business enterprise.

Camel-mounted Muslim Arab warriors first moved into Cyrenaica from newly-invaded Egypt in 642. The following year they crossed the wilderness of the Sirtica, reached and took Leptis (or what remained of it) and then camped in the oasis outside Tripoli. After a month of siege Arab scouts at last noticed that the defences did not extend along the sea front (because sea-borne attack had been thought unlikely) and that there was a gap between the end of the city wall and the water. Taking advantage of this weak spot, the besiegers entered, captured and sacked the city; the small Byzantine garrison escaped by sea and the citizens took to the distant hills. This first Arab invasion seems to have been little more than an extended reconnaissance and pillaging raid. There were further raids in the following years, and the first known Arab governor of Tripoli was not appointed until 666-67.

The Arab conquest of North Africa was opposed by Berber rebellion and resistance; Arab forces were small and widely-scattered; and the processes of Islamization and Arabization were slow and sporadic, lasting centuries, or never wholly achieved in some places. But Tripoli and other towns were fully exposed to the new religious, linguistic and cultural forces, and distinct advantages were offered to those who accepted and assimilated them. Medieval Islam tolerated (even if it taxed) unconverted "People of the Book" (Jews and Christians). Indeed, the survival of a native Tripoline Christian community until at least the tenth century is attested by the discovery of late Christian graves, with epitaphs in crude, misspelt Latin, at Al-Ngila and at Ain Zara on the pre-desert fringes of the Tripoli oasis.

The early Islamic centuries imposed a new world order on the city. Its former political, religious and cultural links with Mediterranean Europe to the north were replaced by new relationships with the Islamic Caliphal Empire, mainly to the east. From its capital cities of varying influence and fortune (first at Damascus, then at Baghdad, and later Cairo) this Islamic entity came to dominate the trade, the communications and intellectual and cultural exchanges between the central lands where the three Old World continents came together. While Tripoli's Mediterranean and

Saharan traffic revived in an Islamic culture with wholly positive attitudes to trade (had not the Prophet himself been a merchant?), the land and sea ways to and from Egypt, the Levant and the Holy Places of Arabia became newly busy and important. They carried pilgrims, trade, influences and ideas between the western wing of the Islamic world (Spain and the Maghreb) through Tripoli to its eastern wing (Egypt and the Middle East). The arrival of the great yearly *Hajj* caravan, escorting Maghrebi, Iberian and (increasingly) West African pilgrims to Egypt and then on to Holy Places of Islam, became an important religious, intellectual, social and business event. The pilgrims' sprawling and prolonged encampment

A thirteenth-century *Hajj* caravan.

outside the city walls almost took on the character of a large, cosmopolitan trade fair, since many pilgrims in effect paid for their long spiritual journey by profitable business dealing (including slave trading) at such suitable halting places along the route.

At about the same time inner, black Africa also took on a new importance. Berber nomads had effectively revolutionized Saharan travel and communications in the early Christian centuries with the sophisticated new organization of the long-distance camel caravan. But the full potential of this new commercial enterprise was realized only after the early Islamic penetration of the central and western Sahara from the seventh century onwards gave inner Africa permanent links with the Mediterranean, opening prospects for wider, intercontinental trade throughout the Islamic world. In the west, the newcomers were drawn by the lure of West African gold, then becoming more readily available through the medium of the black, partly Islamized Empire of Ancient Ghana, on the south-western desert fringes. In the central Sahara, and in the populous lands around Lake Chad, the main exportable commodity was slaves, and especially eunuchs, and women and girls destined for service in the households and harems of the new Caliphal Empire of the Arabs and their Muslim converts. (Eunuchs were particularly expensive because so few boys survived their crude surgical ordeal.) Here was a new, almost urgent demand to be met by regular trading caravans delivering consignments of slaves from the populous lands of inner Africa through the small oasis of Zawila in Fezzan to the port of Tripoli. Some newly-arrived slaves would be sold there to local buyers, but most were shipped across the Mediterranean for further sale in the teeming markets of Egypt and the Levant, or perhaps westwards to Tunis or northwards to Arab Sicily.

Here, then, was the basis of the city's new-found medieval prosperity: a luxury trade in gaggles of enslaved people forced to trudge across the full width of the Sahara to distant markets, where most would be sold into domestic slavery, which implied that they would also be sexually available within the household. Eunuchs and other selected male and female slaves of exceptional skills or appearance (including dwarves) were sometimes brought across the desert with unusual care and consideration for their physical and spiritual wellbeing if they were intended for presentation to a ruler or potentate as part of a larger diplomatic gift, or as tribute or a tax settlement.

All Tripoli's commerce across the Sahara was in effect luxury trade. Raw, unimproved goods (including common trade slaves without skills or remarkable looks) bought cheaply on one side of the Great Desert became exotic luxury goods, and were sold as such, on the other side. Apart from slaves, these goods included a little gold dust (which merchants carried in small leather bags strung round their bodies); skins, hides and leather; small amounts of ivory; kola nuts (a mild narcotic acceptable in Islam); and tiny parcels of precious ingredients for making perfumes and medicines. These included civet musk, a strong-smelling secretion of the perineal glands of the civet cat of tropical Africa.

In many ways, medieval Tripoli was a far more diverse and cosmopolitan trading town than ever it had been in Roman and earlier times. True, it was no longer as important as it had been as an export market for grain and oil from a now more limited and less productive local agriculture; indeed, in bad seasons it was beginning to import emergency grain supplies from Sicily. But it had a new-found role as an import and export entrepôt for richer, better organized and more regular trans-Saharan trade. It had also become a port of call on the two-way overland and maritime trade routes between the two wings of the Islamic world: the great trading caravans that set out at a more or less fixed time every year from the oasis of Sijilmasa in southern Morocco for the new Fatimid capital of Cairo passed through Tripoli, as did their westbound counterparts. And this centrally-placed Mediterranean-Saharan trading counter was also a close and natural business partner of the commercially aggressive Italian maritime republics (Venice, Genoa, Pisa, Amalfi, Gaeta, Otranto and others) that increasingly dominated the general and carrying trades of the central and eastern Mediterranean. But if European Christian merchants were becoming more active and familiar in medieval Tripoli, protected by treaty and establishing their own *fonduks* (secure, combined warehouses and living accommodation) within the walled city, few Tripoli merchants made trading voyages in the reverse direction, to Christian Europe. European and North African Jews also played a large part in this two-way trade exchange, not necessarily as active, travelling merchants, but as international business promoters, investors and financiers. While there were resident Jewish communities even in some sub-Saharan market cities, it is not clear how they got there, since Jews were not usually allowed to travel with the trans-Saharan trading caravans.

The "White City"

Tripoli's medieval slave market dealt without discrimination in white slaves as well as black. In the tenth century this was reputed to be one of the best markets for Christian women shipped from a European continent where slavery and the slave trade were still common social and economic practices. Other white slaves were captured during Muslim raids on the shipping, the islands and the coasts of Mediterranean Europe. Soon after Venice was founded on its remote and protective lagoon in the Dark Ages, its merchants had been exporting Christian slaves to Tripoli from the Dalmatian coast (probably Slavs from which the word "slave" comes) or from Italy itself, and in the mid-eighth century the Pope had tried to stop this traffic. The Church, Venice itself and other Christian powers also condemned Venetian traders who made fortunes by shipping heavy timber, iron and arms to Tripoli and other Maghrebi ports—strategic materials supporting the sporadic Muslim naval and piratical warfare against Mediterranean Christendom.

Tripoli was also an entrepôt for the transit trade of southern Europe, Egypt and the Levant to and from inner Africa. North Africa itself produced little for sale or barter in black Africa, apart from some textiles, and the highly valued Barbary horses. Tripoli re-exported across the Sahara the manufactured products of southern Europe, Egypt and the Levant: arms, armour, textiles, glassware, beads and trinkets, Islamic manuscripts and books. But such traffic was always governed by the limited purchasing or bartering power of Sudanic communities living in naturally impoverished environments who had few desirable or transportable commodities, other than their own people, to trade with outsiders.

Trans-Mediterranean and trans-Saharan trade with the three Old World continents, and especially the slave traffic through Fezzan from inner Africa, brought medieval Tripoli fair renown and prosperity, by the standards of those meaner times. Thus in his *Description of Africa* the tenth-century Arab geographer Ibn Haukal called this "a most wealthy and powerful city with vast markets":

> Merchandise is plentiful there as, for example, local wool and vivid blue and fine black stuffs of great value. These goods are loaded onto ships that call constantly from Europe and the Arab lands with cargoes of merchandise and livestock.

Such accounts should of course be taken with some caution. Even by medieval standards, Tripoli was not necessarily as wealthy and powerful as Ibn Haukal suggested, and its markets were unlikely to have been vast. The city's foreign trade, although impressively wide-ranging, was on a petty scale during the Middle Ages, especially when compared with the burgeoning intercontinental traffic of later centuries. During a trading season usually limited by suitable travelling conditions in the Sahara and sailing conditions in the Mediterranean to the six months from April to October, the city imported and re-exported by land and by sea perhaps a few hundred tons of trade goods, and perhaps, at most, 2,000 black slaves and a few hundred white ones.

This was never an intellectual capital, a place of great and original science, invention or the arts, of religious or secular debate and learning, as were contemporary Fez, Kairouan in Tunisia, or Cairo. It had no Islamic university nor a renowned theological college, and no great library. Yet in the Middle Ages it did produce several Islamic sages with more than a local reputation. This seaport and overland trading city was not altogether an intellectual void, for pilgrims, scholars and men of knowledge would pass through. They brought manuscript books and other materials for study as they travelled from one wing of the Islamic world to the other, perhaps while on a *rihla*, a journey of spiritual and secular enlightenment. Some might even stay for a while to teach, and build a certain local influence and following. Thus when the medieval Tripoline scholar Abu Ishaq Ibrahim ibn Ismail al-Agedabi was asked how he had acquired his wide knowledge, though he had never travelled far from home, he replied that he had learned everything between the eastern and western gates of the walled city—in other words, from those travelling scholars who had arrived there from both directions.

During North Africa's complex medieval history Tripoli was rarely the capital of an independent state, and its political authority and influence rarely extended very far beyond the coastal oasis. It was often caught up in the local, doctrinal wars between Sunni Arabs and Berbers of the heretical Ibadi sect of Islam, or the localized power struggles of rival political dynasties and entities. Berber forces besieged and sacked the city in 811; it was largely destroyed again in 912, and was rebuilt for a second time. Then from the mid-eleventh century on, most of lowland North Africa was overrun by two large, Arab nomadic tribes, the Bani Hilal and the Bani Sulaim, perhaps a million people in all, who spent about a century migrating slowly westwards with their flocks and herds from Egypt to Morocco. This migration eventually Arabized what had until then still been a largely Berber Maghreb in race, language and culture. The newcomers were blamed (fairly or not) by medieval Muslim geographers and historians for what they saw as the destruction of the Maghreb's former agricultural prosperity. The fourteenth-century Tunisian socio-historian Ibn Khaldun compared this mass migration to an army of locusts destroying everything in its path. And the great geographer Idrisi, writing of Tripoli in 1154, complained:

> Before the present time, all the surroundings of the city were well cultivated and covered with fig plantations, olives, dates and every kind of fruit tree. But the Arabs destroyed this prosperity and the people were obliged to abandon the countryside. The plantations were devastated and the waters stopped flowing.[1]

European Interventions

Islam's successes in its early centuries contrasted with the contemporary misfortunes of its greatest and most persistent rival, European Christendom. The prolonged disintegration of the Roman Empire, barbarian invasions, economic and social impoverishment compounded by a harsher climate all contributed to Europe's so-called Dark Ages. But with an improved climate and renewed vigour, Europe was by the eleventh century on the move again, aggressively expanding on its northern and eastern fringes, and into the Mediterranean. The Crusades started at the end of the eleventh century, a decade after the Normans had conquered Arab Sicily. A unique Norman-Arab Sicilian culture then flourished, as did a short-lived maritime empire that turned the central Mediterranean into a "Norman Lake". Malta was taken in 1091, the island of Jerba (then part of Tripolitania) in 1135, and in 1146 a large Norman fleet commanded by a Syrian Christian, George of Antioch, stormed, sacked and conquered Tripoli. Sicilian Arabs were then sent to repopulate and garrison the town.

Although local Christianity was revived and some churches rebuilt, this was no Crusade since, as in Sicily, there was religious, cultural and racial toleration between the Normans and their central Mediterranean subjects. But this imperial experiment in mutual toleration did not last long: after twelve years the Tripolines revolted and ended Norman rule after massacring the garrison. Yet, like the more prolonged Crusades in the Levant, this brief excursion had shown that Europe was again in more confident, expansionist mode, if not yet able to bring any part of Mediterranean Africa under its lasting control. After its brief Norman experience, Tripoli continued to replace its Muslim rulers with fair and confusing frequency: it was an outlying, provincial possession of the Almohads in the twelfth century, and then of the Hafsid Dynasty of Tunis in the thirteenth. But none of these was able to extend its rule or its tax-raising powers very far beyond the city walls, where Berber and Arab tribes remained largely independent of any city-based authority.

That Tripoli was by the early fourteenth century a rich and orderly city is evident from the *rihla* of the Tunisian scholar, Abu Mohammed Abd-Allah Al-Tigiani, who stayed there in 1307-08 while on pilgrimage. As the city could be seen from far off, shining white and brilliantly in the sun, he called it "the white city". He found the streets clean, wider than in other towns, cutting straight through the built-up area, and meeting at right angles, like a chessboard (clearly the legacy of the original Roman street layout). The people were taking much trouble to keep the city walls in repair, but they were unable to make a satisfactory moat (to be filled with sea water) as their diggings kept filling with blown sand. As for the port, Al-Tigiani called it called it "huge and fine" with ships drawn up on shore "like steeds in their stable" (which suggests that they cannot have been very large). The city was well supplied with sweet, fresh water from a group of springs beyond the western city wall (which have long since dried up). There were many cemeteries, with bones and skulls scattered around from the shallow graves. Al-Tigiani particularly admired the arch of Marcus Aurelius (which had resisted recent attempts to demolish it), and he found a Christian who could translate its Latin inscriptions for him. The translator, presumably a European slave, tactfully added on one or two bogus extra lines to his already fanciful translation to the effect that, just as the monument had been completed, news had arrived from Syria that an certain Arab prophet named Mohammed ibn Abdallah had made his appearance in the Hijaz—a sequence of events that had an actual, historical interval of nearly five centuries between them.

Mediterranean ports in general were prone to punitive attacks from the sea, but not so often to capture and full-scale pillage. But Tripoli was especially vulnerable to such assault in the spring of 1355 when it was under the hated rule of "a vile tyrant" who had rebelled against the authority of Hafsid Tunis. News of these troubles had reached Filippo Doria when, as commander of a fleet of fifteen galleys from the Republic of Genoa, he had arrived in Trapani in western Sicily. He loaded up with siege equipment and sailed for Tripoli, entered the port and sent men ashore to buy supplies—and to spy out the defences. Realizing how unprotected the rebellious city was, and that it could expect no relief from Tunis, he duly attacked and captured the place. This wealthy trading city was put to the sack for several days. The Genoese collected an immense booty—collectively and officially reported to amount to 1,800,000 gold florins in goods and cash, and over 7,000 men, women and children as slaves (perhaps one-third of the population of the walled city). But unofficially the booty was far greater because galley officers and crew members gave no account of their own, secret stores of loot.

The Genoese stayed for around six destructive weeks before they restored the city to local Muslim rule for a ransom of 50,000 gold pieces. This act of extended piracy dismayed not only the Islamic world, but also other Italians trading with Muslim ports across the Mediterranean, who had good reason to fear general reprisals. And Genoa itself was so concerned for its own trade relations that it publicly disowned the raiders and forbade their return home, at least until the diplomatic storm had blown over. For years afterwards, slaves of all ages and many different races who had been taken from Tripoli were still being sold from Genoa to foreign buyers, especially from Provence.

Not all foreigners were as badly behaved as the Genoese had been on this occasion, or as rowdy, semi-piratical traders from Pisa and other Italian cities often were. The Venetians owed much of their commercial success to their good manners and careful tact in their dealings with Muslims. As far back as 1350 they had been allowed to set up their own *fonduk* in Tripoli; they were allowed credit on customs dues (instead of having to surrender the sails of their ships, as other traders had to do); they could organize, but never accompany, their own trading caravans into the interior; and they were even allowed their own local mint. Venetian trading galleys sailed regular summer routes, calling at Tripoli twice in the season.

Spain and the Knights

The next big European invasion, some 150 years after the Genoese, was even more destructive, with much greater long-term repercussions. Tripoli found itself in the early sixteenth century a vulnerable prize, and a victim, of a titanic struggle between the two superpowers of the age: imperial Spain and Ottoman Turkey. This was a clash of two opposing civilizations: both were to contest, but neither was to achieve, the ultimate control of the entire Mediterranean—militarily, politically, and thus religiously. The final outcome was indecisive: it left Spain partly in control of the western Mediterranean, Turkey more decisively of the eastern basin, with the centre left as a zone of continuing contest.

In 1492 Spain had completed its centuries of *reconquista* from Muslim occupation with the capture of Granada, the last Muslim outpost in Andalusia, and the expulsion of the last remaining, unconverted Moors. The Catholic monarchy then took this Crusade across into North Africa in the early sixteenth century by occupying strategic points (*presidios*) along the coast, but making no attempt to conquer their hinterlands. In July 1510 Tripoli became Spain's latest target. Besides its strategic importance, the city was then widely reputed to be extremely rich, its peaceable citizens enjoying easy lives. The invasion was launched with crusading spirit from Malta. About 15,000 Spanish troops, with 3,000 more from Sicily and Italy, were packed into a fleet of 120 warships and transports under the command of El Conde Pedro Navarro. On landing on 25 July, two parties were sent ashore, one to take the city and the other to oppose any possible counter-attack by the pre-desert tribes from beyond the oasis. After the walls had been breached, civilians armed with stones and clubs resisted the invaders for three hours, particularly around the Castle and the Great Mosque, but then artillery was turned on them and, as Don Pedro reported,

> There were many dead among the Moors—so many indeed that one could not put a foot down without stepping on a corpse. The Moorish dead are estimated at 5,000 and the prisoners at more than 6,000. The Christian dead are four.

But another eye witness put Muslim losses at 2,000 dead, and Christian losses at 150; and 150 Christian slaves found chained up in the Castle dungeons were freed.

The "White City"

In his official report to the Spanish Viceroy of Sicily, Don Pedro (as might be expected) was most enthusiastic about the city he had just conquered:

> Sir, this city is much bigger than I had imagined and I see that whatever those who praised it had to say, they spoke only half the truth; and of all the places I have seen in this world, I have never found any other city to equal it for strength or cleanliness. It seems more like an imperial city than one that belongs to no sovereign in particular.[2]

But the booty found in the city was disappointing because the merchant community, at least, seems to have been warned of the impending assault and had moved its most precious goods to the villages of Tagiura to the east and Zanzur to the west. Tagiura, indeed, became in effect a small, independent free state throughout the Christian occupation.

There was enormous rejoicing in Christian Europe at the news of Tripoli's capture: in Spain, in Venice, Bologna and Rome, and especially in Sicily and southern Italy, as both had become increasingly vulnerable to pirate raids. These raids were, in effect, a freebooting arm of the rising Mediterranean naval power of the Ottoman Turks. Tripoli was annexed to Spanish Sicily, and Spanish propaganda insisted that its possession was a great advantage since it was "one of the two eyes of Christendom". Although its new rulers ably defended the place against Muslim counter-attacks and tried to rebuild and repopulate it, the economy collapsed, not least because its merchants (and especially the Jews) were dead, had fled, or had been expelled. (Some of those Jews were themselves recent exiles from Spain.) The Venetians, in particular, found that their initial rejoicing at the city's fall had been misplaced, for the Spanish soon discouraged all foreign ships, and especially Venetian ones, from using the port. Instead, the Venetians opened trade relations with the nearby Muslim outpost at Tagiura, or went further along the coast to increasingly busy Misurata; while caravan traffic with the hinterland and across the Sahara similarly avoided an outlet now under alien and hostile rule.

A Venetian engraved print of 1567 suggests that during the Spanish occupation the city was merely a ruined, depopulated space within the defensive walls, with only the moated castle (which the Spanish largely rebuilt from rubble), the Arch of Marcus Aurelius and one or two other landmarks still standing amid an empty waste. It was a panorama of utter devastation more reminiscent of many European cities in 1945 than of the sixteenth century. The travelling Muslim diplomat (later a Christian convert), Leo Africanus, probably never visited Tripoli himself and, as an armchair traveller of the Spanish period, seems to have based his description of the city (published in 1550) on the pre-conquest facts. He might more accurately have written in the past tense when he suggested that "the houses of this city are imposing compared with those of Tunis" and "the public spaces are orderly and are well provided with various trades, most notably weavers of cloth". He also insisted that there was still some Mediterranean trade and that "the yearly visits to the port by the Venetian trading galleys are encouraged". On the other hand, he seemed to be reflecting true contemporary conditions when he noted that "in this same city there used to be many temples [mosques] and some colleges for scholars; similarly there were lodgings offering shelter to the poor and to foreigners".

Significantly, after stating that there was no other city between Tripoli and Alexandria in Egypt, Leo reported that Misurata was doing good business both with the Venetians and into what he called "Numidia" (the Sahara) and "Ethiopia" (the Sudan). They were exchanging Venetian imports for slaves, and civet musk for perfume-making, which the merchants of Misurata re-exported to Turkey (the whole Ottoman Empire)—"so they make profits on both sets of transactions". The implication, of course, was that Misurata was taking every advantage of Tripoli's troubles to take over its Mediterranean and Saharan trades.

As for Tagiura (which he called "Taiora"), Leo Africanus reported:

Tairoa is a locality some three miles to the east of Tripoli, where there are many hamlets and gardens of dates and other fruit. After the Christians captured Tripoli, this locality became quite genteel and civilised because many citizens fled there. But in all the above-mentioned villages or hamlets there are low, ignorant, thieving men whose dwellings are of palm-fronds.[3]

Although Spanish Tripoli gave some in-depth defence to Spanish Sicily and slight protection to Christian shipping in the central Mediterranean, it was soon clear that it was more of a liability than an asset. In 1524 one of the great military and international Orders of the Church, the Knights of the Order of St. John of Jerusalem, were invited to take over the city. The Knights, dedicated to the defence of the faith, were looking for a new base after losing the island of Rhodes to the Ottoman Turks after a six-month siege in 1522. It was suggested that the Knights could regroup in both Malta and Tripoli, and in 1524 the Order sent an eight-man mission to inspect both places. With their recent experience of the Turkish assault on Rhodes, they were not impressed by the city or its defences. Despite the work the Spanish had already done, the walls and the Castle were still in a poor state; fewer than 1,000 civilians (sixty families) were still living amidst the ruins; and the upkeep of the garrison and defences was costing the Emperor Charles V some 12,000 *scudi* a year. Not until 1530, and under considerable pressure from both the Pope and the Emperor, did the Knights reluctantly agree to take on the defence of this troublesome and costly outpost of their new, main base on the Maltese archipelago, some two hundred miles to the north.

This so-called "Christian oasis in a barbarian desert" was not a happy place. The Knights, with few men and resources, tried in vain to revive the civil and commercial life of a city and a port still practically under siege. The few defenders did what they could to rebuild the city walls and the Castle, while beating off intermittent Muslim assaults. Tagiura, at the eastern end of the oasis, was in effect the Muslim capital of Tripolitania and was ruled by a European renegade, Murad Agha, with Turkish support. Then, in the late summer of 1551 a mighty Ottoman fleet tried, but failed, to take the Knights' new stronghold of Malta; so it sailed on to Tripoli instead, landing forces at Tagiura, and at Zuara to the west. Although the defences were weak and defended by only four hundred men, the governor, Fra Gaspard de Villiers, defied the Turks with a message that he intended to defend the city to the death. The historian of the Barbary Corsairs, Stanley Lane-Poole, takes up the narrative:

> Six thousand Turks disembarked, forty cannons were landed, Sinan Pasha [Turkish navy commander] himself directed every movement and arranged his batteries and earthworks. A heavy cannonade produced no effect on the walls and the Turkish admiral thought of the recent repulse at Malta, and the stern face of his master; and his head sat uneasily on his neck. The siege appeared to make no progress. Perhaps this venture, too, would

have failed but for the treachery of a French renegade, who escaped into the trenches and pointed out the weak places in the walls. His counsel was taken; the walls fell down; the garrison, in weariness and despair, had lain down to sleep off their troubles, and no reproaches or blows could rouse them. On 15th August Gaspard de Villiers was forced to surrender.[4]

But once the Turks were let into the city the following day, they broke the terms of the pact that had allowed them in. Murad Agha was made the new Muslim governor in the name of the Turkish Sultan. Europe was shocked by the loss of this strategic outpost, which was not again to come under European rule for 360 years.

Chapter Three
A Nest of Corsairs

God preserve you from the Tripoli galleys.

Tripoli was now on the front line of a mighty Mediterranean and wider confrontation between the forces of a Spanish-led European Christendom on the one side and an Islam newly revitalized by Ottoman Turkish predominance on the other. After their late conversion to Islam, the Turks, originally horse people of the central Asian steppes, had come to power in Anatolia (Asia Minor) in the fourteenth and fifteenth centuries, conquering Constantinople in 1453 and then Egypt in 1517. In the meantime, this land power had become a rising sea power, due in part to the initiative of semi-independent, freebooting corsairs who, acting on the Sultan's behalf, initiated the Ottoman westwards advance into North Africa. The noted Turkish admiral Darghut Pasha became Tripoli's ruler shortly after its return to Muslim authority, and he was to be known as "the Terror of Tripoli" until his death at the Great Siege of Malta in 1565.

While Christian attempts to reconquer the city were unsuccessful, Turkish expansion in the central Mediterranean was decisively checked, first by the failure to conquer the Knights' stronghold at Malta in 1565, and again at the Battle of Lepanto in 1571, where the sea turned red with Turkish and Christian blood. At Lepanto the Turkish fleet of nearly 300 warships was drawn from all the maritime provinces of the empire: Tripoli sent eleven galleys and galleots and lost seven of these ships and 1,200 men in the battle. Although in the words of an eyewitness, Miguel Cervantes, Lepanto "broke the pride of the Osmans and undeceived the world, which had regarded the Turkish fleet as invincible", the Mediterranean was to remain a contested naval war zone for another 250 years. For most of that time, Tripoli and the two other Barbary "nests of corsairs" (Algiers and Tunis) carried on an intermittent war of state-sponsored piracy against Christian merchant shipping and raids against Italian and other south European coastal communities. "God preserve you from the Tripoli galleys" became a common farewell cry to Christian crews and passengers embarking on central Mediterranean voyages.

Strictly speaking, corsairs were not pirates because their activities were recognized, encouraged and licensed by their own city state, and they were as a result judged to be legal by both national and international opinion. The corsair states simply considered their fleets at war with every nation that presumed to sail ships in the Mediterranean without first making a peace treaty and financial arrangements with them. By the seventeenth century the larger European maritime powers—England, France and Holland, later Austria and the Scandinavians—had come to such arrangements with Tripoli. They began to appoint consuls to this corsair state to see that treaty obligations were observed, to protect their countrymen from enslavement and to ensure that an ingenious system of ships' passes really did allow merchantmen protected by treaty to sail on unmolested if challenged at sea by a corsair. But the smaller and poorer Mediterranean maritime powers were unable to afford or enforce such "protection", and their shipping suffered accordingly.

The predatory warfare of the corsairs, with the seizure of ships, their cargoes, and crews and passengers to be ransomed (if rich) or enslaved (if poor), brought Tripoli renewed prosperity. But foreign vessels that put into the port on peaceful business were not always immune from the malign whims of the local authorities. Thus in 1584 the English merchantman *Jesus* (100 tons, captained by Thomas Sanders) tried to leave port after differences with the local Turkish ruler, the *Dey*. With wind and weather unfavourable, the crew had slowly and vulnerably to warp the ship out of port with a cable wound round the capstan and made fast to a fixed point. When the captain ignored blank shots fired as a warning to heave to, the city's gunners were ordered to disable or sink the ship. But as their aim was so poor, and they scored not a single hit, Sebastiano, a Spanish slave who had served as a gunner in Flanders, was unchained and promised his liberty and 100 gold pieces if he could either sink the English vessel or force its return to port. As Captain Sanders later recounted:

> At the first shotte he split our rudders head in pieces, and the second shotte he strake us under the water, and the third shotte he shotte our foremast with a Colvering shot [Culverin was a long-barrel cannon], and thus he having rent both our rudder and maste, and shot us under water, we were inforced to go in againe.[5]

In the event, the master gunner Sebastiano received neither his promised liberty, nor his gold, while the English ship and its cargo were seized and the captain and crew were "condemned to slaverie". (They were eventually released through Queen Elizabeth's personal intervention via the English Ambassador in Constantinople.)

Ten years after Lepanto, a general Mediterranean peace among the Powers ushered in more than two centuries of active corsairing by the ports of Tripoli, Tunis, Algiers, and Salee on Morocco's Atlantic coast. Not one of these was powerful enough to take on the larger European maritime nations, any one of which could probably have ended the whole corsair menace if it had a mind to do so. But the corsairs were useful because they kept in check the smaller Mediterranean maritime states and their seaborne trade, while the larger ones (and especially France), protected by their treaties with the Barbary states, had the advantage of usually (but not always) being able to sail unmolested. It was thus in their selfish interests (and especially those of France) to allow the Barbary corsairs to remain active and to supply them with the materials (iron, ropes and timber in particular) and guns to build, equip and arm their war fleets. These fleets were, moreover, in good part supervised, organized, navigated, rowed and manned by European renegades. Most of these were Greek and Italian former captives, but among them were men drawn from just about every Christian state who had chosen to escape from slavery in Barbary by "turning Turk" (converting to Islam) and were thus free to join a corsair crew, with the prospects of adventure and rich plunder on the high seas.

Tripoli was the least of the Barbary corsair states, and its war fleet was always smaller than those of Tunis and Algiers. In 1612 only four warships were available for winter cruising and three for summer raiding voyages. By mid-century, only one oared galley was in service, but there by then up to nine sailing warships of basic north European pattern with cannon mounted in broadsides. In 1619 a Greek renegade, Mami Rais, had started training Tripoline crews in the unfamiliar arts of sailing ship navigation and warfare, and by the century's end the fleet had grown to about ten sailing ships and a few small galleys (galleots). Some ships in the corsair fleet would no doubt have been captured foreign merchantmen converted as raiders.

The fleet flew "national" flags of various patterns, and a common one was possibly the origin of the (perhaps fictional) international pirates' flag, the *Jolly Roger* or *Skull and Crossbones*. Tripoli's three stars displayed as two above and one below could easily, at a distance, be taken for eye and nose sockets of a human skull; a supine crescent moon below as a mouth cavity; and the crossed Islamic scimitars underneath as the two "crossbones".

Although the port of Tripoli was well placed to raid the rich and busy merchant shipping lanes of the central Mediterranean, and the Ionian Adriatic and Tyrrhenian Seas, its fleet was vulnerable to the counter-attacks of the Christian naval powers. The most aggressive enemies of Tripoline and other Barbary corsairs were the patrolling war fleets of the Knights of Malta and of the Knights of Santo Stefano based at the Tuscan port of Pisa, and also at Livorno (Leghorn) as Pisa silted up. In the cathedral of the Maltese capital, Valletta, is a great, triumphal floor mosaic depicting the "Burning of the Great Tripoli Ship" during a skirmish with the Knights' war galleys.

In summer the Tripoline corsairs preyed on merchantmen in the seas off Malta, Calabria, Puglia, Sardinia and Corsica, and occasionally as far north as Liguria. In winter they lay in wait to plunder the rich merchant traffic between southern Europe, Egypt and the Levant. But they usually fled on sighting a hostile warship. Between 1668 and 1678 Tripoli corsairs alone seized a yearly average of ten Christian merchant ships of which (despite treaties with the France of Louis XIV), one third were French This was always a hazardous business: in 1635 the fleet brought in captured merchandise worth 180,000 *ducats*, and 450 captured slaves; but three years later it lost three ships, 200 men and property worth 100,000 *scudi* in one engagement with the Knights of Malta off Calabria.

Once a corsair and her prize had returned to port with cannon salutes and other public rejoicing, there was an immediate and formal inquest at the seat of government, the Castle of the *Dey*. This assembly decided first on the legitimacy of the capture; then through the protecting intervention of the European consuls, the rights of captives to freedom, slavery or ransom depending on nationality and status; and finally the division of the spoils The booty from these raids was usually divided strictly and fairly in set proportions between the ruling *Dey* and his senior officials, the corsair ship's backers and owners, and its captain, officers and crew. Slaves with useful skills were able to better their lot by using them, especially in the arsenal unskilled men were sent to the quarries, and the women and girls to the harems. "Interesting" slaves with remarkable looks, skills or intellect might be set aside to be forwarded by the *Dey* as a special gift to the Sultan at Constantinople. Any Christian slave could gain his freedom and expect to better his lot by renouncing his faith (and thus his prospects of ever returning home) and accepting Islam. (This was a privilege denied to black African slaves, who had no outside power to protect them or to defend their interests.) The Franciscans set up a mission in the city as early as 1630 to dissuade Christian slaves from becoming Muslims, and to minister to the many who, despite all the pressures on them, still kept their faith.

Most Mediterranean merchant ships, slow, heavily laden with cargo and a supercargo of passengers, and practically defenceless, were usually easy prey if they fell in with a swift corsair predator. While most surrendered to their fate with little or no resistance, a few did fight back, sometimes with surprising vigour. A Venetian merchantman under the command of one Zorzi (George) Tavanelli was set upon by a pair of large Tripoli corsair raiders in January 1749 shortly after leaving the Ionian island of Cefalonia for Crete with a cargo of olive oil and soap. What the corsairs did not know was that this plain cargo ship also carried 16 pieces of medium artillery and 14 heavy muskets, while every one of the 31-man crew had his own gun, as did the 25 soldiers on board. In the ensuing battle the Venetians had almost 100 per cent casualties (killed or wounded) while the corsairs, although finally victorious, also suffered heavy losses. When the Venetian ship was at last towed as a prize into Tripoli, the ruling Pasha went into a mighty rage and threatened hideous punishments—against his own corsair captains, whom he banished from his sight while commending Captain Tavanelli's valour. He had his many wounds treated, and eventually sent him back home to Venice after failing to persuade him to "turn Turk" and to become a corsair captain in his own right with the surviving members of his crew.

European Reprisals

Tripoli, and indeed all the Barbary corsair bases, were always vulnerable to counter-attack by exasperated European naval powers. After a series of outrages at sea, or an especially serious incident, a Christian war fleet would appear off the port to reinforce diplomatic attempts to extract restitution or recompense. When diplomacy failed, the fleet would turn its guns on any corsair ships in port, on the dockyard, the Castle and the city itself. In

1638 a French fleet bombarded the dockyard and the city as a reprisal for corsair raids along the coast of Provence. An English fleet under Admiral Blake assaulted the city in 1654; the French were back in 1660 and 1671; the Dutch followed in 1672. The English returned in January 1676 when a fleet under Admiral Sir John Narborough appeared off the port to reinforce diplomatic demands on the ruling *Dey*. When negotiations broke down, Narborough sent his ships' boats into the port late at night. An English slave in Tripoli at the time, Philip Gell, takes up the story:

> The next morning... about one or 2 of the clocke wee heard severall musketts, and presently after see the light of a greate fire, so [we] presently apprehended that it was the shippes on fire (but at first supposed there had been some rebellion in the towne). In the morning [we] had the news that Sir John had sent his boates and burned 4 of their shippes under the Castell walls and had taken a boate with some men that was upon the watch.[6]

Although the defenders fired "about 9 greate gunnes" on the English boats still in the port as the corsair fleet burned, not one of the attackers was hurt, according to Gell's account. In 1685 and in 1692 the French fleet was back again.

Diplomacy was tried as an alternative to constant warfare and retribution.

The French were the first, in 1630, to sign a treaty with the city-state and to appoint a salaried consul with limited diplomatic powers to oversee the treaty terms. Other consuls of the main European maritime powers followed: the first English Consul, Samuel Tucker, was appointed in 1658 by the Levant Company, which was concerned

Revenge on a Barbary "Nest of Corsairs": Tripoli attacked by a punitive French war fleet in 1685.

for the safety of all its Mediterranean shipping. Later consuls were also granted some juridical and executive powers over their own nationals under the Turkish Capitulations which recognized the special privileges of some foreigners within the empire. But when diplomacy failed, as it often did, it still had to be backed up by cannon.

By the late seventeenth century the power of the Tripoli corsairs was clearly in decline, and continued so until the end of the eighteenth century. In 1765 only four corsair ships were operating, and when five years later the Sultan asked for naval help against Russian expansion into the Black Sea, Tripoli could send him only two rotten hulks manned by mutinous crews. By that time the growing power of the main European fleets and their increasing contempt for the pretensions of the Barbary corsair states meant that the Tripoli fleet was experiencing as many disastrous, unproductive years as successful ones. Nevertheless, the corsairs were to remain as more than an unpleasant pest to the commercial shipping of the lesser Mediterranean powers until the early nineteenth century. And the tribute or protection money paid by European maritime powers to buy immunity from corsair attack continued to support Tripoli's finances until the 1820s. In 1767 the British Consul, The Hon. Archibald Fraser, in a summary of the state's economy, explained that "The General Ballance of Trade against Tripoli is paid off by the sale of slaves [White Christian slaves] taken in their Piracies and the Money spent among them by the Agents and Consuls of the several European powers with which they are at peace." In other words, the activities of the corsairs, or the mere threat of them, were still making an important contribution to the finances of a state of otherwise very meagre resources. And so long as the corsairs continued to do so, the state could afford to project its limited military land power far down the Saharan trading roads towards the tributary province of Fezzan. It thus ensured the protection and continuation of its second main (and equally parasitic) source of revenue—the import and re-export trade in black slaves from inner Africa. This circular system of parasitic state finances only broke down in the early nineteenth century when all Barbary corsair activity was finally and effectively curbed by the main European naval powers.

Although the Barbary states waged vigorous naval war in the Mediterranean for centuries, they failed to develop a parallel merchant marine. The decline of Muslim sea power had started as early as the Third

Crusade at the end of the twelfth century when much of the sea-borne trade of the Mediterranean passed to the Italian maritime republics. The result was that by the mid-eighteenth century Tripoli still had a small war fleet, but its merchant marine consisted merely of a few small coasting vessels, not one of them capable of a trans-Mediterranean voyage. By then the main commercial carriers serving the port (and especially its all-important export trade in black slaves) were French (particularly from Marseille) or from Ragusa (Dubrovnik) in Croatia, Ottoman Greece and even Russia (once it was established on the Black Sea late in the century). The difficulty was that while Tripoli had many skilled European slave artisans and artificers to build and maintain its corsair galleys and sailing ships, and many renegade recruits to join the corsair crews, it had neither a native work force, nor the experienced seamen, to build and man a merchant fleet.

The Spanish and Maltese Knights' military occupation in the early sixteenth century had interrupted normal Saharan trade with Fezzan and the Empire of Bornu to the west of Lake Chad. After regaining the city for Islam in 1551, the Turks had tried to renew this business as essential to the long-term prosperity of their new possession. The trans-Saharan road through Fezzan was equally important to Bornu, as it offered the most direct access to the wider Islamic world outside Africa. Bornu had sent diplomatic-commercial missions to Tripoli during the Christian occupations, with little success, while Fezzan had for some time been a precariously independent province under the Awlad Mohammed dynasty ruling at the new capital and central Saharan market of Murzuk.

For over fifty years the Ottoman regime in Tripoli tried and failed to secure the main trade roads through Fezzan, rather than trust the local Awlad Mohammed rulers to do so on its behalf. Although the Turks occupied Fezzan in 1577 and advanced some way down the Lake Chad road, they could not hold these gains, and they also failed to extract any meaningful allegiance from Bornu. Indeed, its ruler reacted to the Turkish advance by sending an embassy through Tripoli to Constantinople to complain of such interference in his Saharan interests, at the same time requesting Turkish recognition of his rule, and firearms and gunners to ensure Bornu's future military predominance in the central Sudan. Bornu sent periodic official consignments of slaves through Fezzan to Tripoli, either as tribute or as an exchange of diplomatic gifts with the current ruling *Dey*. Thus 100 young men and 100 girls were sent in 1638, and a consignment of 125 slaves, including dwarves and valuable eunuchs, in 1686. The semi-independent regime in Tripoli had recognized the almost equal independence of the Awlad Mohammed dynasty at Murzuk in 1626 in return for a substantial yearly tribute in gold and slaves amounting to a specified sum of 4,000 gold *mithqals*. But because the tribute was partly met as a consignment of slaves determined by their price rather than a specific number, its value in Tripoli seems to have halved in the two centuries of its existence.

For 360 years "Tripoli" (which meant both the city-state and more or less the lands now known as Libya) was considered to be an Ottoman "regency", a province of the empire initially ruled by a quick succession of Turkish governors appointed from Constantinople. But by the early seventeenth century, the city-state became more independent with the rise of a succession of *Deys* of more local and/or renegade origins who seized and kept power through force and skill. But essential shows of tribute and allegiance to the Sultan were always kept up. The most successful of these local, nominally Turkish *Deys* were Mohammed Sakisli (1631-49) and his successor, Osman Sakisli (1649-72). They were renegades and they surrounded themselves with other renegades who formed a military oligarchy to sustain the ruler's uncompromising role as a "strong man" in the traditional Arab-Turkish mould.

Political chaos and Tripoli's slow decline as an active corsair state followed the death of Osman Sakisli in 1672, and over the next 39 years there was a succession of 24 *Deys*, some of whom only very briefly held power. Writing in 1686, a Franciscan observer of the local political scene, Francesco da Capranica, commented sourly on what he saw:

> It is more a republic than a kingdom, and the butchers and cobblers have risen to the highest ranks. The rule of the *Dey* is permanent, but usually it lasts no more than a year because, when he is no longer popular, any drunkard can rouse the city and have the rulers' heads off. Two years ago it so happened that three *Deys* sat on the throne in a single day, and all three were killed.[7]

The good Franciscan also took a poor view of the judicial system, remarking that the courts, without consultation, "straightaway, as it suits their fancy, order the severing of arms, legs, ears, noses or chins, and think nothing more of the matter".

The Karamanlis

This state of chaos ended in a military *coup* in 1711. A class of Turkish professional soldiers, the *Janissaries* had for the past 150 years intermarried with local girls, and the result was a class of racially mixed soldiers and state officials, the *Cologhlis*, generally more popular than the European renegades. A leading *Cologhli* cavalry officer, Ahmed Karamanli, led a successful coup against the ruling *Dey* and had all leading Turks and their supporters massacred. This ambitious and popular officer, who intended to rule independently, then sent his victims' confiscated assets as a necessary tribute and gesture of allegiance to the Sultan, who was pleased to recognize Tripoli's generous new ruler with the more exalted title of *Pasha*. His rank of three horse tails (which recalled the origins of Turkish military prowess) made him equal to the Pashas of Baghdad and Buda-Pest. Four successive generations of Karamanli rulers continued to use the title. (The English in Tripoli always referred to the *Bashaw*, a reflection of the locals' common pronunciation of the Turkish "P".)

Ahmed Pasha Karamanli's ambitions extended well beyond his city-state. In 1716 and again in 1718 he invaded Fezzan, which had neglected its treaty obligations, and also to reassert Tripoli's basic concern to keep the Saharan routes open to two-way trading caravans. As an extension of this policy, he also began to bring Cyrenaica more firmly under his centralizing control, and he started the practice of sending younger members of the Karamanli family to Benghazi to govern that notoriously unruly province. But a secondary purpose was greater control of all trade through Fezzan since merchants at Murzuk were in the habit of diverting some caravans north eastwards to the Augila oases, and so to the Mediterranean outlet at Benghazi, whenever they wanted to avoid trouble, or taxes, on the more direct road to Tripoli.

Ahmed Pasha ruled until his death at the age of about sixty in 1745. He restored the political and economic fortunes of his little state; revived the activities of its corsair fleet in the Mediterranean and of its trading caravans in and across the Sahara; conducted a clever and conciliatory foreign policy with both European and Maghrebi neighbours; promoted the building of the city's handsome Karamanli Mosque and other public works; insisted on a remarkable toleration of slaves and of religious and foreign minorities (Jews especially); and encouraged modest local intellectual and artistic achievement. As his epitaph on his tomb in the Karamanli Mosque complex affirms, he was "Prince of the land which had become happy through his efforts".

He was succeeded by lesser men: his son Mohammed who ruled for only nine years (1745-54), dying at the age of 45. He in turn was followed by his young son Ali who ruled for nearly forty years, until 1793. Ali allowed his city-state to fall into a long depression, losing much of the diplomatic and commercial standing gained in the previous half century. As the French Consul commented towards the end of Ali Pasha's life,

The handsome mosque built in the early eighteenth century for Tripoli's first Karamanli ruler, Ahmed Pasha.

> He rules, but is not obeyed. Master of large estates which yield him nothing, he lives in extreme want, which under a good administration could easily be converted into plenty. Shut up in his harem, where he indulges his lusts with his black women and his craving for drink from his personal distillery, he builds and repairs nothing, but lets everything collapse.[8]

Tully's Tripoli

By the late eighteenth century the city's generally dilapidated and impoverished outward appearance, advertised by huge mounds of accumulated rubbish, seemed to foreign visitors hardly consistent with its role as an international emporium trading by land and sea with three continents, and its command of the diplomatic and tributary attention of leading European powers.

Yet the fact was that this small but still pugnacious Mediterranean and Saharan Islamic city-state was then an extraordinarily fascinating vibrant and intriguingly "exotic" social, cultural and political forum. Such is only too clearly apparent from the evidence of one contemporary foreign witness. Miss Tully (her Christian name is unknown) was the sister of the British Consul in Tripoli, Richard Tully, whom she accompanied on his second tour of duty there (July 1783-August 1793). This acute observer of Tripoline life, society and politics set down her first impressions of the place on sighting it from the deck of the incoming ship with the returning Consul and his family on board:

> Previous to entering the Bay of Tripoli, a few miles from the land, the country is rendered picturesque by various tints of beautiful verdure: no object whatever seems to interrupt the evenness of the soil, which is of light colour, almost white, and interspersed with long avenues of trees; for such is the appearance of the numerous palms planted in regular rows, and kept in the finest order... The land lying low and very level, the naked stems of these trees are scarcely seen, and the plantations of dates seem to extend for many miles in luxuriant woods and groves. On nearer view, they present a more straggling appearance, and afford neither shelter nor shade from the burning atmosphere, which everywhere surrounds them. The whole town appears in a semicircle, some time before reaching the harbour's mouth. The extreme whiteness of square flat buildings covered with lime, which in this climate encounters the sun's fiercest rays, is very striking. The baths form clusters of cupolas very large, to the number of eight or ten crowded together in different parts of the town. The mosques have in general a small plantation of Indian figs and date-trees growing close to them, which, at a distance, appearing to be so many rich gardens in different parts of the town, give the whole city, in the eyes of an European, an aspect truly novel and pleasing.[9]

These gardens were perhaps not as fine and orderly as Miss Tully suggested. A century earlier another foreign witness, Anthony Knecht, had noted:

These gardens with the white walls of the houses in them, shaded with multitudes of date palm trees, yield a beautiful prospect from the town. The Tripolines have little notion... of gardening. There is no regularity, much less elegance in their gardening: fine walks, flowerbeds, groves and other such ornaments is looked upon as a waste of so much useful ground, and regularity in planting and sowing as a deviation from the practice of their ancestors. For in their gardens they have nothing but a confused mixture of date trees and shrubs above, with cabbages, beans, all kinds of greens growing beneath & sometimes barley and wheat intermixed...[10]

The town was certainly not as attractive as first impressions from the sea suggested. As an incoming ship entered the harbour, closer inspection by its passengers showed that many of its buildings were neglected and run-down, and that the place was disfigured by "large hills" of uncollected rubbish.

Despite Tripoli's cosmopolitan character as an intercontinental trading centre and an essential halt for Maghrebi pilgrims travelling to the Hijaz, Miss Tully found that new arrivals still provided a rewarding public spectacle for a crowd of curious onlookers and idlers. As she observed, "The arrival of Christians in the harbour occasions a great number of people to assemble at the mole-end and along the sea-shore, the natural consequence of an African's curiosity, who, never having been out of his own country, finds as much amusement at the first sight of an European, as his own uncouth appearance affords to the newly arrived stranger." Despite the official disembarkation at noon—"an hour when, on account of the extreme heat at this season, no Moor of distinction leaves his house"—a number of the Pasha's chief officers and officials had come to welcome Consul Tully on his return to his post. They were "splendidly arrayed in the fashion of the east":

Their long flowing robes of satin, velvet, and costly furs, were exhibited amidst a crowd of miserable beings, whose only covering was a piece of dark brown homespun cotton... resembling a dirty blanket, but which (by a wretched contrast) heightened the lustre of those who passed among them towards us.[11]

All the great officials and officers of state wore immense turbans, their size increasing according to the rank of the wearer. After a detailed description of the clothes she had seen, Miss Tully confided, "you will conceive that the Tripolitan dress, almost covered with gold and silver, and with so much drapery over them, make a most superb appearance".

She was soon to find out that "they do not excel here in shops, the best of these being little better than booths, though their contents are sometimes valuable, consisting of pearls, gold, gems and precious drugs". There were two covered bazaars, the larger built four aisles meeting in at right-angles. It was fitted up with shops on both sides of the aisles and containing "every sort of merchandise". "Several parts of this place are nearly dark, and the powerful smell of musk makes it very unpleasant to pass through it." The other bazaar was much smaller and had no shops in it: "Thither only black men and women are brought for sale!" And she added, "The very idea of a human being, brought and examined as cattle for sale, is repugnant to a feeling heart; yet it is one of their principal traffics."

There was also the coffee bazaar—"where the Turks meet to hear and tell the news of the day, and to drink coffee: it is filled with coffee houses, or rather coffee kitchens, which within are very black with smoke, and in which nothing but coffee is dressed." The customers themselves never entered these places, but sent their slaves to bring coffee to them outside, where there were marble couches, shaded by green arbours and provided with "the most rich and beautiful mats and carpets". All the principal citizens were to be found at these places at certain hours of the day, each waited on by his own black slaves who stood by "one with his pipe, another with his cup, and a third holding his handkerchief while he is talking". For, as Miss Tully explained in a piece of acute observation of social behaviour, any speaker's hands were "absolutely necessary for his discourse":

> He marks with the forefinger of his right hand upon the palm of his left, as accurately as we do with a pen, the different parts of his speech, a comma, a quotation, or a striking passage. This renders their manner of conversing very singular: and an European, who is not used to this part of their discourse, is altogether at a loss to understand what the speakers mean.[12]

Miss Tully is such a good source of original information because, besides considering the relatively open, masculine side of city life, she was also able o penetrate, observe and describe the tightly enclosed, almost secretive life and society of middle- and upper-class women in the harems. For in the public streets, Muslim and (to a slightly lesser extent) Jewish women were so closely veiled and bundled up in their outer clothing that, as she put it, "it is impossible to discover more of them than their height, not easily even their size" (and such remained the common case until the 1960s, at least). Women "of a middle station of life" could generally go out of the house on foot, but hardly ever without a female slave or attendant. Wrapped up in the *baraccan* (a covering about a yard and a half wide and up to five yards long), which concealed them entirely,

> they hold it so close over their face, as scarcely to leave the least opening to see their way through it. The Jewesses wear this part of their dress to discover one eye, which a Moorish woman dares not do if she have a proper regard for public opinion, as her reputation would certainly suffer by it.[13]

As for the few European women in town, Miss Tully found that it took "some address and resolution" to walk through the public streets, since there were no vehicles to ride in.

> It is only ladies of a Consul's family who attempt to pass the streets in this manner. They are always accompanied by several gentlemen and guards: but these precautions, though they might ensure safety, would not render walking through the streets possible were the Moors inclined to be insolent: on the contrary, however, if the Moors are in the least troublesome, it is from their over kindness and civility.[14]

In April 1785 couriers riding from Tunis spread the plague on their way and brought it to Tripoli. As Miss Tully reported, the symptoms were "that of a person being seized by a sort of stupor, which immediately increases to madness, and violent swellings and excruciating pains in a few hours terminate in death". By June she was writing, "It is impossible to give you a just description of this place at present; the general horror that prevails cannot be described." The only way to avoid the contagion was to confine each household under the strictest quarantine in its own home. The British Consulate was shut up in complete quarantine on 14

June. The Consul himself unlocked the front door once a day to allow fresh food to be brought in with many fumigations and other elaborate precautions that he personally supervised. This quarantine lasted for thirteen solid months.

Miss Tully learned that in the six weeks from the beginning of June 1785, "this dreadful pestilence has carried off two-thirds of the Moors, half the Jews and nine-tenths of the Christians, who could not procure the conveniences necessary for a quarantine". The crisis was clearly worsened by the locals' poor medical knowledge and practice:

> They seem to have but a slender knowledge of physic: fire is one of their chief remedies; they use it for almost everything; for wounds, sickness, colds, and even for headaches they have recourse to a red-hot iron with which they burn the part affected. They perform amputations safely, though in a rough manner; but in all kinds of diseases, such as fevers, etc., it is thought one-fourth die of the disorder, and three of the remedies made use of.[15]

The crisis was also worsened by a famine that had started before the plague and which could not be relieved because foreign grain ships understandably steered clear of this pestilential port. By September 1786 Miss Tully reported that with the plague finally over, "the town was almost entirely depopulated, and rarely two people walked together". Of course it recovered, but it took time; the plague returned in the early nineteenth century, and remained a threat until at least 1850.

In 1795 a new ruler, Yusuf Pasha Karamanli, came to power with great ambitions for his city-state. He claimed the throne after murdering one elder brother and terrifying another into lasting exile. Yusuf was a cultured, ruthless, amiable, cunning and popular tyrant. He had on the one side to resist Turkish plans to regain direct control of his regency that had long been effectively independent of Constantinople, but which had sunk low politically, economically and socially, under its previous Karamanli ruler. On the other side he needed to assert his hegemony over the potentially rival port of Benghazi and its hinterland. He also needed to exert undisputed control of the trans-Saharan trade routes (and especially the slave trading routes) which, since the decline of Mediterranean corsairing, seemed to offer the only means of reviving state revenues. He accordingly put down tribal revolts along the desert caravan roads; curbed the age-old autonomy of the oasis of Ghadames that dominated the south-western trade to and from Timbuctu and the Niger Bend countries; and ended the three centuries of tributary independence of the province of Fezzan, the entrepôt of the central Saharan slave trade. But his ambitions, positively "imperial" in their scale and scope, did not end there, for he believed that he could also project his power fully across the Great Desert to the populous, slave-gathering states of Bornu and "Sudan" (Hausaland).

Yusuf Pasha also found in due course that his corsair fleet was able to take advantage of the Great Powers' preoccupation with the Napoleonic Wars to renew its attacks on Mediterranean merchant shipping, or to extract larger sums of protection money as insurance against such attack. Such renewed activity soon brought both Algiers and Tripoli into conflict with a new sea power inexperienced in the hazards and conventions of Mediterranean mercantile navigation—the young American Republic. Ships from the North American colonies had long been protected by British naval power and diplomatic weight: but after independence United States merchantmen were on their own. Between 1790 and 1800 the Americans paid over two million dollars (an extortionate sum) in safe conduct to the Barbary regencies. In 1801 Yusuf Pasha demanded bigger payments and when the Americans (apparently misunderstanding Tripoli's independent status) refused them, Yusuf Pasha seized American ships and declared war. As the USA then lacked an ocean-going navy capable of facing the challenge even of a power such as Tripoli, it had hastily to build one, including several unusually large frigates of up to forty guns. By 1803 an American squadron of three frigates and other vessels was not very effectively blockading Tripoli. In October the frigate USS *Philadelphia* (38 guns) ran aground on a submerged reef inside the harbour. Immobile, and beset by gunboats and other craft, Captain Bainbridge surrendered the frigate intact, with its crew of some 300 officers and men. *Philadelphia* was plundered as a prize, refloated, and towed to an anchorage off the town.

In that era of much greater social distinction, treatment and fortune, the officers and the crew had strikingly different experiences as captives of Yusuf Pasha. The captain and about twenty officers were brought ashore in a boat and, after being briefly paraded before the Pasha, were confined to the former American Consulate—"a very good house with a large court, and room enough for our convenience", according to the written account of the ship's surgeon. Through the mediation of the Danish Consul, the officers were supplied with fresh provisions "that were tolerably good". They were allowed to walk on the terrace on top of the house, "which commanded a handsome prospect of the harbour, the sea, the town, and the adjoining country".

The wretched American crewmen, by contrast, had to wade or swim ashore and were then, according to the account of the seaman William Ray, marched straight through lines of hostile guards into "the dreadful presence of his exalted majesty, the puissant Bashaw of Tripoli".

> When he had satiated his pride and curiosity by gazing on us with complacent triumph, we were ordered to follow a guard. They conducted us into a dreary, filthy apartment of the castle, where there was scarcely room for us to turn round. Here we remained an hour or two dripping or shivering with the chills of the damp cells, and the vapors of the night. The Neapolitan slaves were busily employed in bringing us dry clothing to exchange for our wet. We... sincerely thanked them for their apparent kindness. We thought them disinterested, generous and hospitable; for we expected to receive our clothes again when dry; but the insidious scoundrels never afterwards would make us any restoration. The clothes we gave them were new, and those which they brought us in exchange were old and ragged.[16]

Another US seaman, Elizah Shaw, described how he and other prisoners were kept in irons overnight, so tightly that "we could not turn our bodies on either side". After about two weeks of this confinement, the prisoners were put to work on rebuilding the city walls, some carrying bags of sand, others dragging a great, clumsy cart loaded with one huge stone weighing up to four tons from the quarries. Guards applied long whips "with an unsparing hand". This imprisonment was to last some nineteen months. In the meantime, the American squadron still at sea had captured a local ketch, which was renamed *Intrepid*. With a picked crew of about eighty men led by Stephen Decatur, *Intrepid* was sent into the harbour at night; *Philadelphia*, lying at anchor by the town, was boarded, taken, and set on fire to prevent such a powerful warship being used against American shipping. Lord Nelson is said to have called this adventure "the most bold and daring act of the age". In a later battle Decatur's younger brother James was killed in action.

Alonzo Chappel's 1858 depiction of the death of James Decatur.

A US-Tripoli peace was eventually made; but even ten years later Yusuf Pasha was seen to receive "with the most visible marks of joy" the news that at the end of the Anglo-American war of 1812-14 British forces had marched into Washington and burned the Capitol and the White House. As for the USA, it has been suggested that its wars on the Barbary coast, and the war with Tripoli in particular, helped to convince Americans that it was a "land of darkness, that abode of slaves" (that is, white American slaves) and undoubtedly contributed to the growth of "spread-eagle nationalism" in the young republic. The Tripoli war also helped to inspire the US Marines' hymn *From the Halls of Montezuma to the Shores of Tripoli*.

By 1815, at the end of the revolutionary crisis of the past quarter century, Yusuf Pasha's prospects as supreme tyrant ruling a small Mediterranean city-state were by no means as promising as they had seemed when he had seized power some twenty years earlier. By the time the Congress of Vienna opened in 1814, and the Battle of Waterloo was fought a year later, the world had changed: balances of political, economic and social power had shifted in ways that, as the Pasha was to learn, were not necessarily in his favour.

Chapter Four
The Gateway to Africa

I think this ought to be the chosen route [into Africa] because practicable into the very heart of the most benighted quarter of the globe. Commander W. H. Smyth, RN

At the opening of the nineteenth century Tripoli was a small, effectively independent and parasitic city-state with a notoriety that still attracted the diplomatic notice of a dozen neighbouring states and Great Powers. But by the end of that century, it was a largely disregarded, almost tradeless and impoverished provincial outpost of the moribund Turkish Empire, known mainly as a place of exile for that empire's political undesirables.

This turn of fortune can be blamed first on the failure of the ruling Yusuf Pasha Karamanli (1795-1832) to come to terms with the realities of the new, post-Napoleonic world order. The greater European maritime powers, and increasingly the lesser ones as well, were by 1815 no longer impressed by the pretensions of this Barbary corsair state, and its claims to regular payments to ensure freedom from attack by its fleet. The greater powers were at last prepared to stop Tripoli's long practice of capturing and enslaving European subjects and citizens as they peacefully sailed the Mediterranean. But then the Pasha's attempts to maintain his capital's reputation as the "Gate of Slaves" by making the trans-Saharan trade in black slaves an economic substitute for his loss of the revenues from Mediterranean corsairing ran up against the new moral, abolitionist outrage of Britain, which began actively to curb even this economic lifeline. In the meantime, the hopes after 1815 that Tripoli, with its command of the main trade routes across the central Sahara, could become Britain's main commercial gateway to the supposed riches of inner, Sudanic Africa foundered in the 1850s on the realization that, with the development of steam navigation and the prophylactic use of quinine, the Niger rivers system actually offered a much easier and safer approach into what was to become British Nigeria. Meanwhile, the overthrow of the Karamanli regime in 1835, and its replacement by the Sultan's direct rule through

Turkish Pashas appointed from Constantinople, denied Tripoli any further, independent control over its own interests and destiny until the early 1950s.

In 1815 the Congress of Vienna, settling the affairs of the post-Napoleonic world, authorized Britain and France to end Mediterranean corsairing and the enslavement of European Christian ships' passengers and crews. In April 1816 a powerful British fleet under the command of Lord Exmouth accordingly anchored off Tripoli and obliged Yusuf Pasha Karamanli to agree to a series of treaties intended to curb the corsair menace, with European captives in future to be treated as "prisoners of war" rather than slaves (which at least meant that they could no longer be bought and sold). When late the following year (1817) a Tripoli corsair brought into port a captured Hanoverian ship (probably not having realized that it sailed under British protection) the Pasha had to pacify the outraged British Consul General, Colonel Hanmer Warrington, by having the corsair captain promptly and publicly hanged from his own mainmast. As the Consul observed, this was a disgrace "which I trust will be an awful and permanent example to these people".

There were further interventions against corsairing, and in 1825 the Kingdom of Sardinia mounted a successful naval assault that enabled it to dictate terms to the Pasha. Two years later the Tripoline fleet at the Battle of Navarino (which pitted the Turks against a combined British, French and Russian force) was dismissed by the Turkish admiral as "a few badly-armed fishing boats". And in 1828 Naples, despite its fleet's inept and ill-aimed bombardment of the town, the dockyard and the Castle, also gained favourable terms from the Pasha. This was to be the last of a series such naval assaults over some two centuries by exasperated powers wreaking revenge and retribution. The fact was that if the corsair fleet then barely existed, not even the city's defences were effective. Although the ramparts still appeared very strong, they were in reality falling to pieces, and most of their few defensive cannon were unserviceable "and more likely to injure those whom they are meant to protect than to annoy an enterprising enemy", according to one witness.

For three centuries Tripoli's extremely narrow margins of economic survival had been broadened by the activities of its small but pugnacious corsair fleet; or, more effectively, by the regency's ability to extract protection money from Christian powers seeking free and unmolested access to the Mediterranean shipping lanes. The notoriety of the Barbary corsairs, and the terror they continued to inspire, may be judged from the fact that even in the 1820s, Holland, Sweden and Denmark were still between them paying to the Pasha as "insurance" against attack a total of $18,000 every year. This sum by then represented about one quarter of the tyrant's total annual income, which in 1822 amounted to barely $70,000 (£14,000).

It has been estimated that, by then, two-thirds of the whole yearly revenue of the regency were spent on maintaining the costly lifestyle of the Pasha and his court, paying the regular troops, maintaining Tripoli's defences and on acts of public charity expected of such a gracious ruler. The remaining third had to meet all other expenses of government. Even as the Pasha's revenues from corsairing dwindled, he had little scope for raising taxes from a rural population reduced by drought for an average of two years out of every ten to the very margins of survival. Nor was there much hope in exacting regular tribute from nomadic tribal groups always jealous of such perceived threats to their freedoms as paying taxes to a central authority that pretended to command their allegiance.

The trade across the Sahara in black slaves from inner Africa thus seemed to offer the best, indeed the only, prospect of increasing the Pasha's revenues from various taxes levied on it. As far back as 1767 the British Consul in Tripoli, the Hon. Archibald Fraser, had drawn attention to the trade's vital contribution to the local economy. In the early nineteenth century an average of about 2,000 black slaves were delivered every year by the incoming Saharan trading caravans. About two-thirds of these unfortunates were women and girls destined for domestic and/or sexual services. About half of them were sold in the Old City's slave market to local buyers; the rest were exported in small sailing craft to other provinces of the Ottoman Empire.

The need to control and protect the desert slaving routes to Tripoli was reflected in the Pasha's vigorously harsh assertion of his sovereignty in the central Sahara between 1806 and 1817. In 1810 he seized control of the ancient and free slave-trading oasis of Ghadames; three years later he ended the three centuries of semi-independence of Fezzan. That southern province was the transit route for most of the slave caravans making for Tripoli and, since the mid-1790s it had also been a base for regular slave-raids into the southern Sahara. Every year these raids brought in hundreds (in some years thousands) of extra slaves to boost the Pasha's revenues. He believed he could gain even more if the raiders, with the advantage of their firearms, were to invade the rich, populous, slave-gathering Sultanate of Bornu, to the west of Lake Chad, Kanem to the east and other such semi-Islamized states beyond the Sahara. This undisguised "imperial" ambition matched similar plans of Mohammed Ali in contemporary Egypt to open up vast slaving fiefdoms in the populous Nilotic Sudan.

The Gateway to Africa

Enter at this stage as British Consul General the imposing, overbearing and deeply patriotic Colonel Hanmer Warrington, his status enhanced by Britain's now convincing predominance in world affairs, and particularly by the new possession of nearby Malta. Warrington, who took up his appointment at the end of 1814, in due course convinced himself, Yusuf Pasha Karamanli and officials in London that Tripoli was the key to Britain's future in Africa, a natural gateway to the inner continent. For the next thirty years he tried to make the central Saharan routes an exclusive highway of British African interests. He believed that if Tripoli's Saharan slave trade and slave raiding were abolished and replaced by alternative "legitimate" business, British exploration, diplomacy, commerce and the processes of "civilization" and "enlightenment" would readily follow. This was not a new idea: in 1788 an Association for Promoting the Discovery of the Interior Parts of Africa (commonly known as the African Association) had been founded in London more or less on these principles, and before the end of the eighteenth century two of its sponsored travellers had tried, and failed, to penetrate the central Sahara from Tripoli.

But times had changed. For Consul Warrington the difference now was his conviction that Yusuf Pasha Karamanli, with his own ambitions on the far side the desert, could become a valued agent and promoter of British interests. This conviction was shared by Commander W. H. Smyth RN, who in 1816 and 1817 visited Tripoli while salvaging Roman remains at Leptis Magna for the Prince Regent. Smyth was hugely impressed by Warrington's obviously dominating relationship with the Pasha, and in an important official despatch to Malta and London he confirmed the Pasha's standing offer to protect any British travellers through and beyond his dominions. As Smyth wrote:

I am becoming still more convinced that here—through this place and by means of these people—is an open gateway into the interior of Africa. By striking south from Tripoli, a traveller will reach Bornu before he is out of Yusuf's influence, and wherever his power reaches, the protecting virtues of the British flag are known... I think this ought to be the chosen route, because it is practicable into the very heart of the most benighted quarter of the globe.[17]

Yet Britain was never able to make Tripoli into another Hong Kong or Singapore between the Sahara and the Mediterranean. The policy of using it as a base for African penetration was founded on delusions and contradictions. The first such delusion was that the influence of Yusuf Pasha Karamanli, as he had claimed, reached across the Sahara as far as Bornu and the great Hausa states. His tax-raising powers in reality barely extended beyond Bani Ulid, about one hundred miles south-east of Tripoli, while his commercial and diplomatic interests were limited, at their furthest, to Fezzan. He had no relations, friendly, diplomatic or otherwise, with any of the black potentates of the Sudan.

The second delusion was that by ending both Saharan slave trading and slave raiding, Britain would be able to foster an alternative, morally-acceptable commerce in the raw materials of inner Africa and in so doing help to promote the economic and social advancement of the continent. While it is true that the abolition of slave raiding from Fezzan would improve general security and wellbeing among vulnerable communities of the southern desert and pre-desert, and restore Tripoli's good name, the abolition of the slave trade itself would in reality be economically disastrous not only for Tripoli, but for the whole trans-Saharan commercial system. This was because the northbound traffic in black slaves was by far the most profitable part of the whole long, difficult and risky desert trading system, and that without the trade in slaves as its mainstay, that system would simply collapse. This is exactly what did happen when European-inspired abolition began to take widespread effect across northern Africa later in the nineteenth century.

Delusion number three was that, apart from its enslaved peoples, Sudanic Africa offered a variety of other rich and desirable raw commodities that were well worth the dangers, troubles and expenses of carrying on a journey of many months across the Sahara to Tripoli. Yet the reality was that, apart from a little gold-dust, tiny packages of the highly-prized ingredients for perfume-making and some ivory, ostrich feathers, and hides and skins, there was little else (apart from slaves) that the traders and merchants of Mediterranean North Africa needed or wanted from the poor natural environment and societies with limited purchasing power immediately to the south of the Great Desert. In modern terms, they were trading with such inherently impoverished countries, as Chad, Niger, northern Nigeria, Mali and Burkina Faso.

Finally, the basic contradiction inherent in Warrington's trans-Saharan policy was that Britain, by now ideologically committed to the abolition of slavery and the slave trade wherever they existed in the world, was in reality hardly a suitable partner to encourage and aid a tyrant such as Yusuf Pasha Karamanli in his ambitions to open up and exploit vast slaving fiefdoms deep in Sudanic Africa.

Nevertheless between 1818 and 1826 three British government missions, through the good offices of Consul Warrington, made Tripoli their base for the exploration and penetration of the inner continent, their first purpose being to establish the course and outlet of West Africa's greatest river, the Niger. The Ritchie-Lyon mission of 1818-20 only reached Murzuk in Fezzan where its leader, Joseph Ritchie died. But George Lyon at least managed to gain much new information about Fezzan and the countries beyond it which he published in his most readable *Narrative of Travels* (London, 1821). The second expedition from Tripoli, the so-called Bornu Mission of 1822-25 (Dr. Walter Oudney, Lt. Hugh Clapperton RN and Major Dixon Denham), was by far the most successful, shedding much new light on the geography of inner Africa and making promising diplomatic contacts with Sudanic rulers. The last mission was the solo journey south-westwards from Tripoli to Timbuctu by Alexander Gordon Laing. He was the first known European to reach that city, a byword for remoteness and still with a commercial and intellectual reputation earned some three centuries earlier, but barely valid by 1825. Laing was killed soon after he set out on his return journey. His story has a particular romantic twist in that during the two months he spent as the Warrington's house-guest in Tripoli, he had found the time and opportunity to woo the consul's second daughter, Emma. On the eve of Laing's departure for Timbuctu Warrington, in his official capacity, joined them in a marriage that he

Starting out from Tripoli, Major Alexander Gordon Laing was in 1826 the first known European to reach the remote, fabulous city of Timbuctu.

would not allow them to consummate.

Further attempts by Consul Warrington up to the mid-1840s to make Tripoli Britain's recognized Gateway to Africa were not a success. He tried for many years to promote rebellious mid-Saharan tribal leaders as the agents of Britain's abolitionist and commercial policies across the Great Desert, and to advance the cause of slave trade abolition and its replacement by other commerce by opening vice consulates at the main slaving entrepôts of Murzuk and Ghadames. But by about 1860 London, at least, had realized that the Sahara, and the lands immediately beyond it, were (with the possible exception of northern Nigeria) not even worth commercial penetration, let alone imperial expansion.

The first known European to cross nearly the full width of northern Libya, from Tripoli almost to the frontier of Egypt, was Paolo della Cella. He was a Genoese who in 1817 served as a surgeon with the army of the Bey of Tripoli (the Pasha's eldest son) led into Cyrenaica to put down a rebellion. In 1821-22 the brothers Frederick and Henry Beechey surveyed the whole coast from Tripoli to Benghazi. After the three great British missions into the Sahara between 1818 and 1825, Tripoli was also the base for the Saharan and Sudanic travels of the anti-slavery agent, James Richardson (1845-46) and the Central African Mission of 1849-55 in which Richardson was joined by the notable German polymath, Dr.

Heinrich Barth, and another German, Dr. Adolf Overweg. Barth's five years in the Sahara and Sudan convinced him (and also in due course his sponsor, the British government) that Britain's most promising approach to the richer parts of inner West Africa was up the River Niger and its tributaries and not across the Sahara from Tripoli: that route could safely be left to any other power that cared to make use of it.

Other nineteenth-century European travellers and explorers who took up the Saharan challenge and continued to use Tripoli as their base for their penetration of the Great Desert and what lay beyond it were mainly French and German. In 1859 the young Frenchman, Henri Duveyrier made important contacts with the Ajjer Tuareg of south-west Tripolitania; the Germans Gustav Nachtigal and Gerhard Rohlfs explored deep into and across the central desert lands from Tripoli in the 1860s and 1870s Rohlfs became convinced during his travels that Consul Warrington had all along been right about Tripoli: that this was indeed the most favoured point of departure for travellers into the interior, and therefore the most promising terminus for the trans-Saharan railway planned from the 1870s onwards to link the emerging French empire in North and West Africa.

The travels of Rohlfs and Nachtigal perhaps marked the end of the "heroic age" of Tripoli-based central Saharan exploration. There were no more original discoveries to be made there by geographical expeditions with underlying diplomatic, political and commercial undertones. The Turkish authorities, increasingly anxious to safeguard their last remaining North African possessions in the face of European expansion, became more reluctant to authorize travel into the interior by foreigners. The few Europeans who did manage to use this Ottoman imperial outpost as a base for their travels were crossing essentially familiar ground already explored, and they had little of substance to add to the findings of the earlier nineteenth-century pioneers.

Visitors to both Karamanli and Turkish Tripoli in the nineteenth century generally agreed that ("for an oriental state") it was relatively clean, orderly, moderately well governed, and usually tolerant of its religious and ethnic minorities, both slave and free. "The present government of Tripoli is very mild," remarked one anonymous witness in 1830, "and even an aggrieved Jew has a chance of obtaining justice." Ali Bey Abbassi, the Spaniard who travelled across the Maghreb in the guise of a Turk, found in 1804 that Tripoli society was "much more free and easy than in Morocco".

European renegades, he wrote, "may obtain the highest rank", and the Christian slaves were well treated and were allowed to trade and open businesses "on condition of giving part of the profits to Government".

As for the ruling tyrant, Yusuf Pasha Karamanli, Ali Bey described him as "a sensible man":

> He... speaks good Italian, and has a fine countenance; he is fond of pomp, magnificence and show, he is endowed with dignity, and his manners are agreeable and polite. He has reigned already about ten years and a half, and the people seem very much satisfied with him.
>
> Sidi Yusuf keeps but two women, the one, his cousin, is of a fair complexion, the other is a negress. He has three sons and three daughters by the former, and one son and two daughters by the latter. He has some negresses for slaves, but no whites. He likes that his women should use all possible luxury and magnificence in their dress and in their houses.[18]

Other contemporary travellers were much impressed by the splendour of Yusuf Pasha's court and his style of dressing—costly silks sprinkled with gems, and an immense turban. Popular and "sensible" though this ruler may have been, he was also an ambitious, ruthless, pitiless and spendthrift tyrant. His lavish personal and public tastes became too much for the slender local economy to support, and after nearly forty years of extravagance, his rule ended in bankruptcy.

As ruler of this small state, the Pasha had, and exercised, supreme and usually unquestioned authority. But he was advised and guided in affairs of state and municipal administration by what in effect was a small council of ministers (*Divan*) whose individual responsibilities ranged from foreign relations and military affairs to the capital's public health and bread supply. The Pasha also administered Islamic civil and criminal law, with appropriate specialized advice. He usually judged serious criminal cases himself. Some crimes were considered capital by law but, according to the British traveller George Lyon, "many are rendered so by the whim of the Bashaw, in which case hanging, decapitating and strangling are used". Whatever its shortcomings, this arbitrary system of justice at least had the advantage of delivering prompt judgements. Verdicts were followed by swift punishments, including death, sometimes inflicted on the spot. Again according to Lyon,

The Moors are never employed as hangman; but the first Jew who happens to be at hand has that office conferred upon him, and is obliged to accompany the culprit to the ramparts over the town gate, attended by the guards and mob, when he puts on the rope well or ill according to his ability, attaching it to a bolt fixed in the wall for that purpose. The unfortunate victim is then forced through an embrasure, and suspended by the side of the gateway, so as to be seen by all who enter or leave the town. When decapitation is the punishment, the head alone is exposed to public view.[19]

The Pasha's guard (in effect, the standing army) consisted of about 100 cavalry (supposedly "Turks" but actually of fairly mixed origins) and 300 infantry, many of them black slaves. They had no uniforms and, with their motley styles of dress, Lyon judged their appearance to be "very curious". When the Pasha mounted a military campaign outside the capital, he would summon the desert and pre-desert tribal sheikhs to contribute the necessary cavalry and foot soldiers, with their mounts, weapons and appropriate banners, to reinforce his small corps of professionals; those who failed to do so in good time risked a punitive invasion of their encampments. (Such a system of tribal recruitment in an emergency was still, even in the Tripoli oasis, an effective, popular military response to the Italian invasion of 1911.)

The corsair fleet was under the authority and supervision of the *Rais della Marina* (or *Kapudan Pasha*)—titles reflecting a historical terminology drawn from a variety of language sources. He worked through the *Taiffa*, the council of ships' captains. The *Rais* was often a European renegade who had "turned Turk" (accepted Islam) to better his prospects on first being brought to Tripoli as a slave, probably many years before. The holder of this prestigious office in the early nineteenth century was Murad Rais (alias the Scotsman Peter Lyle) whose status had been confirmed by his marriage to one of the Pasha's daughters. The *Rais* and the *Taiffa* regulated the seasonal operations of the corsair fleet in Mediterranean waters. In cooperation with the European consuls, they also supervised the strict division of the corsairs' booty from a successful cruise, with captives' fate (freedom, chances of ransom or slavery) decided by their nationality, wealth or status.

During the Napoleonic wars the Tripoli corsairs had taken advantage of the international crisis by reviving the scale and scope of their operations, and by 1804 the fleet counted eleven small ships mounting a total of 103 guns, with two more hulls taking shape in the arsenal. But with the return of peace in 1815 and the powers' new-found determination to end the corsair threat for good, by 1830 Tripoli's only operational warships were a handful of inshore gunboats.

George Lyon, who spent some months in Tripoli in 1818-19 before his journey with Joseph Ritchie to Fezzan, was especially intrigued by the town's *marabuts*. They were, he asserted, of two classes:

> ... idiots, who are allowed to say and do whatever they please; and men possessed of all their senses, who, by juggling and performing many bold and disgusting tricks, establish themselves the exclusive right of being the greatest rogues and nuisances to be met with. There are mosques in which these people assemble every Friday afternoon, and where they eat snakes, scorpions, &c. affecting to be inspired, and committing the greatest extravagancies...
>
> During the time the Maraboots (who are guarded and attended by a great number of people) are allowed to parade the streets, no Christians or Jews can with any safety make their appearance, as they would, if once in the power of these wretches, be instantly torn to pieces; indeed, wherever they show themselves on their terraces or from windows, they are sure of a plentiful shower of stones from the boys who are in attendance.[20]

Lyon reported that two "grand markets" were held weekly—one along the sandy beach every Tuesday (*Suq al-Talat*) and the other on Fridays at the outlying Menscia village named after its market, *Suq al-Giuma*. The covered bazaars in the Old City were open every day:

> The shops of merchants are ranged on each side, and are very small. Slaves and goods are carried about before the traders by auctioneers, who keep up a continual din, each calling the last price bidden.[21]

The Jewish community had its own quarter with its own shops, and was shut off by gates from the rest of the town at sunset. As Lyon reported,

"These people are much persecuted, yet they contrive to engross all the trade and places of profit. They are forbidden... to wear gaudy clothes, and are only allowed turbans of blue."

As for education, Lyon found that there were a few schools at which a little reading and writing were taught "in a very noisy manner":

> A knowledge of letters, however, is by no means necessary to constitute a great man, or to advance him to any post of trust; in this there exists an example in the present minister, Sidi Hamet (who was formerly Rais el Marsa or Captain of the port), and who can neither read nor write.[22]

Drunkenness, according to Lyon, was more common in early nineteenth-century Tripoli "than even in most towns in England":

> There are public wine-houses, at the doors of which the Moors sit and drink without any scruple; and the Saldanah, or place of the guard, is seldom without a few drunkards. The greater part of the better sort of people also drink very hard; but their favourite beverage is Rosolia, an Italian cordial [*Rosolio*, distilled from rose petals], and it is not uncommon for visitors, when making calls, to give unequivocal hints that a little rum would be well received.[23]

There were also many prostitutes who, according to Lyon, had to live in a particular quarter of town under a "Chowse" [*Shaush*] appointed expressly for that purpose. "These women are obliged daily to supply food for the Bashaw's dogs which guard the Arsenal."

As in most oriental cities, the public baths were not only for personal hygiene, but also an important feature of social life. Lyon described the normal routine in such a place:

> The bather, on stripping, is girded round the middle with a linen cloth, and one also is thrown over the shoulders, which is taken off on entering the vapour chamber. This is a large circular room, having a dome, through which the light is admitted by many small holes well stopped by glass, and by which means the air is entirely excluded. The light is much obscured by the vapour, which constantly rises; lamps are therefore kept burning, those who first enter being for a time unable to see their way.

Bathers lay down on broad stone benches raised round the sides of this hot chamber, and water was thrown over them "so as to induce a quicker perspiration". The heat was excessive.

> When a sufficient time has elapsed to produce languor and strong perspiration, an assistant approaches and rubs the skin with a glove of hair, in such a way as to cause the cuticle to peel off in large dark rolls, however clean and white the skin may have appeared previously to this operation. He then proceeds to shampooing... The operations have thus finished, some soap is brought to the bather and he remains sitting under a spout of warm water as long as he pleases. Dry cloths are then brought to him, and being well wrapped up, he is conducted to an outer room, where [water smoking] pipes and coffee are placed before him, with incense to perfume the beard, after which he dresses and sallies out... The men come in the morning, and the women in the afternoon.[24]

The Turks Return

By 1830 the 120-year Karamanli domination of Tripoli and its affairs had reached a state of terminal crisis. The city-state was bankrupt, its coinage debased, its credit exhausted, its foreign debts (notably to Britain, France and Egypt) unpayable, and even extraordinary levies on the Jewish community were no longer feasible. The interior tribes (encouraged, if not armed, by the British Consul) were in revolt and had cut the trade routes to Fezzan; while in the capital Britain and France vied for local primacy. In July 1832, after nearly forty years on the throne, Yusuf Pasha Karamanli abdicated in favour of his son Ali. But the succession was disputed, with the British and French Consuls, the town and the Menscia (the easterly garden suburb) supporting rival claimants. In the midst of this chaos the Ottoman government sent a fleet into the harbour in March 1835 to depose the last of the Karamanlis and to re-impose the Sultan's direct authority from Constantinople.

After the French occupation of Algiers in 1830 and Mohammad Ali's achievement of near-independence in Egypt, the Turks' clear motive in returning to Tripoli was to prevent further loss of nominally Ottoman territory in North Africa. But a succession of Ottoman governors (with the title of Pasha) found like the Karamanli Pashas before them that the tribes, while duly paying their homage to the Sultan, were quite unwilling to pay his taxes or to submit in any way to his authority unless persuaded to do so by superior force of arms. The result was that Tripoli became the forward Turkish military base for a long, brutal and bloody war of conquest that only brought the desert and pre-desert tribes to order in 1858.

The undisputed possession of Tripoli and its hinterland was to remain a prime Turkish objective for the next 75 years. While north-west Africa (the Maghreb) eventually came under French and some Spanish control, Britain became predominant in Egypt and the Nilotic (Anglo-Egyptian) Sudan. Between these two great power blocs, Turkey's renewed tenure of Tripoli seemed to provide a secure basis for the Ottoman Empire's claims, based on the hinterland principle, to vast, if undefined and internationally unrecognized possessions reaching even as far as the rainforests of equatorial Africa. In modern terms, these claims included the whole of the Chad Republic and parts of Algeria, Niger, Nigeria, Cameroon and the Central African Republic. But only at the beginning of the twentieth century did Constantinople make any realistic attempts to establish such claims on the ground by planting small garrisons at a few almost unknown oases in what is now northern Chad to protect the caravan routes to and from the Mediterranean coast.

Yet it can be argued that the accepted Turkish possession of Tripoli in particular, and the at least nominal possession of what is now Libya in general, did much to preserve a certain local popular awareness of Islamic identity, culture and self-reliance well into the twentieth century. The people's recognition of the Ottoman Sultan's role as Caliph of Islam reinforced a continuing sense of Muslim political and religious solidarity throughout one of the last regions of Africa to face the European imperial challenge.

Tripoli seems indeed to have inspired its succession of modern rulers, at least, with the Turkish conviction (or delusion) that they should possess and dominate much more of the African continent than the actual, recognized territory of what is now Libya. Thus, in the early nineteenth century Yusuf Pasha Karamanli had his own trans-Saharan "imperial" ambitions in the central Sudan, as the Ottoman Turks later staked claims extending to the Congo watershed. The Italians still hoped in the early twentieth century that their possession of Tripoli would give them strong territorial claims and rights of access towards Lake Chad. Colonel Muammar Gaddafi, from his Tripoli redoubt, put such ambitions into actual, if ephemeral, military practice through the Libyan invasion and occupation of the northern third of the neighbouring Chad Republic in the 1970s and 1980s; and in the same spirit he later cultivated an image as a leader of popular, pan-African significance and influence.

By the 1850s the town and port of Tripoli were in continuing economic trouble. This was mostly because the Saharan slave trade which the Turkish rulers had positively encouraged as the mainstay of local prosperity, and most reliable source of taxation, was being curbed by European (mainly British) moral pressure. Caravans that used to deliver an average of up to 2,000 black slaves to the town every year were now diverting their business to places where the trade was still either encouraged—notably Morocco and, to a lesser extent, Egypt—or was quietly tolerated, such as the smaller and less noticed Turkish outpost of Benghazi. In Tripoli the Turkish authorities had as yet found no comparable substitute for this formerly lucrative trade. Then Wilhelm Heine, a German artist who visited the town in 1859 (to prepare for the US government a series of paintings depicting the naval war of 1801-05) found that

> Another blow to trade has been a famine which has lasted for several years, and the resultant prohibition of exports of cattle for slaughter, and cereals, which used to be shipped in large quantities to Malta [for Royal Naval and garrison victualling]. And to judge by the slackness in taking measures to avoid another such shortage, once it takes effect there seems to be no prospect of a return to previous prosperity.

Nevertheless, Heine still found that

> There are many bakers in town. But because of the shortage of wood, they try to save fuel by just one baker undertaking to light his big oven, and whoever else wants to use it pays to bake his bread. So in the morning one sees semi-naked men running from all directions balancing on their heads long bread trays filled with unleavened and unsalted flat bread, all the time crying out *balek, balek* to avoid collisions with the passers-by.[25]

Other foreign visitors were intrigued by the strange arrangement of the traditional Tripoli bakery shops. Swainson Cowper in 1897 explained:

> These are situated in the open street, right on to which the oven mouth opens, while the baker stands before it in a sort of pit, so that his chest is about on a level with the street. To insert and withdraw the loaves he uses a sort of shovel with an immensely long handle, which when he draws them out, is brought a long way across the street, so that the passers-by are compelled to wait until it can be removed.[26]

According to Wilhelm Heine in the 1850s, because there was no running water, the flour-mills scattered around the town were worked by camel power:

> Large groups of women and children gather before the buildings housing the machinery, each one with their basket full of the grain to be milled. This is poured onto the mill-stone, which the camel then turns round, pulling on a cross-bar wedged in the stone. If the animal is not already blind with old age, he is fitted with blinkers of woven straw. A little bell, activated by the motion of the mill, provides the music these animals love. The miller himself contributes an accompaniment of strange melodies on a small wooden flute. Each customer collects his flour in a bag placed under the mill-stone, and when the process is finished, gives some of it to the miller as payment.[27]

Bread was also sold in the seaside market outside the Castle where, according to another visitor, "hundreds of Arabs crouch all day under their barracans in the hot sunshine, keeping guard over loaves of bright yellow and other tints, unhygienic but artistic".

As for the local medical services, Wilhelm Heine was informed that the town's physicians were of two types: those who *let* their patients die and those who *made* them die—"and as the latter resolved the crisis more quickly, they were more highly regarded by the public".

Heine found the lives of expatriates in this remote imperial outpost to have been very restricted:

> Horse rides along the beach in the cool of the evening are a universal relaxation, and often donkeys, big and fine with a more

easy gait, are preferred to horses. Sunday is a day for the exchange of visits, for dinner and supper invitations. As in most places rarely visited by outsiders, new arrivals are given a warm welcome, and there are indeed few of them who cannot have a grateful memory of the open and cordial hospitality enjoyed during their stay.[28]

The evenings were enlivened by performances by the Turkish garrison band in front of the Pasha's Castle. But Heine judged that

> Its purpose seems to be not so much harmony as bedlam, and as some of the musicians apparently try to finish their own parts as quickly as possible, so the resultant concert is not particularly pleasing.[29]

Nevertheless, Tripoli seems to have pleased its foreign visitors. The travelling Dutch heiress Alexine Tinne, who arrived in 1868, was able to write:

> Here I have found again something of the *bonhommie* of Egypt, which even fanaticism cannot check. The people seem happy and healthy, and where are seen the awful scarecrows that shocked one's sight in Algeria? Great cordiality seems to exist among the natives and the Europeans... and the people are most kind to me.[30]

A view of Tripoli, 1871.

Miss Tinne startled Tripoline polite society by importing "a velocipede of the latest Parisian manufacture" but (according to *The Times*) "not finding it adapted to the sands of the Great Desert, she presented it to the Pasha of Tripoli".

At about the same time the great German traveller Gustav Nachtigal warned

> In visiting an oriental town the traveller must become accustomed to disappointments. The cleanliness and glitter seen from a distance became, when viewed from within, dirt, decay and misery. Tripoli, too, did not live up to its promise without, however presenting such an impression of decline as do many of its sister towns on the Mediterranean coast.[31]

Foreign travellers were particularly struck by the filthiness of the Jewish quarters and their inhabitants in the Old City, and of the largely Jewish village of Amrus, in the eastern oasis. Significantly, perhaps, one of the sharpest critics of these places was the Jewish traveller and *savant*, Nahum Slouschz, who between 1906 and 1909 made three visits to Turkish North Africa. He described Amrus in unflattering terms:

> In the foreground, two streets formed a sort of bazaar, occupied chiefly by Jewish blacksmiths and, huddled about this, were groups of hovels in filthy alleys, littered with the debris of food trampled into the mud and forming a hideous swamp. And the swarming humanity about us was, sadly enough, in perfect keeping with the picture—in unwashed bands they beset us and kept pace with us. True, they were robust and well-built, fine specimens of humanity, but—and may the God of Israel pardon this offence—the one idea that possessed me was how to keep them from getting too close to me.[32]

In the later nineteenth century the Turks did make some belated efforts to reform and modernize this, their last possession in North Africa. They improved the municipal administration and services of their imperial outpost—some streets were actually paved and "faint lamps, fed by petroleum, were set here and there in gloomy corners". Measures were taken to curb the continuing, clandestine trade in slaves, to encourage trans-

Saharan business in such goods as hides, skins, ivory and ostrich feathers, to found a local newspaper, *Trables*, and from the 1860s to encourage the export of esparto grass (*alf-alfa*) which grew wild in the hills of northern Tripolitania. The Turks also founded a military school in Tripoli, which by the early twentieth century had ten instructors and 150 students. In addition to the traditional Koranic schools, there were two primary schools (one for girls), an intermediate school and a teacher training institute. The Jewish, Italian and French communities had schools of their own.

Of course, remarked a British visitor in 1897, "in Tripoli anything that requires any head work is in the hands of Europeans". He elaborated:

> There are the quarantine and the lazaretto, which are under a sort of international board; the lighthouse is French; there is the Eastern Telegraph Company; and although there is, of course, a Turkish post office, the Italian one is much more important. To show the management of the Turkish post, it may be mentioned that on a mail day, it was found on inquiry that the postmaster had a stock of only fifteen stamps for foreign countries, but he thought that if he sent round the bazaars he might raise a few more. His applications to Constantinople for a new stock had been repeatedly disregarded.[33]

As a relatively remote outpost of the Ottoman Empire, Tripoli and its hinterland were "a sort of colony for political suspects", as an early twentieth-century American visitor put it. She reported that "a good many exiles lived in the white city who brought the very atmosphere of Constantinople with them, the elegance, the grace of living which no transportation could disguise..."

> Many other interesting exiles were banished from Constantinople for they knew not what imaginary offense or suspected crime, but their loyalty to the Sultan seemed unshaken and their almost daily hope of return pathetically unquenched.[34]

Such political exiles in the provincial capital were clearly much better off than those unfortunates who found themselves banished to such really isolated and unhealthy places as the oasis of Murzuk in Fezzan, which was known as "the Turkish Siberia".

Towards the end of the nineteenth century two new types of travelling inquirer started to arrive in Turkish Tripoli. The first were scientists, commercial agents, nationalists and journalists from the newly-united Kingdom of Italy, eager to probe and assess the resources and potential of this neglected Ottoman territory as a future Italian settler colony. They saw its main port as a strategic naval base protecting Italian maritime interests by its command of the southern shore of the central Mediterranean. The city itself had potential as a revived trading centre dominating the shortest and most direct overland routes to central Africa, while its hinterland was judged to have huge agricultural potential.

The other group of travellers consisted of moneyed, leisured European and American tourists armed with cameras, notebooks and water-colour sketch-books. They were fascinated by Turkish Tripoli, its various peoples and its surroundings as original and exotic curiosities, as yet barely touched by the intrusions and influences of the modern world. The titles of some of the books recording these tourists' adventures seem to reflect a collective romantic vision: *The Gateway to the Sahara*; *Tripoli the Mysterious*; *The Country of the Moors*; *The Magic Gate of the Sahara*. To one early twentieth-century American visitor, Mabel Loomis Todd, this was a town of "a radiant vision". Indeed, writing in 1912, just after the Italian invasion, she recalled that it had been

> more picturesque under Ottoman rule than it can ever be again— dreamy, dirty, sordid, exquisite, noisy, enthralling, beautiful, unsanitary,—the strange city gripped one's affections... Whatever it may have been, Tripoli was a city of enchantment, white as dreams of Paradise, fringed by palms and olives, and steeped in memories of the centuries.[35]

Chapter Five
Italian Tripoli

Why on earth have they sent us here to die for the sake of seizing these deserts?
Soldier Donato Magro

Italy is your father because it has married Tripoli, which is your mother.
General Caneva

Splende la pace in Tripoli latina. Gabriele D'Annunzio

Tripoli—the city, the port and all the land now called Libya— was by the early twentieth century destined for a new and more prestigious role. No longer was it to be a neglected outpost of a slowly disintegrating empire, significant only as the left-over space between British-occupied Egypt to the east and the French protectorate of Tunisia to the west. Rather, it was to become the credential, the physical affirmation, of young Italy's claims to Great Power status. In the decades after her own unification and independence of 1861, the Kingdom of Italy had acquired an unpromising colony on the Red Sea (Eritrea) and another on the Horn of Africa (Somalia), while in 1896 an Italian army attempting to conquer the Ethiopian Empire had been soundly defeated in battle at Adowa. And historically, strategically and commercially, East African colonies were remote from modern Italy's natural spheres of interest.

Tripoli (in its fullest geographical sense) was by contrast the obvious first objective (after Tunis) of Italian imperial expansion, and it was as yet unclaimed by any other European power. Strategically, its possession would reinforce Italian naval control of the narrow seas between Sicily, Malta and Africa, as well as the central Mediterranean triangle whose base was defined by the line of ports from Tobruk to Zuara, its second side reaching from Zuara up the south-east coast of Sicily to Albania, and the third side linking Albania to Tobruk. Then, at a time when hundreds of thousands of landless peasants (Italy's greatest resource) were migrating every year in search of a better life in the Americas and elsewhere, Tripoli was seen as an agricultural colony of magnificent potential where settlers would keep their *Italianità* while working to their own and the Mother Country's benefit. Hence the vision of the poet Giovanni Pascoli of Italy as a "proletarian nation", its people bestirring themselves for their North African venture. And, of course, once Italy was installed in Tripoli, and the desert trade routes had been secured, the wealth of inner Africa would readily find its way across the Sahara and the Mediterranean to Italy whose own, belated industrial revolution would supply the manufactured goods Africans would be eager to accept in exchange.

Such visions were promoted in the early twentieth century by an active nationalist lobby. Visiting journalists and other investigators sent home highly coloured, misleading and often downright mendacious reports of a neglected but rich agricultural potential which the touch of Italian skill and hard work would release in all its abundance. Tripoli was presented almost as *un paese di Bengodì* (a mythic Land of Cockaigne). Giuseppe Bevione of the Turin daily *La Stampa* found the Tripoli oasis to be "a little paradise". It was said to have two million palm-trees which, he affirmed, "were a sign of water at a little depth and an essential condition for the life of more tender vegetation". That was fair comment so far as this particular limited area was concerned, but it was certainly not true

Long Live Italy! A 1911 postcard sent from newly-occupied Tripoli.

hat endless stretches of both Tripolitania and Cyrenaica rested on "an uninterrupted stratum [of water] sometimes one or two metres below he surface". Nor was it true, as Bevione insisted, that the Libyan people detested their Turkish rulers, would welcome the Italians with open arms as liberators and would be happy to sell them the best land near Tripoli and other towns "for a few *lire* a hectare". And as for ownerless tribal lands, they were there for the taking! In September 1911 the *Giornale di Sicilia* went further, insisting that "the people of Tripoli are favourable to the Italians... there will be no objection to a foreigner occupying Arab land". "Arab hostility", according to Giuseppe Piazza of *La Tribuna*, was "a Turkish myth". Even the popular songwriters joined the chorus, their biggest hit being *Tripoli, bel suol d'amore (Tripoli, Beautiful Land of Love)*. It concluded with the reassurance that *Tripoli, terra incantata,/ Sarà italiana al rombo del cannon* (The enchanting land of Tripoli/Will be Italian at the roar of the cannon).

Confident in such delusions, Italy at the fiftieth anniversary year of its own unification and independence declared war on Turkey on 29 September 1911. It did so on the very flimsy pretext that the small Italian communities in Tripoli and other places were in danger. Three days later a large Italian battle fleet appeared off the port: there were three new 12,000-ton battleships with twelve-inch and other guns, three heavy cruisers and protecting screens of destroyers and torpedo boats. While talks were opened to save the city from a destructive bombardment, the Italian community of about 1,200 people was ferried to safety. The city and its oasis were defended by five Turkish land forts equipped with outdated short-range German artillery. Naval bombardment of these outlying strong points (from many miles out to sea) started in the afternoon of 3 October, ceased at dusk and resumed the next morning. Fort Hamidie (the former English Fort) on the coast east of the city was spectacularly destroyed when its magazine blew up. On 5 October 900 marines went ashore, secured the heavily-damaged Turkish forts and raised the Italian flag over them; later the same day 1,700 sailors occupied the city.

Tripoli had apparently fallen without a fight: a short naval bombardment without risk to the attacker had seemingly prepared the ground for the mere "military parade" that had been expected against an inept Turkish defence. As one newly-landed foot-soldier wrote home:

Italian troops enter Tripoli.

Just to let you know that we have landed at Tripoli... all the people are for us. There are even Tripoline *Carabinieri* [paramilitary police] who have taken an oath to serve Italy. And every day they shout "Long Live Italian Tripoli!" even saying it in Italian... In Tripoli three-quarters of us are Italian troops and the rest are natives... The Turks have retreated from the coast and have left all their stores and stuff behind them—heaps of grain, flour, sugar and coffee. They have abandoned all their fortifications, which by now have been destroyed by splendid Italian shells—walls down, boats sunk, torpedo boats, warships, which actually seems rather a shame.[36]

Another squaddie of the regiment of *Bersaglieri*, (distinguished by their plumed helmets and marching at the double), one Donato Magro, took a rather more cynical, or perhaps realistic, view of the military prospects:

As soon as we landed here we saw a beautiful city with fine buildings, which was Tripoli. But we landed on the beach because there's no port... It seems to be all sand and trees. At my first sight I declared, "Why on earth have they sent us here to die for the sake of seizing these deserts?"

But then we began to discover the beautiful country beyond Tripoli, rich in all kinds of produce: olives, oranges, lemons and many other varieties I cannot describe. And I was sorry for having called it a desert.[37]

The Turkish commander, meanwhile, had made an orderly withdrawal into the oasis with fewer than 5,000 men to spare the city from destruction. There he was surprised when his regulars were joined by hundreds, and then by thousands, of armed tribesmen, accompanied by women to cook, tend the wounded and to lay out and mourn over the dead. The tribespeople, far from welcoming the Italians, had ridden to support the Turks in their defence of this *Dar al-Islam* (Land of Islam) against the Christian invader.

Rather than mount an immediate offensive against this hostile build-up, the outnumbered Italians chose to start digging in outside the city walls and await the arrival of their main expeditionary force, which sailed into the port from Naples and Palermo a full week after the first shore landings. Thirty-eight steamers escorted by warships brought in 20,000 troops with heavy artillery, horses, mules and waggons, as well as motor transport and other new weapons of war: barbed wire, machine guns, searchlights, wireless telegraphy and aeroplanes and airships. Tripoli in 1911-12 was to be the first active theatre of the new semi-mechanized warfare of the early twentieth century. Here, three years before the First World War began, the Italian military anticipated, rehearsed and tested some of that war's battlefield innovations. Yet, even with these weapons and large reinforcements, it failed to attack decisively, preferring to dig into fixed positions covered by heavy artillery, barbed wire and machine gun nests in a defensive semi-circular perimeter beyond the city walls. Senior commanders still recalled the battle of Adowa only fifteen years before, and lesser East African military setbacks: but desert warfare is essentially a campaign of movement, not fixed positions.

In the meantime, there were similar amphibious landings at Benghazi, Tobruk, Derna and Homs, where small bridgeheads were well defended by the great naval guns offshore. But, as at Tripoli, attempts to break out and advance inland were soon halted by counter-attacking Turkish regular and Libyan irregular land forces.

Back in Italy these seemingly successful landings were celebrated with banner headlines. Newly-published postcards showed sailors raising the national flag over the ruins of Tripoli's Turkish forts and (particularly significant) the Roman Arch of Marcus Aurelius; they were overprinted with slogans such as "Dreams of Glory" and "Long Live Italian Tripoli". One of the most striking images of the war was a widely-reproduced painting by Fortunino Matania making the point that Italy had returned to North Africa to reclaim the legacy of Rome. It showed an Italian sailor, newly-landed on the shore of Tripoli, with the national flag furled under his left arm, while with his right taking up the untarnished sword from a Roman Centurion's skeleton lying in the sand: "Young Italy has dared once more to draw the sword of the Caesars in North Africa".

All such easy illusions were thrown into confusion when, less than three weeks after the first landings, Italian fixed positions at Henni, Sciara Sciatt, Sidi Mesri and other points on the east of the Tripoli oasis were counter-attacked and overwhelmed. The fact that supposedly loyal and pacified local people had taken up arms and joined the Turks in this fighting prompted especially harsh counter-measures against these "traitors" in the oasis and in the city itself. Many locals found with weapons were hanged, shot or deported to small Italian offshore islands. Such a panic-stricken reaction reflected badly on the military, which for the past half century had been taking similar draconian measures to suppress so-called *banditismo*—effectively, popular revolt—in the Italian *mezzogiorno* and islands. It also suggested to foreign observers, at least, that Italy would find it no easier than had the French in Algeria since 1830 to conquer and pacify the people of North Africa—not even with an overwhelming superiority in modern arms.

The War in the Air

The most strikingly dramatic of these arms were undoubtedly the Italian airships and the aeroplanes, which went to war for the very first time over the war zones of Tripoli, Benghazi and Tobruk in the autumn of 1911, only eight years after the Wright brothers' first powered flight. A *Flottiglia Aviatori* of ten newly-qualified officer-pilots with nine French and Austrian aeroplanes and supporting ground crew arrived in Tripoli with the main expeditionary force in early October. They set up a military airfield near the Jewish Cemetery, to the south-west of the city walls. On 23 October the commander of this air detachment, Captain Carlo Piazza, became the first airman to fly over enemy lines when he made a one-hour reconnaissance flight from Tripoli to and from the main Turco-Arab camp at Azizia, some thirty miles to the south. The next day Captain Ricardo Moizo flew as far as Garian, around fifty miles south of Tripoli, and according to the local Turkish commander, inspired the Berber tribesmen of the Western Gebel to believe that a noted *marabut*, Sidi Abd-al-Rahman, had miraculously flown to their support. During later propaganda flights leaflets were dropped on enemy lines (despite the illiteracy of most of the intended recipients) and pilots also began target-spotting for the land-based artillery and the naval gunners offshore. At first they used a simple system of visual signals; but wireless trials, supervised at Tobruk by Guglielmo Marconi himself, soon followed.

Then the aircraft itself became a means of attack, with pilots dropping crude two-kilo bomblets the size of an orange onto enemy positions below. The first such raid was on 1 November 1911 when Lieutenant Giulio Gavotti, piloting an Austrian-built *Etrich*, dropped one bomb on the Turco-Arab camp at Ain Zara, at the edge of the Tripoli oasis, and three more on the camp at Tagiura. The start of this dramatic and alarming new form of aerial warfare was announced with banner headlines in the Italian press, and it at once caught the imagination of the populace and the leading contemporary poet, Gabriele D'Annunzio. This *vate* (poet of national significance) was (from his safe bankrupt's exile in France) already contributing a series of verses on the Tripoli war in Dantesque *terza rima* to the Milan daily *Corriere della Sera*. Now he had an inspiring new subject and dynamic poetic images of the pilots on their "flimsy ramparts" to play with. In *La Canzone della Diana*, published in the *Corriere* of 23 November, he imagined how

S'ode nel cielo un sibilo di frombe
Passa nel cielo un pallido avevoltoio.
Giulio Gavotti porta le sue bombe.

A rushing sound of siege catapults is heard in the sky.
A pale eagle passes across the sky.
Giulio Gavotti is carrying his bombs.

The poet later went on to imagine how the pilot's heart must have exalted at the subsequent explosion on the ground.

So what of these pioneer airmen in the war-zone around and beyond Tripoli and its oasis? One of them, Captain Piazza, later described what it was like for him and the others to take it in turns to fly over enemy lines. They, of course, met no opposition in the air, but they were vulnerable to the thousands of enemy marksmen on the ground:

> We are up there, alone in the immensity of space, without a friend of any sort who can see us and report on how we die. The noise of the engine blots out everything. All around and below us is a flowering of little white cloudy puffs: they are shots aimed at us; we can only indistinctly make out those who are firing them, and there is no possible response we can make... If the engine gives out, we will end up doing the most beautiful gliding flight into the very midst of gentlemen who will finish us off in the most refined manner, such must be their hatred for us devils who fly over them, spy on them and endlessly torment them without their being able to bring one of us down. Yet one bullet for us, hitting us or the plane, will either end in a crash or in an idiotic descent, as pointless as can be, right into the midst of them.[38]

In the event, when an Italian pilot did eventually crash-land amidst the enemy, he was soon treated with respect and courtesy, as Captain Ricardo Moizo later related:

> At 0620 hours on 10 September 1912 I took off from Zuara airfield on a fifty horsepower *Nieuport* monoplane to fly to Tripoli, and to make a reconnaissance on the way of all the intervening coastline.
>
> A little before Zavia the engine cut out completely. I was at 400 metres, and flying a little out to sea, to avoid being shot at. In spite of my efforts, I could not get the engine going again and I had to land not far short of our trenches fronting the sea.
>
> I saw some enemy cavalry hurrying up, arriving in time to halt a few dozen metres off and open fire; but before the aircraft had come to a complete halt, the engine came to life again and I was able to take off. I got up to 200 metres and had covered

several more kilometres when another breakdown forced me to land some 300 metres from the coast. It was now 0650 hours. As soon as I was on the ground, the engine restarted, but it ran so irregularly that I could not get off again.

So, taxiing the aircraft, I tried to reach some rather more level ground that seemed to offer a better chance of take-off. Rifle fire was now coming from individual Arabs, and others in small groups. But rolling up a slope, I found broken ground at the top that tipped the aircraft entirely over. A little knot of Arabs had fired on me a few seconds before. I emerged from underneath the plane and saw a head and a rifle appear behind a mound about fifty metres off. Certain that I had no chance of reaching our trenches, I went towards the Arab (at that moment the only one to be seen) before he took it into his head to shoot. At a few metres he signalled to me to halt. Other Arabs, some of them armed, some unarmed, lost no time in hurrying up. After a prolonged discussion, they signed to me to start walking.

Up to then, they had all looked at me from a respectful distance with a mixture of wonder and wariness.

To make me walk in the right direction, one of the Arabs took me by the sleeve, and when I objected, another took the other arm. Meanwhile a crowd collected, enlivened by the "show". They relieved me of everything I had; only my wrist watch escaped from the pillage because it was covered by the sleeve of my flying jacket. I received several buffets from behind, happily absorbed by my flying helmet and my clothes. Foot soldiers and cavalry were arriving from the nearby oasis. I then observed that one Arab horseman, finely attired, was riding close in front of me with the evident intention of keeping the over-excited elements away from me. Another horseman dressed as an Arab (actually one Lt. Raghib Effendi of the Turkish infantry) said some kind words and did the same thing. When we arrived at the oasis, the "show" reached its climax. I was made to enter the first house to the north of the road. From then on I was treated by the Turks with every consideration, while from the Arabs I had to endure nothing worse than intrusive curiosity.[39]

The popular Sunday review, *Domenica del Corriere*, published this highly fanciful cover showing Captain Ricardo Moizo's crash-landing in Arab-Turkish lines outside Tripoli in September 1912. The artist clearly knew nothing of Libyans' dress and appearance.

After aeroplanes, the Italians introduced another new weapon. At the beginning of March 1912 a report reached Turkish headquarters that the enemy were amusing themselves flying kites. These games were actually to test the wind around and over Tripoli in preparation for the flight of dirigible airships. Three Italian-built dirigibles had been tested over Venice in 1911; one was sent to Benghazi and two were shipped to Tripoli in December. But not until March 1912 was the Tripoline weather judged right for flight trials of these cumbersome machines. One of them was at last seen rising over the city like an "indistinct moon", according to the *Central News* war correspondent, H. C. Seppings-Wright, who covered the war from the Turkish lines.

Because they carried a crew of several men, were more stable than aeroplanes and could hover over areas of interest for close observation, airships were well suited to reconnaissance; they were also used to launch shrapnel bombs onto Turco-Libyan positions below, as Seppings-Wright reported:

> The various villages and camps were all systematically reconnoitred and attacked, with more or less disaster, Zanzur [west of Tripoli] being the greatest sufferer, for we counted 20 or 30 reports on each occasion, and we heard afterwards that this was the number of bombs carried by the ships.

Seppings-Wright gave a graphic account of the uncommon experience of being bombed in the desert by airships:

> The two ships were headed direct for us, swerving very slightly at times. The steady, deliberate approach was fascinating to behold, and we watched it with helpless interest as they manoeuvred to get into a favourable position for their fell purpose...
>
> The most minute details of the ships focussed themselves on my mind. I tried to make out the number of men upon each, the colours of the flags at the stern, and calculated the height at which they were sailing.
>
> Somehow the undulations of the envelope seemed to give them a more terrible and more realistic appearance, almost as if they were panting to attack and destroy us. A slight smoke wafted from their sterns, and caused me to wonder if they carried guns as well as bombs.

They then rose higher and higher, until the figure of the pilot was no longer discernible, but all the time they were drawing nearer and nearer to a position immediately above us...

Suddenly, very faintly, the curious humming caused by the passage of the bomb falling through the air broke the silence and broke the spell. I could almost feel the sob of relief from a thousand breasts, before the crash of the explosion took place, as the missile buried itself in the earth about 50 yards from where we were standing... The ships veered off after dropping 15 bombs amongst us. Immediately they exploded we ran like excited children to look at the holes they had made in the ground, and to secure such portions as remained as trophies of our bombardment.[40]

In his many hundreds of published verses on the war, D'Annunzio did not have very much to say about the fighting in and around Tripoli and its oasis. But in *La Canzone dei Trofei* (published in the *Corriere* of 12 November) he did suggest that the names of some of the city's little-known suburbs (Bu Meliana, Sidi Mesri, Sciara Sciatt and Henni) had been mightily aggrandized by the (Italian) heroes who had fought there:

> ... *Par che al lauro si mariti*
> *La palma. Tutta l'oasi è un'ara fumante.*

It seems as if the laurel is wedded to the palm.
The whole oasis is a smoking altar.

D'Annunzio stopped writing about the war early in 1912. So far as he was concerned, Italy had by then done all that was needed to claim her new place in the world, and so command the respect and acceptance of fellow Great Powers. And the ambition of providing the nation with a "Fourth Shore" on the Mediterranean Sea—that is, the Tripoli shore—had been achieved:

> ... *novel tumulo ad eroi novelli*
> *diamo, oltremare, su la quarta sponda*

We will raise new burial mounds to new heroes,
over the sea, on the fourth shore.

and:

ella [gloria] fa dell'Italia dai tre mari
la grande patria dalle quattro sponde.

She [Glory] makes Italy of the three seas
the great Fatherland of the four shores.

Then there was the phenomenon of the Futurists. Their over-excited contempt for history and "culture" in the broadest sense was summed up by their founder, Filippo Tommaso Marinetti, with the assertion that the clamorous automobile that seemed to be running on shrapnel was more beautiful than the Classical statue known as *The Victory of Samothrace*. As for war, it was, according to Marinetti, "the hygiene of the world"; and in 1911 he went to see it for himself in Tripoli, as a correspondent for the French newspaper *L'Intransigeant*. His collection of published reports later appeared in a book *La battaglia di Tripoli* (The Battle of Tripoli), which included a startling piece of contemporary symbolism, *L'orchestra delle trincee notturne (The Orchestra of the Night-Time Trenches)* in which he used a very broad metaphorical canvas (bringing in as spectators the desert, the constellations and the whole universe) to underline the essential theatricality of disciplined military heroism under the spotlight of war.

In January 1912 the Commandant in Tripoli, General Caneva, had issued a naively hopeful proclamation to the citizens, reassuring them that "Italy is your father because it has married Tripoli, which is your mother". D'Annunzio (who never visited the war zones he celebrated in verse) had already envisaged Peace "shining out in Latin Tripoli" (*splende la pace in Tripoli latina)*. The war with Turkey officially ended in October 1912 when under the terms of a peace treaty signed at Ouchy, near Lausanne, Italy was left in nominal control of Tripolitania and Cyrenaica. In fact, such was local resistance to this arrangement that the full and harsh conquest and "pacification" of the country was not completed for another twenty years. Many thousands would die in Italian concentration camps. During the year-long Italo-Turkish war, the Italian army (still mindful of past disasters in East Africa) had shown itself to be cumbersome, over-cautious and essentially irresolute. The navy had fought a more dashing war against the Turks in the Dardanelles and elsewhere, while at Tripoli and the other bridgeheads on the Libyan coasts aircraft had proved themselves as promising battle machines and as valuable extensions of land and naval forces. They had been tested in a wide variety of roles as the fighting had suggested new uses. By the end of the campaign, Italy had gained more valuable practical experience of air warfare than any other nation at that time, although one important missing element was any comparable enemy opposition. But the British war correspondent G. F. Abbott (who covered the campaign from the Turkish side and was always critical of the Italians) was not impressed by this new form of fighting: "Personally, after having seen both aeroplanes and airships at work, I have conceived a very poor opinion of the scouting utility of the one and the destructive capacity of the other." *The Times,* however, disagreed, noting that "the practical results of the frequent and regular aeroplane flights by the Italian forces had been inestimable".

In 1912-14 Italian forces did break out of their bridgeheads at Tripoli, Benghazi and elsewhere to conquer large swathes of northern Tripolitania and Cyrenaica, and even sent an expeditionary force into distant Fezzan. But their hold on these territories was uncertain, and lines of communication were overstretched. Even before Italy entered the First World War on the Allied side against Austria in May 1915, daring counter-attacks by tribal forces were driving the invaders back to the coast. By August the tribes were receiving help from Rome's enemies, Turkey, Austria and Germany. The only places then still under Italian control in Tripolitania were Homs, Tagiura and Tripoli itself, where there were 40,000 troops to man the artillery emplacements, the machine gun nests and the stout new defensive wall protecting the city and its outer suburbs. Thus Tripoli had the distinction of remaining under Italian control for longer than any other place in Libya: from the time the Turks abandoned it early in October 1911 until it fell without a fight to the British Eighth Army late in January 1943. And the Italian imprint during those 31 years and nearly four months was profound.

Italian Outpost

There had been Italian influences in Tripoli long before 1911. Italian, which had been the diplomatic language of the Turkish Mediterranean well into the nineteenth century, was widely, if imperfectly known. A resident community of over 1,000 Italians, with its schools, trades and businesses, had a certain social, cultural and economic imprint and influence on this small Turkish outpost (and especially on the Jewish and Maltese communities); even Roman Catholic festivals, with their music, processions, illuminations and fireworks, were tolerated in this Islamic milieu. Then, with Italy's formal annexation of Tripolitania and Cyrenaica in November 1911 Tripoli's role as an Italian city was no longer in doubt. Its administration, society, economy, language, culture, buildings, infrastructure, appearance, services and a host of other features were then transformed to reflect its new political status as first port and capital of Italian Tripolitania. The city's important Jewish community, in particular, largely welcomed these changes because they seemed to offer greater political, economic and social equalities and freedoms after centuries of inferior status under a succession of Muslim regimes. Similarly, many of the city's Muslims saw new opportunities for their own economic and social advancement through constructive cooperation with the new rulers. But many other Libyans outside Tripoli did not share such views.

Gathering momentum in 1911-15, such transformations were slowed down, but never ceased, while Tripoli and its oasis were effectively under siege by armed tribal "rebellion" during and after the First World War. After the Liberal government in Rome tried, but failed, in 1919 to come to peaceful, constitutional terms with the Tripolitanians, Governor Giuseppe Volpi in Tripoli anticipated Fascist colonial policy by several months when, early in 1922, and almost on his own initiative, he started the military re-conquest and pacification of this disorderly territory. Volpi's policy was continued with renewed vigour after a Fascist government led by Benito Mussolini came to power in Rome in October 1922.

Tripoli's leading role in Fascist colonial ideology was reflected in the status of the governors appointed there from Rome after Volpi's retirement in 1925. First came General Emilio de Bono (1925-29) one of Mussolini's three closest early associates. Then came the Marshal of Italy, Pietro Badoglio, who at Vittorio Veneto in 1918 had redeemed all Italy's recent setbacks on the Alpine war front. He was succeeded in 1934 by Air Marshal Italo Balbo, another close associate of the *Duce*, pioneer aviator, Air Minister and creator of the modern Italian air force.

Arriving there in 1930, the remarkable Arabic-speaking Danish Muslim, Knud Holmboe, found that "all Tripoli was intoxicated with Fascism, even though we were in Year VIII [of the Fascist era]". This city, together with Benghazi on a lesser scale, became an ideological, and especially an architectural, showplace of the Fascist colonial achievement (see Chapters Nine and Ten). Tripoli (but never Addis Ababa) was the Jewel in the Crown of the New Roman Empire, proclaimed in 1936 after the swift, if superficial, conquest of Ethiopia. The hostile international reaction to Italy's Ethiopian venture (1935-36) helped put Libya in the forefront of defiant Italian strategic (Mediterranean) and imperial (African) policy. It prompted the building of the great coast road, the *Litoranea*, a strategic highway linking Libya to Egypt and Tunisia; an increasing military presence; and the mass settlement of thousands of landless Italians on agricultural settlements in both Tripolitania and Cyrenaica (seen also as potential local recruits in the event of war).

During the Balbo years Tripoli became a ceremonial city. This was a forum where the achievements and benefits of militant Fascism were constantly extolled and promoted in such public events as fairs; military, civil and youth parades and rallies; official visits by the *Duce* (1937), the King-Emperor (1938) and high Nazi officials Hermann Goering and Hitler's deputy, Rudolf Hess (1939). There were frequent visits by

The *Duce* in combative mode in 1938. The slogan urges Italian agricultural colonists, just landed in Tripoli, to start their new lives by vowing to be worthy of Mussolini.

arge German cruise liners, with organized tours to newly-uncovered archaeological sites. Then there were the sporting fixtures: equestrian trials, air displays and the Tripoli Grand Prix: with a stand to hold 30,000 spectators and a purse of over one million lire, this was billed as "the richest auto race in the world". In October 1938 the city turned out to welcome 20,000 newly-landed, state-sponsored settlers. On other ceremonial occasions selected Libyan soldiers, public servants and others who had closely identified with the regime were publicly granted Special Italian Citizenship. All this rhetorical, theatrical ceremonial, this neo-Roman Imperial *kitsch*, was played out against a background of huge posters and banners showing the *Duce* in glamorous guises. The role of a leader who declared himself to be "always right" was underscored by public display of his more striking slogans (just as the many guises of Muammar Gaddafi, and his distilled wisdom, were to be publicly paraded across revolutionary Tripoli fifty years later). New public buildings of Italian Tripoli were adorned with the *Fasci* (the bundle of rods and axes symbolizing the Roman Lictors' authority), with the post-1922 Fascist year of their completion commemorated in Roman numerals.

Tripoli itself had few recoverable Roman remains and monuments. But with its many new hotels and the state encouragement of tourism, it was a congenial and convenient base for trips to the outstanding Roman sites at Sabratha, some forty miles to the west, and Leptis Magna, about eighty miles eastwards, as well as settlements in the Gebel Nefusah hill country to the south (with their characteristic structures both above and below ground), and the distant Saharan oasis of Ghadames. The 1929 Italian Touring Club Guide Book urged every tourist not to miss Sabratha, while Leptis was presented as "the city whose Roman character is confirmed at the most overpowering level". By then, with tourist coaches and good roads, each Roman site could be "done" within the day from Tripoli. The state ensured that both were being fully and lavishly excavated and restored—even over-restored in some places. Fascist ideology demanded such photogenic and startling archaeological spectacle as the rebuilt theatre at Sabratha or the Severan basilica at Leptis as concrete evidence (often indeed sustained by new reinforced concrete) of Italy's historical claims to this particular stretch of North Africa. So the world could learn how the New Roman Empire was revealing and repeating the achievements of Imperial Rome 2,000 years before.

Governor Italo Balbo was the dynamic manipulator of such public works and public opinion, and if he could make Italy and the wider world aware of his pride in the achievements in Libya in general (united as one colony) and in its capital, Tripoli, in particular, then some of the reflected limelight would surely shine on him as well. Balbo wanted to show that this was not *uno scatolone di sabbia*—a crate of sand, or as the British observer Elizabeth Monroe termed it: "a slice of territory which imagination depicts as limitless, useless, and yellow". In Balbo's words this was no longer "a contemplative oriental country, but a shop-floor where one *works*". As for Tripoli and the facilities it now offered, some visitors judged it to be "the Cannes of North Africa" or "better than the French Riviera".

Tourists of the 1930s to the city and the colony of Libya were advised that

> A sporting costume of good khaki cloth with leggings (preferably with buckles) can be worn at all seasons because it is by far the most practical, shows less wear, and is more resistant to the inevitable perspiration. It should be borne in mind that one has to be sure to be well covered, whatever the season. Always wear a woollen stomacher which should be in place on arrival in Tripoli and never abandoned if stomach complaints are to be avoided. For anyone not used to the climate may suffer from the frequent changes in the weather and humidity. In any case, do not forget a woollen vest. A pair of ground sheets will always prove useful, together with an overcoat in winter and a travelling cloak in summer. Also in summer the classic pith helmet should be worn, or better still a wide-brimmed Panama hat, or at least a Boer hat in light felt.[41]

Balbo gave marvellous late-night receptions at his official residence with its luxuriant gardens. A German journalist who was invited one of these in 1938 was clearly enchanted by what he saw:

> Among the thousand or more guests were the leading officials of the colony, all in brilliant uniforms, such as the officers of the air force, navy and army; all the leading and decorated public personalities; a large group of the colony's lower-grade officials and professionals; the leading native notables in European dress

with the typical fez, or in splendid oriental dress; all the Fascists completely in black. The gentlemen were in the company of large numbers of beautiful ladies, exquisitely coifed. There was dancing on two open-air floors...[42]

Mussolini visited Tripoli twice, the first time in 1926 when he was largely concerned with colonial agriculture, and then with much greater spectacle and impact in March 1937. He arrived in the capital after first visiting Cyrenaica, where he had opened Fascism's foremost public work in Libya, the great coast road from Egypt to Tunisia, passing through Tripoli, Benghazi and nearly all the main population centres. The climax of the *Duce's* Tripoli visit was the extraordinary ceremony on a selected sand dune outside the city. Astride a chestnut stallion, and accompanied by 2,000 Libyan cavalrymen, he accepted from two Libyan heroes of the recent Ethiopian war the sheathed *Sword of Islam* to the massed war-cries of his escort and the boom of cannon in the background. With his unsheathed sword and his escort he then galloped back into Tripoli where, in front of a vast crowd in Piazza Castello, he proclaimed his intention to become the "Protector of Islam". This was a role that seemed to promise all Muslims a striking (yet in reality undefined) alternative to current British and French policy in India, the Middle East, North Africa and elsewhere.

There was another striking public ceremony in 1938—Tripoli's official welcome for the newly-landed *Ventimila*. These were the 20,000 Italian state-sponsored colonists who had been chosen to settle on prepared farms around a dozen new village centres in Tripolitania and Cyrenaica, for it had been recognized that this was probably the only realistic way of making Libya a viable agricultural colony. Accompanied by military bands, the 20,000 men, women and children marched from the ships that had brought them from Italy. For two hours this mass of people filed into the Piazza Castello, where there were two ceremonies. Knowing that the colonists (even from such "red" regions as Emilia and the Veneto) were at heart better Roman Catholics than Fascists, the authorities had first arranged a priestly blessing of the new arrivals and symbolic sheaves of wheat. Fascism then came to the fore, with Balbo making a short speech of welcome and unveiling an equestrian statue of the *Duce* flourishing the *Sword of Islam* presented to him the year before. The colonists were then invited to enjoy themselves with free access to the city's kiosks, bars, cafés and cinemas, before being driven in army lorry convoys to their prepared farms the following day.

All these efforts, all this hard work, these hopes and expectations were undone and were finally lost with the rest of the Italian African empire as a result of Italy's disastrous involvement in the Second World War as an ally of Nazi Germany. The military planners had long assumed that, in the event of war, Italy would be engaged on two fronts in Libya—against the British in Egypt and the French in Tunisia. But with the collapse of France in June 1940, Italy's declaration of war against Britain and France on the tenth of that month soon left only the British in the field, in Egypt. This meant that Tripoli, far from being the frontline base it would have been in any fighting on the Tunisian front, was now securely separated by many hundreds of miles of desert from the Anglo-Italian (and later Anglo-Axis) battle zone in the Western Desert of Egypt and in Cyrenaica. And so the city and its port, while vital supply-points for the Axis war effort in North Africa, were largely spared the destruction that over 1,000 air raids and five military occupations and evacuations brought to exposed Benghazi between 1940 and 1942. Tripoli, shabby if largely intact, was for British forces a distant, seemingly unattainable prize for some thirty months of warfare.

Chapter Six
War, Liberation and Independence

In the swaying battle of the desert, Tripoli... for two and a half years appeared as a mirage that grew strong and now faded away again, and was for ever just beyond the Eighth Army's reach. Alan Moorehead

Three months exactly after the start of the Battle of El Alamein, and after a westwards advance of 1,400 miles, the British Eighth Army entered Tripoli. Fortunately for the city and its people, the retreating Axis forces of 76,000 men had decided not to waste time and resources in defending it "house by house", as some had wanted to do. Instead, they made good their escape westward into Tunisia (where they fought on for another four months). The civil population had been awaiting the British arrival for two fearful days when, very early on 23 January 1943 British armour, with Highlanders riding on the hulls, rolled into the sleeping city and woke it with the rumble of tank tracks and the skirl of pipes

For the British, at least, the fall of Tripoli was a turning point: the first substantial success in a long land campaign that had been going on for over two and a half years, and a seeming vindication of the whole war effort since September 1939. This is how the war correspondent Alan Moorehead saw it:

> At last, after thirty months of warfare, the ragged and dishevelled desert soldier stood with wonderment and emotion beside the playing fountains. If one excepts the entrance of the Germans into Paris, of the Japanese into Singapore, and the return of the Russians to Stalingrad, there can have been no moment in the war equal to this one.[43]

Significantly, the news from Tripoli came on the last day of the summit conference between Prime Minister Winston Churchill and President Franklin D. Roosevelt at Casablanca, Morocco. After the disastrous loss of Tobruk seven months earlier, the news seemed to justify all Churchill's efforts to reassure the Americans of the true value and effectiveness of the whole British war effort to date. For the city's fall could still be presented as the outcome of a wholly *British* (and Empire) campaign, and (not yet) of an Anglo-American partnership. Yet, on the war's wider world stage, the surrender a few days later of a German army to Soviet forces at Stalingrad was to be of still greater, long-term significance.

Another British ally, the Free French, also gained from Tripoli's fall. Soon after the British rolled in, there appeared a fantastic force that had battled its way across the Sahara from the colony of Chad (the first in French Africa to declare for the Gaullist Free French cause in 1940). It had captured from their surprised Italian garrisons both the Saharan province of Fezzan and the Kufra oases of southern Cyrenaica. As the war correspondent Alexander Clifford described their arrival,

> They came in filthy, rackety trucks tied together with wire, unkempt men incredibly sunburned, with great, bushy, shapeless beards. Their own mothers could never have recognised them. But their trucks flew the tricolour of France and the Cross of Lorraine.[44]

On the morning of 23 January General Bernard Montgomery met the Vice-Governor of Libya, the Prefect of Tripoli and the Mayor at the Porta Benito crossroads on the eastern outskirts of the city to accept its formal surrender. Montgomery said there was to be no violence from troops; private property was to be respected; the Italian police were to remain in control; the civilian population was to be wholly loyal; and there was to be no obstruction or treachery on the Italian side. He invited the Italian civil administration to remain at its posts to help the people by continuing its normal functions. The Italian officials listened to Montgomery impassively and had no questions.

Reporting the surrender, the *Tripoli Times/Corriere di Tripoli* (which first appeared on 25 January as a single-page broadsheet in English on one side and Italian on the other) then continued:

> Back in the piazza [Castello], near the harbour, two Highlanders climbed to the flag post and hoisted the Union Jack. For a moment, it caught in some wire, fluttered free, spread and waved

triumphantly. To the crowd below who looked up and saw it flying over the statue of Romulus and Remus being suckled by the wolf, it meant the end of an epoch.

While Mussolini insisted that Italians had accepted the fall of Tripoli "with manly and Roman courage", the priority for the British military was to bring the port back into working order. It had been bombed by the RAF, and two days before abandoning the city, German engineers had blocked the entrance with sunken wrecks, blown up the tall, elegant

Newly-arrived British armour, lined up in Tripoli's Piazza Castello in January 1943, three months after the Battle of El Alamein.

lighthouse and fired warehouses full of stores and munitions. For the British this was a vital forward supply base for the campaign against the Axis forces regrouping in Tunisia. In fact, after a "scandalous delay", it was only fully working again in mid-February, when Churchill sent a message for the troops working there: "Tell them they are unloading history!"

In the meantime, despite the many difficulties of setting up a military administration in this colonial capital of mixed Italian and Libyan population, the authorities considered it necessary to make a priority of that peculiarly British concern for the welfare of animals. Within hours of Tripoli's occupation, a public proclamation forbade members of HM Forces to hire public vehicles (*gharries*) drawn by ill-fed or otherwise maltreated horses. Under the extraordinary military, political, social and economic circumstances of the moment, the point at which the Second World War was just beginning to tilt in the Allies' favour, this order affecting animal welfare must have seemed a preoccupation, an order of priorities, well beyond the understanding or experience of anyone unused to British ways.

Churchill arrived in Tripoli, after flying a long detour from Casablanca on 4 February. So far, the British had not put on grand parades to impress the locals, but they did put on a "decent show" for Churchill. According to his biographer, Martin Gilbert, "Tears ran down his cheeks as he took the march past of the 51st Highland Division and other Allied units, 40,000 men in all." He, at least, fully understood the importance to British and Allied morale of the fall of Tripoli, this "noble possession" as he had called it under very different circumstances a generation earlier, in 1911.

Britain had not fought in North Africa since June 1940 to conquer an Italian colony as such, but first to defend the Suez Canal and the approaches to the Middle East and its oilfields, and then, by finally and decisively occupying Tobruk, Benghazi, and finally Tripoli in 1942-3, to gain strategic control of the southern shore of the central Mediterranean. But the status of Libya in general and its cities in particular as Occupied Enemy Territory meant that military administrations had to be set up to govern them (under the terms of the Hague Convention of 1907) on a "care and maintenance" basis until the end of the world war. Laws and institutions at the time of occupation remained in effect, but purged of their obviously Fascist provisions. The British Military Administration based in Tripoli (there was a separate administration in Benghazi and

French one in Fezzan) thereby found itself the new ruler both of the colony's former rulers (the conquered Italians) and of the ruled, the native Libyans, who tended to be seen as passive allies. As an official commentator put it,

> In this territory, where the British conquest ended a regime widely hated by the indigenous population, BMA is forced to play the double role of liberator of the ruled, and of steward of the old rulers, a contradictory task which ill accords with smooth administration.[45]

The British administrators found that "there was no doubting the joy with which the Arabs welcomed the British occupation of Tripolitania in January 1943... though they gave little active help to our forces". At the same time, the Italians "showed little resentment at our occupation; not because they liked the British, but because of war-weariness. The universal desire was to get back to normal as soon as possible." Although trade was at a standstill, according to the military authorities, "the population very soon realised that a minor boom was in progress and lost no time in fitting themselves into the best points of vantage in order to extort money from an over-generous and numerically great body of British and Allied troops". By April 1943 Tripoli was indeed returning to some normality: shops had reopened, the port was busy, and farmers, back in their fields, were starting (with good weather) to make an essential contribution to the local market and economy. The artificial boom lasted until most of the free-spending Allied troops left to invade first Sicily, and then mainland Italy. But then many skilled and unskilled labourers were able to find work in the port or on large Allied military projects in and around the city.

The British administration later attributed much Italian tranquillity in the first year of occupation to the influence of the Church, and particularly the Bishop of Tripoli, Monsignor Camillo Vittorino Fachinetti, a self-confessed Fascist and friend of Mussolini and other Fascist *gerarchi*.

> The Bishop has always adopted a most correct attitude of cooperation with the Administration and has instructed his clergy to do the same. His sermons... were at all times an appeal to the Italians to cooperate with the Administration and to refrain from

any kind of political activity, their value cannot be over-estimated. The Bishop has been an excellent link between the Administration and the civil population.[46]

As in every other place directly or indirectly caught up in the world war, Tripoli in 1943 was a disturbed, confused and troubled city. Many of its people and communities, new and old, were displaced, deported, dispersed or evacuated to a greater or lesser degree and were trying, or hoping, to return to their families, homes and familiar surroundings. Earlier in the war, the Axis forces had herded several thousand Libyan Jews into a concentration camp at Giado in the uplands about one hundred miles south-west of Tripoli. As the BMA reported, "typhus and over-crowding in conjunction with the bad conditions, reduced their numbers. When the Allied troops arrived, they found desolation." The camp's inmates were slowly returned to their homes in Tripoli and elsewhere.

Some idea of the human chaos at the time can be read in the series of other repatriations of survivors to Tripoli under British supervision in 1943 alone. Among the first to be brought back, in February, were Libyan prisoners of war who had served in the Italian Army and whom the British had been holding in Egypt: their families were by then almost destitute. Next came about 1,000 Jews (French subjects) who had taken refuge in Tunis. In August, hundreds of Tripoli Maltese (British subjects who had been interned in parts of Italy now liberated by the Allies) came home. At the same time, a few Italian evacuees to Sicily tried to return to Tripoli: most were rounded up on arrival and interned. But as the war came to an end, thousands more Italian evacuees (including some former settlers from Cyrenaica) sailed across the central Mediterranean to Tripoli in small and often unseaworthy boats—the reverse of the migration of African "boat people" from Libya to Italy and its islands in the twenty-first century. The British authorities did not encourage Italian returnees and even after the war they tried to restrict numbers by a policy of "one in one out", with returns supposedly balancing departures.

The BMA found at the start of its occupation that "the elaborate colonial social structure remained more or less intact... but without the vast [Italian] financial resources upon which it had previously depended". But so long as the Allied military needed labour, "Tripoli acted as a magnet to the rural Arab and large numbers were drawn to the capital in search of well paid employment". The result was a ten per cent increase in the city's population by 1947, compared with 1938, with most of the new arrivals housed in festering shanty towns on the outskirts.

These labourers, both skilled and unskilled, found work on Allied military sites. In 1943 the US Air Transport Command took over and began expanding the former Italian airfield at Mellaha, east of Tripoli, and within a year was employing nearly 3,000 locals. By 1945 spending on the 1,300-acre site had reportedly reached $100 million. This first permanent US air base in Africa marked the extension of American military activity into an area long dominated by Europe. The British, for their part, needed local labour for the reconstruction of Tripoli port and at military bases and barracks in and around the city, including the expansion of the Italian airfield at Castel Benito (later Idris Airport) in the plain to the south. But when these works were finished, and Allied forces moved on, local unemployment quickly rose as the economy again collapsed.

Many Italians in and around the city (who complained that their wages had fallen to "Arab level") were also having difficulties in making ends meet. In several respects the Jewish community (despite its sufferings) was seen as better organized and materially better off than others. Here, together with the local spread of Zionist propaganda and Tripoli Arabs' sense that the Jews enjoyed special British favour, was the source of some of the resentments behind violent anti-Jewish rioting, murder, looting and arson in and around Tripoli and other places over four days in early November 1945. About 130 Jews were killed and property damage was enormous. The British military was culpably slow in restoring law and order, and the Jews of Tripoli and the Tripolitanian hinterland began to sense that migration to Palestine offered the best chances for their long-term survival.

The very ancient Jewish communities of Tripoli and its oasis villages thus began to sail for Palestine after the 1945 disturbances. Many more followed after the State of Israel came to independence in 1948. In what was almost a mass migration, more left in 1949, when they were joined by many thousands of refugees from Jewish communities in Cyrenaica and inland Tripolitania—more than 30,000 people in all. But some Tripoli Jews who stayed put were joined by others members of ancient Tripolitanian Jewry. Together they formed a fairly tight-knit community of about 6,000 people in a city where Jews had lived and prospered for centuries, and where they still believed in their future safety and wellbeing.

What that future might be was an unsettled question for several years after the war—to the evident frustration of all Tripoli's communities, and of the British, who still had the thankless task and expense of administering them. During their many post-war meetings and debates about the future of Italian colonies, the "Big Four" victorious Allies (Britain, France the USA and the USSR) proposed various forms and combinations of trusteeship under UN supervision. (Among these was Moscow's demand for trusteeship in Tripolitania, immediately seen in London as a Soviet ploy to secure a naval base at Tripoli.)

During these years of debate, Tripoli in particular and Libya in general have never known such free and diverse political expression as the British allowed, or such a free and vigorous press in Arabic, Italian and English. Overt political activity was on a fairly limited scale, and many of the political parties and groups that emerged at this time in reality had few paid-up members. But at one or two vital junctures, Tripoli did witness mass demonstrations and other forms of protest (which the British authorities did not ban) against unpopular proposals thrown up by the international debate on Libya's future, and in particular a suggested Italian trusteeship over Tripolitania. But without "Big Four" accord, and with the Libyans themselves unable to agree on their own future, the United Nations eventually stepped in and decided in November 1949 that Libya, comprising Tripolitania, Cyrenaica and Fezzan was to become an independent and sovereign monarchy by 1952, with a UN commissioner to help and advise in the state-making process. Britain and the United States came to welcome this solution, since it enabled them to continue to use their military bases in an independent state which would not have been possible under a UN mandate.

Independent Tripoli

Libya duly emerged in December 1951 as an independent federal kingdom one of only seven independent Arab states. It was largely dominated by Cyrenaican Sanussi interests that had been the mainstay of resistance to the Italian conquest, and King Idris was a firm ally of the British. Tripoli was denied its obvious role as national capital when, to appease Cyrenaica it was named joint federal capital with Benghazi. This cumbersome arrangement meant that the king, parliament, the federal government and ministries, and the diplomatic corps, were expected to shuttle back and forth between these two widely-separated cities every few months, while maintaining appropriate working and domestic accommodation in both.

The first US Ambassador to the new United Kingdom of Libya, Henry Serrano Villard, found that

> To take up residence in Tripoli in no way implied that one was domiciled at the permanent seat of government. The federal offices might be situated in Tripoli, but the King lived in Benghazi. Parliament was to open in Benghazi but expected to move almost at once to Tripoli. Whether the Cabinet remained in Tripoli or functioned for a year in Benghazi depended on the whim of the King.
>
> I was soon to discover the awkwardness of this arrangement, which entailed more hours of flying between the cities than I cared to contemplate... I lost count thereafter of the number of trips I was compelled to make over the desert reaches in order to conduct the affairs of my office. Federal officials remained in Tripoli for the first year of independence but moved to Benghazi, files and all, for the second year. Then they moved back again to Tripoli.[47]

Tripoli and Benghazi remained joint capitals even after the almost unworkable federal system was ended with the creation of a unitary state in the early 1960s. Indeed, had the Sanussi monarchy survived beyond 1969, the small town of Baida, in the uplands of Cyrenaica four hours' drive from Benghazi, and site of the first Sanussi mission in Libya, might—as intended—have become the national capital.

In its early years the destitute little Kingdom of Libya could only hope to survive by "living on its geography"—by allowing Britain and the United States the use of military bases in return for generous aid and support. This western military presence was especially evident in and around Tripoli in the 1950s and 1960s. All three British services, with their personnel, barracks, transport, support services, family quarters, recreation sites and British Forces' Radio, were openly present there. The Americans, after practically abandoning the Mellaha airfield by 1947, had later refurbished and expanded it with "phenomenally long runways" to take the largest nuclear bombers, and renamed it Wheelus Field. Reportedly the largest American base outside the United States, Wheelus was a link in the chain of US bases extended around the Sino-Soviet bloc as the Cold War deepened. Wheelus became in fact the second-largest source of the kingdom's income and employment before the oil boom and, according to Ambassador Villard, writing in the 1950s, "an air of permanence surrounds this transplanted offshoot of the American way of life". With ancillary USAF facilities and ranges elsewhere in Tripolitania, Wheelus was especially useful as an all-year training ground for American fighter crews normally based in West Germany.

As Ambassador Villard also pointed out, in the city of Tripoli the Libyan state inherited "an attractive, ready-made metropolis"; indeed, it inherited with it a magnificent, modern colonial infrastructure that Italy had built and paid for, and had been forced to abandon after the war. Long after Independence the Italian influence was still plain to see: this was, in many ways, still an Italian provincial city. The more conspicuous reminders of its Fascist past were removed, notably the statues, the carved *Fasci* and the Fascist year in Roman numerals on buildings and other public places. The Roman *Lupa* atop her harbourside column was replaced by an Arab horseman. Various Italian streets were given new names more appropriate to a Libyan Arab joint capital; but many more were left unchanged, and on its plinth the fine statue of the locally-born Roman Emperor Septimius Severus continued to dominate the main entrance to the old, walled city.

Most of the 25,000 or more resident Italians still in Libya lived in and around this joint capital, and particularly in the new quarters that had grown up outside the walls in the 1920s and 1930s. They provided the active, middle management of the modern, local economy and, with local Maltese, much of the skilled workforce. English was only slowly replacing Italian as the city's second working language. The *Municipio* (the city administration) although staffed by Libyans, still worked largely in Italian, and to Italian systems. Italian banks, shops and businesses (and those of Italian-speaking Maltese and Jews), schools, cinemas, restaurants, cafés, bars and one daily newspaper continued to give the city as strong an Italian as an Arab identity. Beer was still brewed by the Birra Oea establishment, local vermouth was produced by the Carlo Curti concern, and the city was well supplied with red and white wines of varying quality produced on the working Italian agricultural concessions in the nearby countryside. The continuing Italian presence was confirmed every evening by the *passeggiata* of strolling couples and family groups along the main, arcaded shopping streets; by the swarming presence of small schoolchildren in their black and white apron uniforms (*grembiuline*); by the Sunday crowds outside the city and suburban churches and the dominant Cattedrale del Sacro Cuore di Gesù; and by public and processional Roman Catholic ceremonial. Thus as late as 1966 the centre of this Muslim Arab city was closed to traffic for an afternoon to allow the annual *Corpus Domini* procession to pass from the cathedral through streets decorated, according to proper Italian custom, with carpets and other bright stuffs draped from overhanging balconies. Sunset in central Tripoli was marked, first by the tolling of great bells from the cathedral's *campanile*, and then, soon after, by the *muezzins*' penultimate daily calls to prayer from the city's minarets. So did the distinct communities of Muslims, Christians and Jews live together in reasonably tolerant respect and harmony in this cosmopolitan metropolis of the independent Libyan kingdom. There were, it is true, serious disturbances in the city (with at least a dozen deaths) after the first parliamentary elections in 1952, and further troubles in 1964; but neither of these outbreaks was directed against the Italian or other foreign communities.

Visitors in the 1950s and 1960s were struck indeed by how quiet, orderly and clean the city was:

> There are no whining beggars, importunate shoe-shine boys, or pestering merchants demanding attention. To anyone familiar with any Mediterranean seaport, the quiet of Tripoli comes as a shock... Tripoli is not only quiet: it is undoubtedly the cleanest city on the Mediterranean... Gardeners are continually working on the public gardens, cutting the lawns, raking the paths, and sprinkling the flower beds. Tripoli is one of the truly beautiful cities that border the Mediterranean.[48]

Or, as another contemporary traveller put it, "I do not think it is an exaggeration to say that Tripoli has become the cleanest and most attractive town on the whole North African coast"; it had "a beauty and dignity that is lacking in any other town we passed through on our route". But the women of the Old City, "who occasionally venture forth into the modern town, are the most heavily veiled in North Africa". Many indeed were still as closely wrapped up in their all-enveloping *baraccans* as Miss Tully had described in her celebrated letters nearly two centuries earlier (see Chapter Three).

Libya at independence was one of the poorest countries in the world, subsisting mainly on the charity of others. Yearly per capita income was estimated at $35. Exports were worth barely one quarter of imports. Shipments of hides, skins and peanuts were just about enough to pay for imports of Libyans' staple drink, tea. But in the 1950s Tripoli itself presented a rather less desperate face to the world. This was, after all, a seat of the Tripolitanian provincial government and, for at least half the time, the federal government as well. It was the kingdom's main port, handling about four-fifths of all foreign trade; a centre of industry, such as it was (mainly food, drinks and tobacco processing) employing about eighty per cent of the nation's industrial workers; a main market of the agricultural zone of northern Tripolitania; and it served the kingdom's main concentration of British and United States military bases. The city's relative wealth attracted more rural migrants, driven by the pressure of continuing drought (1955-59) and by the prospect of new jobs. As the suburban shanty towns grew, so a city centre building boom gathered place.

In 1955 the federal government passed its first petroleum law. It was designed to attract the international oil industry to prospect in the kingdom—unknown territory perhaps, but one removed from the troubled Middle East, protected by Western military bases and with open Mediterranean access to the fast-growing oil markets of Western Europe. By the beginning of 1957 about a dozen companies had been awarded some sixty exploration concessions. Even their work of merely prospecting for oil, let alone actually *finding* and developing it, was enough to start a rapid transformation of an otherwise largely destitute economy.

As the International Bank for Reconstruction and Development described this process in a report of 1960:

> The indirect impact of oil company operations on the economy is to be observed, particularly in Tripoli, in the sharp rise in prices of housing rents, hotel accommodation and other services bought mainly by foreigners, in the almost equally sharp rise in wages

and salaries paid to skilled and semi-skilled Libyan workers, in the establishment of many new Libyan and foreign trading and construction enterprises catering for oil company requirements, in the acceleration of the drift of labor from the land and in the general boom in trading and servicing activities of all kinds. There is already an acute shortage of skilled and semi-skilled workers.[49]

Oil was struck in the Cyrenaican Sirtica in abundant commercial quantities in 1959, and many more large finds soon followed. Crude oil exports started in 1961, and by 1969 yearly exports of over one billion barrels were bringing in yearly revenues of over one billion dollars. This oil was exported through specialized tanker terminals on the Gulf of Sirte and at Tobruk: Tripoli remained the main entry point for the cornucopia of foreign goods and services that the new national oil wealth could readily buy.

An American resident of the 1960s described the city's resultant transformation:

> The prosperous modern shopping district is gay and tempting with imports from Italy, France, England and West Germany, and a fortune may be spent on toilet goods, female beautifiers, lingerie, gowns and shoes. Along the arcade-covered walks stroll individuals of every faith, colour, race and political conviction. Sidewalk cafes are crowded with a galaxy of races, and mostly men, who sip espressos, suck lemon sodas, dandle cigarettes between fingers which glint with heavy rings, and ogle svelte *signorinas* who saunter smartly by.[50]

By the mid-1960s Tripoli's population had doubled since the war and was approaching a quarter of a million. Out in the oasis, the stands of palms, the groves of olive and fruit trees, the irrigated gardens and the sandy lanes with their hedges of prickly pear were cut down, grubbed up and flattened to make way for new suburbs to the east, west and south of the municipal core. A new half-ring road was a concrete indication of how and where the metropolis would further spread in the decades to come. The expatriates, the military service families, the oil men and the salaried foreign staff of air-conditioned offices made their homes on the western outskirts, and particularly in Giorgimpopoli, an unplanned sub-American sprawl along the main coast road to Tunis. The English-language *Sunday Ghibli* (with tongue in cheek as usual) always called this "the fashionable oil man's suburb". With their drab patches of garden, the depressing concrete duplex bungalows, which only air-conditioning made habitable, were ranged along unpaved, treeless and nameless side tracks. Expatriates gave the most prominent of these tracks the unofficial name of California Street, but attempts to call others Utah, Idaho or Texas were discouraged. As one former resident recalled life in 1950s Giorgimpopoli:

> The streets had no names, the houses had no numbers, it was dusty in summer and boggy in winter, the lights went out with each wind, and we cooked with bottled gas. The only clue to where you lived was your own sense of direction, and a plan drawn up for your friends. It was considered quite daring to live so far out of the city...[51]

A busy store in one of the shanty towns that grew up in the city suburbs after the Second World War. Several men wear the traditional *barracan*.

War, Liberation and Independence

The city's other immigrants, the rural poor, also lived in the outer suburbs, if under rather different conditions. Their festering, rubbish-strewn, flyblown shanty towns were without power, light, water, drainage or any other services. In 1954 it was estimated that at the very least 25,000 people lived in the Tripoli shanties; ten years later the estimate was nearly double, or perhaps one in five of the city population. Although it was said that the appearance of these unofficial settlements "indicates a terrible poverty", the fact was that by the mid-1960s there were fair numbers of new cars and light trucks parked in and around them, and new consumer durables could be glimpsed amidst the squalor. Clearly, despite obvious corruption in high and middle places, some of the new oil wealth was beginning also to filter down to the poorer levels of society. In 1965 the state eventually stepped in with the Idris Housing Scheme, which was to replace such dwellings with 100,000 new cheap, concrete homes over the next five years. (But shortly after coming to power in 1969, the new revolutionary regime decided that 150,000 families nationwide *still* urgently needed decent housing; it condemned the Idris scheme as "futile" and ordered many of its gimcrack little houses to be demolished as substandard.)

In the meantime, Libya in general and Tripoli in particular were slowly acquiring the infrastructure and services of a modern welfare state, with free education from primary to university level, free health and other social services. The new University of Libya, with departments in both Benghazi and Tripoli, not only supported its students with free tuition, books and maintenance, but actually *paid* them a monthly stipend for attending their studies.

In the mid-1960s Tripoli, and the kingdom as a whole, seemed content to bask in growing and tranquil prosperity under a moderately benign regime, corrupt certainly, but subject to the rule of law, tolerant of its racial and religious minorities, and gradually loosening its Western defence and other ties. Thus the events of 1967 came as a double shock, destroying the mood of quiet optimism and giving clear notice that the regime faced a significant political challenge. When Israel went to war with the Arab states on 5 June, mobs urged on by Cairo Radio took to the streets of Tripoli to kill Jews and loot and burn their property. British and American interests in both Tripoli and Benghazi were also attacked. Quite apart from Israel and the Tripoline Jewish community, and the burnt-out city centre shops, stores and homes, the other obvious targets of this violence were the regime and its pro-Western policies. Within two days the government had collapsed and, with the country reported to be "on the verge of revolt", the situation remained tense for many weeks. Government and order were eventually restored, but it was clear that the regime faced an acute crisis of confidence (which it never really regained) in its domestic, Arab and foreign policies.

Although Tripoli's resident Italian and Maltese had not been singled out for attack, many saw the events of 1967 as fair warning of trouble to come, and their confidence in their long-term security was undermined. Those who could began quietly to sell up and return to Italy or Malta, even if they had been born in Tripoli, had passed all their lives there and considered it their home. Within two years the Italian community in and around the city had fallen from over 20,000 to probably barely half that number.

Chapter Seven
Gaddafi's Tripoli

When he looks more closely, the visitor finds that much of this handsome city is falling apart. Justin Marozzi

Revolutionary Tripoli was for 42 years (September 1969-August 2011) the focus of Colonel Muammar Gaddafi's political, economic and social experiment known as the Socialist People's Libyan Arab Jamahariyyah. This last word, Gaddafi's own invention, is usually translated as "State of the Masses". In this recent phase of the city's long history, much of the outside world viewed its apparent role as a "base for terrorism" with the same distaste, outrage and often the pure loathing that it had earned in the centuries when it was one of the Barbary "nests of corsairs". With his unopposed, unquestioned and unaccounted access to the national oil wealth, "Brother Colonel" had the means during most of his four decades of uninterrupted power to pursue a provocative foreign policy that was widely seen (especially in the West, in the Arab world and in parts of Africa) as malign, if not downright dangerous. As the seat and symbol of the regime, Tripoli itself earned by association an almost equally disreputable character, becoming a synonym for all the perceived provocations, terrorism, outrages and shortcomings of the Gaddafi state. As such, it was the prime target of the armed retribution of an exasperated United States in 1986, and of the vicious forces of regional rebellions which in 2011 finally overthrew Gaddafi and the Jamahariyyah system that he had created, sustained and still personified. As for the domestic policies of the State of the Masses, over four decades they left their own particular marks on the city's appearance, its infrastructure, economy, institutions and society.

The people of Tripoli and other Libyans outside Sanussi-dominated Cyrenaica had been broadly inclined in 1969 to applaud the overthrow of King Idris' lacklustre Sanussi monarchy and its replacement by young army officers with a clear mission to put the world to rights and bring this new Arab republic more decisively into the Arab fold while loosening its Western ties. What was not understood at the time was that this change of power, planned and led by the young Captain Gaddafi (self-appointed to the rank of colonel), was no opportunist military *coup*. Rather, it was the start of a thoroughgoing political, economic and social revolution that he had been planning for years—just how thoroughgoing, Libya in general and Tripoli in particular were to find out over the coming decades.

By birth and upbringing, Gaddafi was alien to Tripoli. He was not a townsman of any sort, not even the child of any settled community. Rather, self-defined as "humble", he was seen by many as an upstart, the son of a tent-dwelling family of semi-nomadic herders of a minor and largely disregarded Arabized Berber tribe (the Gadadfa) of the northern Sirtica. As such, his closest tribal, ancestral, and cultural ties were neither with Cyrenaica nor with Tripolitania, but rather with the greater Sahara itself. Once in power, he immediately denied Cyrenaica its predominant Sanussi royalist role and Benghazi its status as co-capital when he made Tripoli the sole national capital. He based his new administration and personal quarters at the Bab al-Azizia barracks in the southern suburbs (which in the course of the following years was to become this "popular" leader's fortified redoubt). In doing so, he seemed to reinforce his credentials as the first truly Libyan leader ever to emerge from the open, common space of the Great Sahara to take over and dominate this urban and alien centre of power, built, ruled and exploited by a long historical succession of foreigners and foreign interests. Yet Gaddafi, according to one of his biographers, "hated Tripoli". It housed an army of bureaucrats whom he always regarded as parasites; another army of greedy merchants; and also those last, despised elements of the old, royalist middle class. He had no sympathy for, or understanding of, this pre-revolutionary, historical and still very Italian Tripoli. He always felt more secure, more protected, among his own tribespeople, and his planned sites for a new national capital included, first, the Giofra oasis, centrally located in the Sirtica, about 150 miles from the Mediterranean coast, and later the wayside coastal village of Sirte, near his pre-desert birthplace.

Gaddafi and his eleven young officer associates on the ruling Revolution Command Council very quickly began to change the character of their new Arab nationalist and republican capital. Early decrees in 1969 were intended to erase the more obvious and intrusive symbols of the discredited royalist regime, and the nation's subservience to "colonialism and imperialism". This meant that the prominent, domed Royal Palace with its opulent contents (originally built as the official residence of Italian governors) was thrown open to the public and renamed "the People's Palace". It also meant the closing of such reminders of foreign influence as the dominating city-centre Cathedral, its deconsecration and conversion into a mosque commemorating the Egyptian nationalist President Gamal Abd-al-Nasser (the Romanesque *campanile* made an unconvincing minaret); the closure of other (but not all) churches; banning nightclubs with their "unseemly displays" of near-naked women; pulling down street and other signs in Latin script; and forbidding the production and sale of alcohol. The new regime then turned its attention to the nationalization of foreign (notably Italian) banks and the evacuation of British bases (all by then only in Cyrenaica) and the USAF base at Wheelus Field within sound, if not sight, of the capital. The Americans quit Wheelus in June 1970, leaving behind not only its vast military infrastructure but also radar, electronics equipment, ammunition dumps and other facilities, a hand-over which the new regime duly heralded as the "victories over imperialism" that had eluded the royalist regime. Within weeks of the change of power, Tripoli turned out to greet a visiting Arab nationalist who would never had been officially welcomed there before: President Nasser of Egypt, the leader who had long indirectly influenced the young Gaddafi's political development.

Although Gaddafi intended to make Libya a "State of the Masses", not all the masses were to be allowed a part in it. His vision encompassed only those who might be called "Sunni Muslim Arab" without undue offence to other native Muslim communities, such as Berbers (including the veiled Tuareg of the south-west), the Tebu, and other black Fezzanese. The Italian and Jewish communities of Tripoli and its surroundings were, as "Fascists" and "Zionists" respectively, certainly not eligible to be part of this future utopia. In July 1970 Gaddafi started accusing the Italian community of serving an imperialist aim: "We shall not accept the presence of a Fascist or an imperialist intruder in our land." A two-week anti-Italian campaign reached its climax with the announcement that all Italian property—including buildings, plantations, installations, movable and immovable equipment, means of transport, animals and all fittings and attachments—were to "revert" to the state (the implication being that they had all been in existence and in place before 1911 and had thus been stolen from their original owners). The confiscation of property, nearly all of it within or close to Tripoli, combined with other restrictions, meant in effect that the whole community was expelled without compensation over the next two months. By then this community amounted to fewer than 13,000, some 10,000 having quietly sold up and left while still able to repatriate their assets in the three years since the 1967 disturbances. In a typically Italian gesture, even the bones of the dead were repatriated from Christian cemeteries in and around Tripoli. At the same time, the seizure of the assets of about 600 Jews (officially called "Israelis") still living in the city left the very last remnants of that ancient, pre-Arab community with no other option than immediate flight to Italy or Israel. By October Gaddafi could proclaim the end of what he called "a Fascist Italian colonialism in every sense... like a cancer in the body of the country".

Lost Italian skills and expertise were made up for by an influx of tens of thousands of Egyptian and other Arab workers; but without its long-term resident Italians and Jews, Tripoli lost much of its cosmopolitan cachet, while its economic, cultural and social life were never to be the same again. And the puritanical prohibitions and prejudices of the new regime did little to make the city an attractive and welcoming place for visitors, or even for many of its own residents. A published contemporary comment by a leading cartoonist under the cynical title "Tripoli after Eight at Night" showed a deserted, moonlit townscape with a solitary passer-by shinning up a palm tree to escape a pack of ravening wild dogs below.

Tripoli in the 1930s had served as a public showplace for the achievements of Fascism under a leader who declared himself to be "always right". So it was that forty years later its blank walls and its public spaces were again filled with the super-size posters and graphics extolling the virtues of the populist revolution under the guidance of "Brother Colonel". Just as Mussolini's *obiter dicta* had been written large throughout Fascist Tripoli, so were Gaddafi's slogans spelled out across the revolutionary city. They were drawn from his basic revolutionary text, *The Green Book*, a short and artless work explaining how he believed a people's democracy, economy and society should work. Similarly, as Mussolini, *Il Duce*, had been shown in many outsize and glamorous guises in the 1930s, so Gaddafi was represented from the 1970s onwards as the revolutionary guide and leader with an extensive wardrobe of unlikely costumes in which he fulfilled a series of striking public roles: as, for instance, a colonel n a dazzling white uniform with full military decorations; as an Arab horseman; as a bulldozer driver demolishing slums; as an intellectual thinker-leader; as a desert falcon; and as what seemed to be an aging pop-star embarking on a come-back tour...

With the publication of the Leader's distilled thinking in the three parts of *The Green Book* in the later 1970s, largely apathetic Libyans were expected to study and learn from these ingenuous (and mercifully brief) texts. There was no excuse for not doing so, since in Tripoli, as in other towns, there was a *Green Book Centre* with numerous copies freely available in most of the world's main languages. The Tripoli Centre, in the words of a British correspondent, was "a conical structure with green-tinted windows, which looked like nothing so much as a spacecraft which had unexpectedly landed from above". Inside, an eerie green light shone over a pool of green water with a globe in the middle. Around a circular inner hall there were individual study rooms, all with the pervasive little green books matching the green upholstery and decor.

Modern totalitarian regimes need a wide, open urban space where an appreciative populace can be made to parade, march and demonstrate its official enthusiasm for the leadership: a Red Square for Comrade Stalin; a Tiananmen Square for Chairman Mao; the facilities of the Nuremburg rallies for Adolf Hitler. In 1930s Tripoli, Piazza Castello was considered a sufficiently central, monumental and extensive urban space for the assembled citizenry (on separate occasions) to greet Mussolini, Italo Balbo, the King Emperor and 20,000 newly-landed farming colonists. Early in 1941 it was quite large enough for units of the Afrika Korps to parade, and two years later for the victorious British Eighth Army to march past and salute Winston Churchill in person. But in the 1970s something still more extensive than this *Maidan as-Saraya* was needed to accommodate the Jamahariyyah's appreciative masses when they assembled before their "thinker leader" and visiting foreign (mostly African) notables. The site of the former Miramare Theatre on the seaward corner opposite the Castle had been vacant for years; the demolition of two more blocks of buildings (including the little Italian-built Mosque of Sidi Hamuda that mysteriously "fell down" one night) opened up an even bigger space that also took in the former Piazza Italia (renamed *Maidan ash-Shuhada,* Martyrs' Square). This new *Maidan al-Akhdar* (Green Square: Green to stress the regime's Islamic credentials) was an open-air forum,

A modest Gaddafi poster adorns the wall of the Castle in 2006 commemorating the 37th anniversary of the September revolution.

a disproportionately wide space, three times larger even than the Fascist piazza of the 1930s, where the revolutionary masses could assemble in far greater numbers to demonstrate their support for the regime (or, in 2011, to rejoice at its hideously bloody overthrow).

By 1975 Tripoli had about 570,000 people, at a density of nearly 2,300 inhabitants per square kilometre. The population had thus more than doubled in ten years; but "Greater Tripoli", which took in places as far off as Azizia and Zanzur, was approaching 750,000. By 1980 the built-up area was more than six times greater than it had been in 1966. In its sheer size this city had now come to dominate the nation in a way that few other capitals do: about one-third of the nation's entire population of 1975 was concentrated there; and indeed the proportion remains roughly the same today, even if the overall figures have more than tripled. So the conurbation still kept some of its unofficial role as a city-state, seemingly almost a separate political, economic and social entity in its own right. Even Colonel Gaddafi himself complained in a speech in January 1981 that the concentration of the national administration in Tripoli was such that the only way to solve the problem was to remove the city's status as capital. He would have liked to (but never did) transfer the capital to Sirte. This former township had by the twenty-first century grown in prestige, and to a population of 100,000, under Gaddafi's personal regard. If nothing else, it at least had the advantage of being roughly mid-way between the main population centres of Cyrenaica and Tripolitania.

But Tripoli grew, and continued to grow, through both natural population increase and migration. Its people had, and were encouraged to have, large families. The modern city has been filled with young people: in the 1970s, children of 5-14 years outnumbered young adults (25-34) threefold. Due to oil wealth, better social services and higher standards of living in general, infant and child mortality fell sharply. There was no national family planning programme, and no political, economic, social or cultural pressures to counter the official encouragement of large families to expand a small national population.

The city and its surroundings were also swollen by uncontrolled migration: half of all those who moved from the interior to the coast in the 1960s and 1970s settled in or near the capital. Then there were the arrivals from other Arab countries: even in 1973 there were 80,000 legal Arab migrants and an unknown number of illegals in and around the city. Later still, even more destitute people began to arrive overland from sub-Saharan Africa, expecting either to find work locally, or a sea passage to Europe—just as incoming black slaves had done in past centuries. Other coastal towns (notably Misurata and Benghazi) had similar problems, and even in such a totalitarian state, there seemed to be no effective measures, sanctions or incentives that would end this lopsided overpopulation of the capital and a few other coastal towns offering social and economic advantages over the rest of the country. Such change and over-development was largely the result of state intervention through massive, ill-considered investments in the economy and infrastructure with little regard for the constraining social plans and guidelines drawn up in the 1960s by the despised royalist regime. And the weak, state-subsidized urban economy proved especially vulnerable to periodic fluctuations in oil revenues, and to the harsh economic climate of international sanctions in the 1990s. There were echoes here of the city's fortunes of earlier centuries based on the unstable returns of the essentially parasitic activities of the trans-Saharan slave trade on the one hand and Mediterranean corsairing on the other.

So Tripoli expanded further—outwards across its own oasis, absorbing into concrete super-suburbs the palm groves, the irrigated gardens and the simple whitewashed villages and other settlements of the past, while turning the sunken, sandy lanes and byways into streets and highways. And it expanded upwards, into the tower blocks of offices, hotels and popular housing perceived as the standing symbols of any modern metropolis. But small, balconied apartments planned around the lifestyles, habits and needs of Western two-children families were suited neither to fecund Tripoline families of five, six or more children, nor to a social culture traditionally confining women to the seclusion of a low-built house lacking outside windows, but with rooms opening onto an internal courtyard, and thus allowing free movement within the home. Then the often delayed, or simply disregarded, need for regular and competent building and services maintenance all too often made everyday domestic life difficult in tall, modern blocks beset by such defects as lifts or air conditioning out of order, water pressure insufficient on the higher floors and fittings and fixtures insecure or dangerous.

But the city's real housing crisis was caused when the views of the Leader on property ownership were put into practice. As *The Green Book* asserted, "a house is for its inhabitants". In practice this meant that by the late 1970s the payment of rent for property had been outlawed; private property had been nationalized (confiscated without compensation); and tenants were forbidden to pay rent to landlords. The crisis was deepened when long-term interest-free building loans were suspended. Families who had invested heavily in property for want of any other worthwhile savings outlets were particularly hard hit—unless they had unmarried children old enough to wed promptly and thus able to take over otherwise forfeit family dwellings. And would-be house builders naturally declined to invest in projects with such troubled prospects. Utter confusion was finally ensured when the regime ordered the destruction of many thousands of the city's private property deeds.

By the early 1980s even the terminal of Tripoli International Airport was more a squalid example of an uncaring lack of supervised maintenance than of competent "revolutionary" efficiency. This was despite the fact that by then most newly-arrived visitors gathered their first impressions of the State of the Masses at its airports, and the fact that the new Tripoli terminal, in an appropriate green and white colour scheme, had been pen for only a few years. In 1984 a newly-arrived BBC correspondent described it as "the epitome of modern neglect: contemporary furniture (broken), conveyor belt (unmoving), glass display cases for duty-free goodies (none visible), immigration/visa office (man asleep amid filthy coffee cups)."

As for the revolutionary city at the end of the airport road:

> The vista was a symphony of the twentieth century on the slide. Modern scruffy apartment buildings set amongst broken pavements and dusty rubbish-strewn yards. Untended patches of grass with half the railings missing. Roads that started—and went nowhere. Vaguely Soviet, but baked in the sun, so saved from dark ugliness and looking merely tatty.[52]

Another contemporary writer described the opinions of expatriate residents: "They set out into the city's familiar chaos, with all the opportunities it offered Westerners for self-complacency and contempt." Such opportunities included the sight of "the balconies of a new block of flats... crowded with animals—including one baby camel—of the peasants who occupied them". Then there was "a car which had mounted another as if in an act of copulation; thus joined, the cars had embedded themselves in the wall of a house".[53]

The city was finally spruced up for the twentieth anniversary of the revolution in September 1989. "Messy, corroded by sand and salt, long littered with rubbish", it had, according to the Italian journalist Bernardo Valli,

> now been repainted white and green, and shone immaculate under the sun. In the evening, a million little lights twinkled along the fronts of houses, illuminating the fountains and the motorways, the balustrades and the lawns of the lungomare. Thousands of South Koreans had waved the magic wand and in a few months had transformed decrepit Tripoli into an overdressed metropolis, into a stage set on which the people moved in an uncertain manner, pleasantly overwhelmed, as if at a parade.[54]

Before Gaddafi, the city had for centuries had been a local, regional and international forum of private trade and business, and a centre of limited, pre-industrial processing and manufacture for local and some foreign markets, particularly in Sudanic Africa. Suddenly in the 1970s private enterprise was stopped from doing any of these things as the business community found itself officially pilloried as "exploiters". The Leader then called for self-managing worker committees to take charge of public and private enterprises in which there should be neither employers nor employees, only partners. Workers hurried to take over companies with more than five employees, with inevitable confusion and disruption of output (although the key sectors of oil, banking and insurance were in practice untouched). As the exercise of "people's power" began to transform wholesale and retail trade into state operations, importers and traders in Tripoli, where most of the nation's foreign goods and services were delivered, were suddenly put out of business. Conventional shops were closed and even merchants in the ancient, characteristic *suqs* of the Old City pulled down their shutters for good when they were no longer allowed to trade. As a British commentator put it, "Much of the spice and fun of life in an Arab country which, after all, has traditionally been centred round buying and selling, has been removed."

Libyans, then had no choice but to do all their shopping at a very few, large, state-run "People's Supermarkets" (the first was ceremoniously opened by the Palestinian leader Yasser Arafat) which were intended to eliminate "exploitation" by private traders supposedly only interested in profit-making. The suburban supermarkets, which did generally offer lower, subsidized prices, were filled with goods that state bureaucrats had decided the people needed, rather than those they actually wanted; and these sole retail outlets were thus beset by periodic gluts of goods that would not sell, and prolonged shortages of those that would have done.

In the era of the Barbary corsairs, and particularly in the seventeenth century and the early decades of the nineteenth, Tripoli was attacked many times by fleets of various European maritime powers outraged by the assaults and depredations of the Tripoline galleys on their Mediterranean merchant shipping and seacoasts. Avenging cannon fire was mostly aimed at the Castle, the city's defensive walls and the corsair fleet in the port but mosques, houses, commercial buildings and their occupants were also at risk from what is now known as "collateral damage", if not intentional retribution. Twentieth-century Tripoli was bombarded as a passive target in others' wars—in 1911 by an Italian fleet intent on expelling the Turks ind occasionally during the North African campaign of 1940-43 by the RAF aiming to damage this main Axis supply port, or by the Luftwaffe once the British arrived in 1943. But in 1986 the exasperated US Reagan Administration brought down more direct retribution on the city, its people and their leader (and also on Benghazi) in response to a series of perceived terrorist provocations by the Gaddafi regime—an episode in many ways reminiscent of European reactions to the corsair menace of earlier centuries.

After several years of deteriorating relations between Washington and Tripoli, and a series of terrorist attacks for which the Gaddafi regime was blamed, on 15 April 1986 the United States launched air assaults on selected targets in Tripoli (including Gaddafi's home in the fortified Bab al-Azizia complex), as well as Benghazi. A BBC correspondent who was in the central Tripoli Al-Kabir Hotel on the night of the raid described how

> At two in the morning, the growl of aircraft, the first explosions and an eruption of chaos in the hotel sent me straight to the balcony looking south over the city. I could see the planes, they were so low, and a second explosion, a pink-orange glow growing like a ghastly sunrise behind the dark building, produced shock waves that made me hang onto the balcony rail. The Hotel Al-Kabir is a large, ten-storey building. It shuddered as the bombs detonated, and although I have been under both Russian and Israeli bombing, this was the most severe I'd experienced.[55]

Gaddafi's home was hit; his "adopted" daughter, Hannah, was killed; but not the leader and his other children. Residential quarters were widely damaged, with many civilian casualties. The city's anti-aircraft defence had been almost wholly inept. But the raid, although widely condemned in the Arab world and elsewhere, did not in the long run reinforce Gaddafi's leadership. On the contrary, the people of Tripoli, in particular, expressed their growing sense of apathy and political disengagement simply by declining to join official public demonstrations of outrage: "One saw more demonstrators in Khartum and Tunis than in Tripoli, where the numbers of foreign journalists outnumbered the locals."

The damage inflicted on Gaddafi's family home in the Bab al-Azizia complex was carefully preserved as evidence of American aggression. A

British visitor who was there some years after the raid reported that the compound was surrounded by a fifteen-foot wall that was supposed to be impenetrable. The wall had few entrances, and was protected by heat sensors, remote-control cameras and alarm systems linked to an internal control desk. Visitors passed through three sets of doors, each vacuum-sealed, with groups of men (presumably armed) on guard at each one. The visitor asked himself,

> All this to protect the Leader of the Revolution and his family—but from what? To shield him from the People, from imperialist aggressors, or to give him privacy? Or, perhaps, time to take control in the event of an attempted coup...

But on its inside, the compound was

> not like an army barracks at all, more like a country club or a vacation camp, with houses spaciously positioned apart, orchards, lawns, vegetable gardens, two tennis courts, a soccer field, and plenty of trees and greenery to shield all the defensive hardware.[56]

A process of some political liberalization in the late 1980s was characterized by the release of many political prisoners. In March 1988 Gaddafi himself used the surveillance tower of Tripoli's central prison as a platform to make a scathing verbal attack on those who abused the revolution for their own ends. He then, typically, took part in the prison's demolition and supervised the destruction of thousands of citizens' personal security files. But a more telling, and lasting, symbol of regime oppression in the capital was the notorious Abu Salim prison where many more political prisoners were held for years on end, with its very name, according to one correspondent, being "synonymous with torture, starvation, sickness and death". A riot in 1996 was only put down after the guards turned their guns on the inmates, killing over 1,200 of them. Their deaths were never reported or acknowledged; thus some families continued for years to make a long journey to Tripoli to entrust the guards at the gate with parcels of clothes and food for a relative who had long been dead.

By the 1980s Tripoli had become a byword for all the perceived misdeeds of provocative and adventurous foreign policies attributed to the Gaddafi regime by the United States in particular, the West in general and other sectors of the international community. The imposition of economic sanctions, first by Washington in the 1980s, and then a series of far more draconian measures by the United Nations in 1992, made life extremely unpleasant for ordinary people in Tripoli (one-third of the country's total population), and in the rest of the country. The next ten years were probably the most difficult since the North African campaign of 1940-43.

> A people exhausted by more than two decades of constant revolution lived under persistent and insidious economic and social pressures more typical of conditions during a total war. They included corruption, profiteering, black marketing, currency collapse, unemployment, falling living standards, a sense of isolation, moral insensibility, intellectual stagnation, low morale and loss of civic pride. Visitors were particularly struck by the visible increase in prostitution in the towns and the filth, untidiness and uncollected rubbish even in Tripoli, which up to the 1960s, at least, had kept up Italian Fascist standards of municipal cleansing.[57]

A visitor at the turn of the millennium felt that there was "something unmistakably forlorn and beautiful about this city, a sense of wistfulness and a largely unspoken resentment". He elaborated: "Thirty years of the revolutionary regime had almost brought the city to its knees—cars fell apart, homes crumbled away, roads rotted—and now sanctions held the city in a tight and unforgiving embrace." The same visitor sensed that there was then "an unmistakable whiff of Orwell's *1984* about Tripoli, an Oceania on the shores of the Mediterranean, a city whose people just about get by... when he looks more closely, the visitor finds that much of this handsome city is falling apart."[58]

Yet some people, and particularly some of the younger generation, had not altogether lost the sense of the adventurous business ethos that had once made their city an intercontinental emporium. Until nearby Malta joined the European Union in 2001, Libyans did not need visas to go there. Many enterprising young dealers would ignore sanctions on air travel by taking the boat to Valletta, illegally exporting Dinars (and thereby risking the death penalty) to buy hard currency on the Maltese black market. They could then shop in Valletta for the latest European and American fashions for resale on Tripoli's unofficial markets: but they still ran the further risk of losing everything as they passed through Customs on their return to Tripoli. And their enterprise also aroused the resentments of state employees committed by their employment to supporting the regime's draconian economic restrictions while trying still to live on meagre salaries frozen since the 1980s.

The End of Gaddafi's Tripoli

Yet things began to improve markedly in 2003-04 when the regime cleverly brought about its own timely international rehabilitation, and started moving closer to the West. International sanctions were lifted, and political, economic and social reform seemed to be in the air. Tripoli was able to turn out to welcome such visitors, among many others, as French President Jacques Chirac and the British and Italian Prime Ministers (Tony Blair and Silvio Berlusconi) as they flew in to flatter Gaddafi by conferring with him in his elaborate "Bedouin tent" pitched in the Bab al-Azizia complex. By the end of 2004, foreign visitors found that the capital was again booming, as it had not done since the 1960s and the early revolutionary years of the 1970s.

> The lobby of the country's first five-star international hotel, the Corinthia, was filled on a continuous basis with a frenzied bevy of Libyan and foreign businessmen trying to strike deals as the government moved closer to announcing new oil contracts and continued to liberalize the country's economy.
>
> To anyone who had known the country during the austere years of its revolution when virtually all private business had been abolished or withered away for lack of provisions, the city's streets had been transformed beyond recognition. Many of the revolutionary slogans that had once punctuated urban and rural landscapes alike were giving way to commercial advertising signs. The once ubiquitous portraits of the Leader now vied for attention alongside commercial dioramas that touted an array of products Libyans once could only dream about—most dramatically, advertisements for airline destinations outside the Jamahiriyya.[59]

New shopping malls in Hay al-Andalus were filled with luxury goods and the latest electronics; new private supermarkets were overflowing with imported food and drink; property prices in the capital were quickly rising. But, as one foreign visitor noted at the time, the fact that the Corinthia Hotel was the only place in all Libya where a credit card was accepted "was a small but telltale indication of the backwardness of the country's economy, and of the isolating impact of some of the earlier economic sanctions". And the apparent economic transformation to be witnessed in Tripoli could not disguise new and deeper divisions in this urban society. Here was a city where state employees still found it difficult to make ends meet, and where ubiquitous African immigrants (who, like the black slaves of the past, did the hard, dirty work the locals would or could not do) were clearly on the lowest social strata in a State of the Masses still supposedly based on the principles of equality and equity. In practice, moreover, the leadership was incapable of reforming the political, economic and social life of the Jamahariyyah in ways that might have at least partly calmed the people's resentments and satisfied their expectations.

In the meantime this Central Mediterranean port found a new role as a trans-shipment terminal for thousands of African and Arab migrants who saw no future in Libya but were prepared to pay dearly for passages to the European Union by way of Italy and its islands. They did so at clear risk to their lives on board small, hideously overcrowded, under-provisioned and unseaworthy craft which traffickers would launch at all seasons and in all weathers. Not even the slave traders who operated the Mediterranean "Middle Passage" from Tripoli in earlier times were so careless of human life and welfare. This transit traffic continued, indeed increased, after the fall of the Gaddafi regime.

Thus by the time open, popular rebellion broke out, first in Tunisia to the west and then in Egypt to the east in the spring of 2011, Libya was more than ready to make its own, unique contribution to what was popularly known as the "Arab Spring". The origins and the development of Libya's bloody counter-revolution were not in Tripoli, still the main (if not the most favoured) public seat and forum of the Gaddafi cult. Rather, it was in distant Benghazi, long neglected and deprived of its former royalist role as joint capital, that the rebellion emerged under the red, white, green and black banner of the former Sanussi monarchy. Benghazi's uprising inspired a series of other, distinct rebellions in towns and districts across Cyrenaica and Tripolitania where the broad hostility of the "masses" to the regime was reinforced by particular, long-suppressed regional, tribal and other local resentments. Throughout the confused and bloody summer of 2011, when the intervention of NATO aircraft to protect rebels from the regime's threatened retribution became seemingly a means of regime change, Tripoli still declined openly to rebel. This inactivity suggested that the capital still needed the protection of its apparent and frequently-demonstrated loyalty to the regime, at least until late August when disparate fighting militias which had made their own successful rebellions on their own terms elsewhere in Tripolitania advanced on the city.

Tripoli's Reluctant Revolt

All Libya's attempts to free itself from the Gaddafi tyranny could only be fully successful if Tripoli joined in as well. With one-third of the national population, its prestige as capital and seat and centre of the regime, this was almost the last and, second only to Gaddafi's eventual overthrow, surely the greatest prize of the collective rebellions of 2011. There were some early, small and ineffective popular disorders in Tripoli in support of Benghazi's initial uprising. But the capital declined for months (February-August) either to demonstrate its solid support for a regime from which many of its people still benefited, or to revolt against a tyranny that oppressed and terrified them into cowed submission. Here, as across the country as a whole, there was no third, middle way out of the crisis, no prospect of formulating or presenting a coherent agenda for negotiation or compromise with a regime that could accept no possible alternative to its own prerogative. And, again, as in Libya as a whole, there was widespread foreboding (based perhaps on historical memory) that any regime change might well lead to something even worse.

The capital's most solid support for the 2011 revolts was mainly in the run-down and disregarded eastern suburbs and settlements, notably Tagiura and Suq al-Giuma. Historically these had long been places of political refuge from, and subversion or revolt against, central authority within the city itself. Many of the professional and business classes dispossessed by Gaddafi's draconian redistributive policies of the 1970s had relocated to these outer eastern suburbs, still nursing their personal and collective grievances. But in broad terms the rest of the city was more inclined fatalistically to support and cooperate with a regime from which it had gained some material benefits over several decades. Moreover, Gaddafi's complex security apparatus was much more in evidence and in much more effective control here than just about anywhere else in Libya. The regime's main power base was, after all, at the Bab al-Azizia barracks complex in the south of the city, and most of those who lived and/or worked under its wide shadow did so in a strict security zone; they seemingly supported the regime by conviction or necessity in a society where any contrary opinions were best left unexpressed in word or deed.

Gaddafi's son Saif al-Islam, with his more "modern" and sophisticated understanding of Libya's underlying problems, and of the wider world, was very briefly seen by the rebels as a possible moderating intermediary with the leader. But when on 20 February he went on television to dash all such hopes by repeating the father's threats to crush the rebels like rats, protesting mobs for the first time took to the streets of eastern Tripoli, and even managed briefly to occupy the recognized, official forum of popular expression, Green Square. Such spontaneous public reaction was soon discouraged when the security forces started shooting to kill protesters, especially as they emerged from mosques after Friday prayers.

Thereafter, Tripoli's own revolt developed more cautiously, with diverse and mutually suspicious revolutionary cells only slowly coalescing into larger if barely compatible groups. A seemingly unhurried process of preparation, organization, arms stockpiling and training filled roughly the six months (February–August) when Benghazi, Misurata, Zawia and other places were desperately fighting for their own revolutions on their own terms, aided and supported by NATO and Arab and other foreign interests. Tripoli's special difficulty was that it was never able to present anything like a united rebel liberation front. Thus by late summer the best that had emerged from the springtime chaos were two rival and mutually hostile networks, one "secular" and the other "Islamist", that were to outlast the capital's eventual fall.

Meanwhile, the city's singular and culpable failure to rise in coordinated revolt prompted other, neighbouring and successful rebellions to intervene, in the hope of moving or shaming it to bolder action. While Misurata delivered smuggled arms, some of Tripoli's own rebel recruits were trained and equipped in already "liberated" zones of the Western Gebel. But when the city was at last ready to rise in revolt on the appointed day, it still failed to do so itself and on its own terms. Rather, the uprising set for 20 August was in effect started by fighters from Misurata and the Gebel who, after their own successful revolts, advanced on the capital and blockaded it on the landward front.

Only when mosque loudspeakers had broadcast the evening call to prayer, and the *takbir* (the hypnotic, ululating glorification of God), Tripoli was at last ready, willing and able to erupt spontaneously. While the centre and the areas around the Bab al-Azizia complex still flew the green flags of the State of the Masses, the elaborate security services that had sustained the regime for decades were steadily overwhelmed in hundreds of small, separate engagements with the rebels across the city. It is not clear when and how Gaddafi and the members of his family still with him decided to quit their urban stronghold for safer and more sympathetic refuges elsewhere. But senior state officials and other close servants and supporters of the regime were already bolting towards the airport or the limited safety of Bani Ulid, to the south-east. On 21 August fighters from Misurata and the Gebel burst into the city and added their weight to its uprising. Within two days they and Tripoli's own forces were converging on the three most prominent symbols of the Gaddafi state: the Bab al-Azizia complex, Green Square and, most hated of all, the Abu Salim prison. When the rebels forces were in sufficient control the urban mobs finally turned on these symbols of 42 years of uninterrupted one-man rule. The Bab al-Azizia complex was stormed and the Brother Leader's fortified homes and the luxurious kitsch of their contents looted, vandalized, put to the sack. The notorious Abu Salim prison was thrown open and its wondering prisoners released from their cells into the free light of day. Down in Green Square the thinker-leader's giant public portraits, and the oversize posters carrying his slogans, exhortations and words of distilled wisdom, together with the ubiquitous green banners of his revolution, were torn down, defaced, burned, trampled underfoot. Through the smoke of these bonfires of vanities prolonged, joyous but perilous small arms fusillades acclaimed the disappearance and evident if not yet complete rout of a leader whom Tripoli had late in 1969 acclaimed as one of its own.

The city had been spared the long, bloody street battles that had been greatly feared. But commanders had lost control of many Gebel fighters, who seemed more eager for loot than revolution. While there were immediate disputes over who should announce, and claim credit for,

A popular poster shows the former Brother Leader as a rat being exterminated by the 17 February uprising. It parodies Gaddafi's threats to hunt down and destroy "like rats" those who had risen against him.

the capital's "liberation", huge tensions erupted into violence between the main and uncontrolled armed groups at large in the streets. None of this boded well for the future.

A National Transition Council had been formed in Benghazi soon after the February uprising started there. It was an interim administration representing a coalition of rival rebel interests, and in due course it gained international recognition. Soon after Tripoli's "liberation" it moved there, thus confirming that despite all Benghazi's efforts, Tripoli was to remain the sole capital. After all, it was here that Gaddafi had concentrated all political, economic, commercial and social power in his stateless "State of the Masses", and there was no denying the city's overwhelming national predominance.

On 20 October Gaddafi's squalid public death at Sirte, near his pre-desert birthplace, and his children's deaths, capture or flight marked the end of his era. In late November a temporary Cabinet of Technocrats, including a fair range of competing and other rebel regional interests, was formed in Tripoli. Over the next several months Libya in general and the capital in particular enjoyed a brief taste of proto-democracy, with freedom of expression, an active civil society and, in July 2012, the first free government elections since 1952.

Yet Tripoli was still so insecure that, even with their elected and popular mandate, government ministers, deputies and officials were at the mercy of armed rival militias contesting their every proposal and decision. In 2013 even the Prime Minister was not immune from (temporary) kidnap from the supposed safety of the Corinthia Hotel. Soon after, Libya found itself with two rival governments, one sitting in Tripoli and the other in Tobruk, at the far eastern end of the country.

Tripoli's continuing state of insecurity and chaos was one legacy of all the practical shortcomings and eccentricities of the Gaddafi era. Like other national participants in the 2011 "Arab Spring", Libyans had discarded a hated and moribund regime; but they then alone faced the dilemma of inheriting no coherent, functioning state to take over and adapt to a new and "democratic" form of government. The country and particularly the capital were faced in 2011 with political, economic and social voids that were the inevitable outcome of Gaddafi's unique and profoundly disruptive policies over 42 years of power. Then there was the further challenge of Islamist interventions largely alien to the Libyan experience and practice of "moderate Islam". And once again the capital had to contend with the basic historical contradictions between re-emerging and opposing social, cultural and therefore political forces in Tripolitania itself. On the one hand was the customary tribal society of the Arab-Berber hinterland, and on the other the cosmopolitan urban society of the Mediterranean coastlands dominated by the overwhelming presence of Tripoli itself. This fundamental social and cultural divide between Sahara and Mediterranean has been evident at many previous historical moments—particularly during foreign invasion and regime change—and it still confounds and inhibits Libyans' attempts to build their own civil state and society.

Chapter Eight
The Trading City: Between Sahara and Mediterranean

The citizens are most of them merchants; for Tripolis standeth neare unto Numidia [the Sahara] and Tunis, neither is there any citie or towne of account between it and Alexandria: neither is it farre distant from the Isles of Sicilia and Malta: and unto the port of Tripolis Venetian ships yeerly resort, and thither bring great store of merchandize. Leo Africanus (Pory's paraphrase, London, 1600)

For over a thousand years, trade with the three Old World continents brought Tripoli some moderate local prosperity. Such business was largely the import and re-export of goods and produce from and to markets on the far side of the Sahara in one direction, and on the northern and eastern shores of the Mediterranean Sea in the other. For this town and its hinterland, like North Africa as a whole, usually made or grew little that was wanted elsewhere, or was worth carrying across the sea or the desert.

One exception was horses: for centuries the North African Barbary breed was a highly-valued trans-Saharan import in the Sudanic lands where the local breeds were small and puny. Local rulers needed these imported horses to wage cavalry warfare on the flat, open lands of the Sudan. These bigger and heavier mounts showed off their full advantages when they were equipped with imported stirrups and saddles that gave the rider greater security and stability, particularly when wielding weapons. In the sixteenth century the Muslim traveller Leo Africanus told how in Bornu "they exchange horses for slaves, and give fifteen or sometimes twenty slaves for one horse". Three centuries later the British traveller George Lyon still found roughly the same exchange rate of slaves for horses in the Fezzan. Such rates partly reflected the costs and difficulties of taking horses across the Sahara: as a general rule, one horse had to be

131

accompanied by three camels loaded with the food, and especially the water, it needed on each stage of the journey.

Camels were much more useful than horses in the Sahara. By exploiting the unique long distance endurance of the acclimatized Asiatic camel, Saharan Berber tribespeople had mastered trans-Saharan travel by the early Middle Ages. Arab Muslim expansion then furthered this revolution by providing the necessary business incentives of open access to the intercontinental markets of the Islamic Caliphal Empire. While the medieval western Maghreb prospered mainly on the flow of gold from inner West Africa, black African slaves became the mainstay of trade on the central Saharan roads. Tripoli's trans-Saharan trading partners in the central Sudan had little exportable gold, and few other raw products worth the time, risks, effort and expense of carrying across the desert. But they had many slaves considered surplus to the needs of their host societies, and they could profitably be exported into distant lands. Medieval Islam believed the Sudan (in its widest geographical sense) to be truly vast and populous ("of all peoples, they are the most prolific", according to the twelfth-century Arab geographer, Al-Idrisi) and easily enslaved. Slaves were readily available for export in the main wholesale marshalling centres and markets of the central Sudan, where they had been collected from wide swathes of inner, tropical Africa. But the number of slaves that could be brought across the Sahara in any one year was always limited by the size and frequency of camel caravans, and their capacity to carry large loads of food and water for hundreds of hungry and always thirsty slaves on the march.

In the Middle Ages, most black slaves were brought up to Tripoli by the ancient Garamantian road from Lake Chad through the small oasis of Zawila in Fezzan. Zawila was known for centuries throughout much of the Islamic world as a source of slaves, and was especially famed for the eunuchs needed in the harems of the rich and powerful. Although Fezzan was the main crossroad of the central Saharan trade, with its oasis of Murzuk later predominant, some slave caravans from the south and the south-west passed instead through the oasis of Ghadames, as an entrepôt serving both Tripoli and Tunis.

Only valuable slaves (eunuchs, dwarves, girls with remarkable looks or skills, or a selected group intended as a gift or tribute) were allowed to ride across the desert: the common trade slaves, including little children, had to walk all the way, some bearing loads on their heads. Yet most (eight or nine out of ten) survived this horrific trek of three, four or more months in the care of whip-wielding slave-drivers who had themselves to put up with all the dangers, difficulties and discomforts of Saharan travel. Disasters sometimes overwhelmed an entire slave caravan: the failure of a vital well; a particularly violent sand storm; an outbreak of disease; extreme heat or cold. Two out of every three slaves in the Saharan caravans were women and girls destined for domestic and sexual services in the Muslim households of North Africa and the Middle East. They usually survived the desert crossing better than the men and boys, generally taking a quieter and more positive attitude to their ordeal, and to their prospects. George Lyon, the British traveller who in 1819 returned all the way from Murzuk to Tripoli in the company of a slave caravan, noticed that "the females were much less exhausted by travelling than the males: the women and girls walked together and sang in chorus nearly the whole day, which enlivened them and beguiled the way".

On arrival outside Tripoli, slaves' treatment showed a marked change for the better. Here, by the Mediterranean, they were rested and prepared for market. They were decently clothed; their skin was oiled to give it a healthy-looking "sheen"; their hair was dressed; they were encouraged to

A slave caravan rests on the long road from sub-Saharan Africa to Tripoli in the mid-nineteenth century. (Richardson, 1848).

rest and put on some weight; and they were taught the basic principles of Islam and the few words of Arabic that would raise their sale value since there was little or no demand for a pagan slave with no known speech. About half of any consignment would be sold to local buyers with the rest exported on a further journey by sea. In the Middle Ages black slaves were exported mainly to Egypt and the Levant, and also to Tunis and Sicily; but with the rise of the Ottoman Empire in the eastern Mediterranean, Tripoli began supplying the slave markets in the great cities of Constantinople, Smyrna (Izmir) and Thessalonika, as well as Turkish markets in Anatolia, Crete, Cyprus, the Aegean islands and the southern Balkans.

Historically, the size of the trade is uncertain, for there are very few reliable statistics before the nineteenth century. But even by the thirteenth century it is likely that 5,000 black slaves were, on average, delivered every year by all the Saharan roads, probably reaching an average yearly peak of 7,000 in the eighteenth and nineteenth centuries. In all cases, at least half those slaves were probably brought to Tripoli and other ports in the Regency of Tripoli (Misurata, Benghazi and Derna).

While not necessarily North Africa's largest single slave market, Tripoli was for many centuries the main African slave outlet on the Mediterranean. This was the point at which this intercontinental trade was transformed from an overland caravan traffic out of Africa into a Mediterranean seaborne "middle passage". British consular figures show that in the eleven years 1846-56, a yearly average of nearly 1,100 slaves were shipped from this one market, with several hundred more sold there every year to local buyers.

Foreign observers as far back as the seventeenth century had remarked on the essential contribution of the black slave trade to the Tripoli economy. The armchair traveller John Ogilby, in his *Africa*, published in London in 1670, recorded that "the chiefest Trade is now in Blacks and Negro's [*sic*] which were formerly sold in *Sicilia* but now in *Turky*". A century later the British Consul General, the Hon. Archibald Fraser, similarly underlined the essential contribution of the slave trade to the town's economic wellbeing and balance of payments. In an official report on its international trade for 1767, he noted that 1,000 black slaves had that year been brought across the Sahara—800   through Fezzan and 200 via Ghadames. He valued these slaves at a total of 40,000 *Barbary* or *Tripoli Sequins*: at an average exchange rate of 2.35 *Sequins* to the Pound Sterling, this amounted to £17,000, or an average price of £17 a head. Fraser assumed that all these slaves were re-exported across the Mediterranean, thus overlooking considerable local demand. Perhaps he thereby over-estimated the trade's true contribution to the city-state's balance of payments: he put it at about forty per cent by value of all exports in 1767. But if Tripoli then had a trade deficit on the year of 22,000 *Sequins* (almost £9,000), this was fully met by the continuing activities of the corsairs, and particularly by foreign powers' payments for immunity from corsair attack. As Consul Fraser put it:

> The General Ballance in Trade against Tripoli is paid off by the sale of slaves [White Christian slaves] taken in their Piracies and the Money spent among them by the Agents and Consuls of the several European powers with whom they are at peace.[60]

Fifty years later, another British Consul General, Colonel Hanmer Warrington, also officially noticed the black slave traffic in the context of the local import and export trades. In 1818 he reported the arrival of a large caravan from Fezzan bringing a total of 1300 slaves worth an average of one hundred Spanish Dollars each—about £20. But a few years later the prices listed by the Swedish Consul were considerably higher—$400 a head for eunuchs, $120-$150 for women "according to beauty" and $100 each for "grown men and just nubile girls".

By the early nineteenth century, following the effective ending of Mediterranean corsairing, the black slave trade was Tripoli's most valuable business, and it was actively encouraged by the Karamanli Pashas, and also by the Ottoman Turks after they re-imposed their direct rule from Constantinople in 1835. The Turks, indeed, treated this trade like any other, subjecting it to all necessary tax, health and other government controls. In 1846, the total value of slaves shipped from this port (60,000 Spanish Dollars - £12,000 Sterling) was two and a half times the value of all other exports. Even so, there was still a large trade deficit, due in part to continuing drought and famine which meant that the town was importing food from abroad, rather than exporting it (especially to Malta).

The slave trade was clearly a rewarding business, the mainstay of the northbound Saharan traffic. For the slave-makers, the slave-drivers and the traders and financiers, it generated profits that justified the expenses and risks of bringing gangs of enslaved men, women and children across the full width of the desert to Tripoli. Occasionally there were devastating losses, as in August 1849 when all 1600 slaves in a large caravan imprudently travelling up from Lake Chad at the hottest time of year died of thirst when a single well failed. But the good profits to be made on successful journeys more than compensated for such losses. A young girl bought for $32 at the slave marshalling centre and market at Kano (now in northern Nigeria) in 1850 could be sold for around $85 at the mid-Saharan market of Murzuk, and for $100 in Tripoli. Her value increased by a further $30 when she was sold to her final purchaser in the great slave market at Constantinople, or in Smyrna. An adolescent boy, bought for as little as $10 at Kano, could usually be sold for four times as much at Murzuk, for $60-65 at Tripoli, and up to $100 to his final owner in Constantinople or Smyrna. Indeed, the trade in men and boys became relatively more profitable the further they were removed from tropical Africa; but they were much more trouble to bring across the desert than the more docile, amenable women and girls.

These gains were all *gross* profits, and the *net* profits of the mid-nineteenth century tell a rather different story. The costs of bringing a slave of either sex across the Sahara at that time included deaths of between five and twenty per cent on the road; food, water bags and the hire of camels to carry them; government taxes at various points on the journey; the payment for "protection" to tribes and peoples along the way; and the costs of presenting slaves in decent condition at successive markets up to the point of final sale. As the total costs of moving a slave across the Sahara and the Mediterranean were about the same for both sexes (about $40 from Kano to Constantinople via Tripoli), women and girls usually earned higher net profits than the trade in men and boys.

In the mid-nineteenth century some of the biggest slave dealers in Tripoli were Turkish government officials who would take every opportunity provided by their short posting to this international slave market to buy slaves and make quick profits by shipping them off for sale in Turkey. This officially-sanctioned trade continued quite openly in Tripoli until the later 1850s when, under British pressure, the Turkish government began to take measures that gradually curbed it over the next twenty to thirty years.

Black trade slaves on their long trek across the Sahara were in different ways treated as badly as were slaves on the notorious Atlantic passage between Africa and the Americas. The first European travellers who penetrated the Great Desert from Tripoli early in the nineteenth century were horrified by the casual inhumanity and the prodigal indifference of the slave traders (whether Tripoline Arabs or such desert peoples as the Tuareg and the Tebu) towards their charges. Most slaves were as yet unconverted pagans, and as such were considered even in death to deserve neither respect nor burial: most dead slaves were simply abandoned where they had fallen on the road, or at resting places at mid-desert wells.

But, as we have seen, most slaves' fortunes changed for the better once they reached the Mediterranean at Tripoli. This was the point at which most of them left behind them their more horrific mental and physical experiences of recent months. By the Mediterranean they might at last begin to experience something of the vaunted mildness of the Islamic (or Jewish) systems of domestic slavery. For many slaves prospects were no worse, and often better, than a life of free drudgery and bare subsistence in central Africa.

Slaves were usually brought to Tripoli and other North African ports in the April-June quarter. Caravans thus avoided crossing the Sahara in the hottest months of the year, or during the desert "winter" with its frigid nights and mornings: both seasons could be fatal to many near-naked, ill-fed and exhausted trade slaves. Caravans were also timed to take advantage of the Mediterranean sailing season from April to October when slaves could be sent off to other destinations with better chances of safe voyages.

Most such slaves were embarked on small sailing cargo boats—brigs, schooners or typically Mediterranean *polaccas* or *poleacres*, all of around 100 tons. These small merchantmen, usually already heavily laden with the low-grade pastoral and agricultural produce of Tripolitania (barley, olive oil, hides and skins), had been neither designed nor adapted to carry a supercargo of human passengers (as were slave ships on the Atlantic run). Many of them sailed out of Tripoli harbour with barely enough food and water for the slaves sitting, squatting or sprawling on the general cargo in the hold. Thus the Ottoman brig *Messaoud*, of around 85 tons, perhaps fifty feet long and with a crew of a dozen men, sailed regularly in the 1840s between Tripoli and the port of Mytilene on the Aegean island of Lesbos, and then on to Smyrna or Constantinople, with miscellaneous cargoes and black slaves. She normally loaded about 85 slaves at Tripoli; but in May 1847 she left port with 31 male slaves, and 327 women and girls, a total of 358 slave passengers. There is no record of how this pitilessly overloaded little craft (barely bigger than a barge) fared on her voyage of about 1,000 miles across the central Mediterranean and the Aegean, with the island of Crete a likely and very necessary landfall about two-thirds of the way across.

If all went well, if wind, currents and weather behaved as expected in the summer sailing season, these little boats setting out from Tripoli might reach Malta in a few days (although any slaves arriving in *British* Malta would be freed) or Crete in a fortnight or so. There fresh supplies would be taken on and some space cleared when some slaves were sold off to local buyers. A further voyage of a week or more might bring these little slave ships safely to the coasts of Turkish Greece or Albania, or to Smyrna, Constantinople, or Thessalonika in north-eastern Greece. There the slaves would be sold off to their final owners, far removed in time, space, climate, disease environment and culture from their places of origin in inner, tropical Africa.

This long-established route out of Tripoli took on a new and rather bizarre aspect when Turkish government steam ships came into service in the central and eastern Mediterranean about 1840. Turkish steam warships were used to ferry contingents of troops to and from tours of duty at this imperial outpost (which had also recently become an important central Mediterranean coaling station). There was usually room on the steamers' return voyage to Turkey for consignments of slaves handled by regular dealers, or sent by government officials and military officers on their own account for sale in Constantinople, or which they would take with them to sell at the end of their tours of duty. Although the costs of this modern form of transport were higher, the larger and better-appointed steamers offered the advantages of much faster voyages (five days against three or more weeks by sail), smoother and more regular passages, and slaves were delivered to market in better condition than at the end of a long Mediterranean voyage in a small, cramped, ill-equipped and badly-provisioned sailing boat. When government steamers dropped anchor at Tripoli in the 1840s and 1850s, the town crier would be sent round the markets and "other places of public resort" to proclaim that the ship would be available to carry slaves to Constantinople for a fare of about five *nahboobs* a head (a little under £1). One such government steamer, the *Esseri Jadid* (New Creation), had room for up to 400 market-bound slaves on every homeward voyage.

But there was one particular difficulty with this convenient arrangement: the on-board engineers, who alone understood, operated and maintained the British-built marine engines and other steam-powered machinery, were British. They were therefore subject, wherever they were, to recent British law on participation in the slave trade for which the penalty, as for piracy, was death. Several British engineers serving on government steamers sailing from Tripoli were to find themselves on arrival in Constantinople closely questioned by the British Consul General on the status of the many blacks who had been embarked at the beginning of the voyage. The engineers had to defend themselves from a possible charge of slave trading by reasonably declaring that from appearances they had been unable to tell whether they were slaves, or the legitimate servants of the officers they served. But the Foreign Secretary, Lord Palmerston, had on more than one occasion in 1849-50 to take up with the Turkish government such cases of possible British marine engineers' involvement with the Turkish slave trade out of Tripoli. The Sublime Porte in due course forbade the embarkation of slaves on *steam* ships of the Turkish navy, while apparently leaving government *sailing* ships still free to carry them. Nevertheless, as late as November 1856 the Turkish "war steamer" *Sayik Shadi* carried eighty slaves on one voyage from Tripoli to Constantinople.

The Turks were not the only ones shipping slaves across the Mediterranean on both sailing boats and steam ships. Some European shipping lines in the mid-nineteenth century (notably Italian and Austrian) were in the habit of embarking black people under the pretence that they were free "servants" of various passengers, when it was generally understood that they were in fact trade slaves being shipped to market. Some European consuls in Tripoli could easily be persuaded to issue "certificates of manumission" for black slaves being shipped overseas, such certificates having been "lost" by the time their holders disembarked with their human charges at the final Ottoman destination.

No foreign visitor has left a full description of the Tripoli slave market. But it is on record that common trade slaves were sold openly and without ceremony to the highest bidder in the covered but airy market in the *Tariq* al-Halqa (The Street of a Link [of a chain]) at the eastern edge of the Old City's business quarter. According to the British traveller George Lyon, individual slaves were offered for sale at a sort of mobile auction. The auctioneer, with one or two of the slaves he was selling trotting behind him, would solicit bids for them from likely buyers in the marketplace. A slave, standing or kneeling, would be scrutinized in public and on the spot by a potential buyer: the feet would be examined, and then the head, the eyes and the insides of the mouth and nostrils; the slave's age and origins (rarely precisely known) would also be discussed. If no satisfactory bid was forthcoming, the sales tour of the market would resume. Undisclosed physical and moral defects in newly-bought slaves could result their return to the seller within three days. Such defects included epilepsy, leprosy, flat feet, insomnia, anorexia, "dissolute habits" and a tendency to alcoholism or absconding. A buyer also had a right of redress if a newly-bought female slave was found to be pregnant. The more expensive slaves would not be hawked around the streets, but were offered by dealers to selected clients during discreet meetings in private houses.

One of the main demands for slaves in places such as Tripoli was for young girls, even children, who could be easily assimilated and trained up as servants in the domestic routines of traditional Muslim (or occasionally Jewish) households; they would also become sexual partners. Black women were considered to be docile ("born to slavery") and to make excellent wet-nurses. But any slave who did give birth to a child would be freed (although likely to remain a household dependent), for, unlike American practice, in Islam no free father could have a slave child.

Besides the routine domestic chores that middle- and upper-class Tripoline housewives could or would not do, black slaves made other useful (but not essential) contributions to the local urban society. In addition to the Pasha's corps of black slave guards, black male slaves provided much of the basic heavy labour around the town and in the port, the dockyard and the stone quarries. A few with special skills and business aptitude might become the trusted assistants and agents of traders and entrepreneurs.

Slaves were usually better treated in such Islamic environments than they were in the mines and plantations of the Americas. But, unlike the prolific slave communities of North America in particular, the pool of slaves in places such as Tripoli was constantly eroded by low reproduction rates, early deaths from disease and manumission. Slaves raised in the tropics suffered in the cold, damp North African winter, and lung infections were a common source of premature death. It has been estimated that the average "service life" of a slave in Tripoli—the interval between sale to a final owner and death or manumission—was a mere seven years. Thus the trans-Saharan slave traffic was largely a replacement trade, maintaining a more or less constant population of slaves in and around the town, with any unwanted surplus exported across the Mediterranean. But there is little historical evidence that the slave trade itself, and this local, largely social rather than economic exploitation of slave labour, ever had much lasting impact on the long-term prosperity, capital accumulations or self-sustaining economic growth of Tripoli—as, for instance, the Atlantic slave trade had on eighteenth-century Bristol and Liverpool.

Apart from gangs of their own people who by one means or another had been reduced to slavery, the countries of the central and eastern Sudan produced few other unprocessed raw materials that were worth carrying across the full width of the Sahara to the markets of North Africa. Goods in this trade had to be imperishable and able to withstand the heat, the dust, the long, harsh conditions and daily jolting and mishandling of the desert journeys. They had to be bought cheaply on one side of the desert, to be sold dearly as exotic luxuries on the other. Such goods included gold and gold dust; ostrich feathers; ivory; hides, skins and leather; kola nuts (a mild narcotic acceptable in Islam); senna; natron; dates; gum Arabic; and the ingredients for perfume-making in tiny but very valuable parcels.

Merchants carried gold, either as dust or made up into rough little rings, in dirty little pouches hidden in their clothes, hoping to evade its discovery either by desert marauders, by tax officials at mid-Saharan oases or at Tripoli itself. Civet musk, as an essential ingredient of the perfume-maker's art, was carried across the desert in small leather boxes, a tiny quantity at certain times and places fetching half as much minted gold by weight as the weight of musk. This musk (still used in modern perfume-making) is produced by the civet cat of tropical Africa. The cat's most notable feature, its musk, is a foul-smelling secretion of the perineal glands produced by both males and females. Highly valued both as an ingredient and stabilizing agent in perfume-making, this *civettone* is collected either by killing the animal and extracting the musk from its glands, or by periodic scraping of the living animal's musk secretions. (In the past, so familiar was civet musk as an essential ingredient of the perfume-maker's art that "The Civet Cat" was a common shop-sign of chemists, druggists and perfumers in eighteenth-century London, and presumably elsewhere in contemporary Britain and Europe.) The British explorer of the Lake Chad area, Dixon Denham, considering the prospects of British trade with Bornu through Tripoli in the 1820s, noted the brisk local market in civet musk "which brings an uncommon price in Europe". At the end of the nineteenth century it was reported that some caravans crossing the Sahara from the Sudan to Tripoli were bringing as much as fifty to eighty kilos of civet musk, which seems an excessive amount, even if it was regarded as an acceptable substitute for the by then increasingly proscribed black slave trade.

When brought safely across the Sahara, caged live civet cats were also extraordinarily valuable. At the beginning of the nineteenth century George Lyon found in Fezzan that one "savage old cat will produce ten or twelve dollars' worth [of musk] in three heats", while the animal itself could be worth as much as three or four common trade slaves, each of them then valued at perhaps £10 on the local market.

Ostrich feathers were carried across the Sahara from the Middle Ages onwards. Although demand (driven mainly by European courtly fashion) was spasmodic, it became much stronger and more regular in the nineteenth century, again in response to European and American demand. Ivory, although bulky and heavy, also became a more important item of trans-Saharan trade, especially as a substitute for the slave trade. But the trade in all these raw and unprocessed materials, including hides and skins, natron, senna and gum Arabic, became increasingly vulnerable to international economic competition, trade forces and cycles in the later nineteenth century.

Tripoli's main European Mediterranean trading partners were Marseille, Livorno (Leghorn) and Venice. Malta emerged as an increasingly important trans-shipment port after it became a British possession in 1800, when it also began buying cattle and grain from the Barbary coast for the Royal Navy and the military garrison. While Marseille dealt largely in French imports and exports, both Livorno and Venice were trans-shipment ports. Livorno was an entrepôt for the distribution of British goods throughout the Mediterranean, while Venice re-exported the products of northern Italy or goods carried across the Alpine passes from landlocked central Europe. Venice itself was the source of a staple product traded for centuries with sub-Saharan Africa: coloured glass beads of many different colours, sizes and patterns, mass-produced on the Venetian island of Murano. These "beads for the natives" were always cheap to buy, easily transported in bulk, and usually had a popular appeal in inner, tropical Africa that ensured good profits for traders who shipped them from Venice to Tripoli and then across the Sahara. Indeed, Venetian glass beads often circulated as currency in central Africa. Yet the market for such trinkets also fluctuated, and by the nineteenth century there is evidence that wearing beads was no longer as fashionable among "the belles of Timbuctu" as it had once been. About 1880 an Italian traveller in Libya lamented that Venetian beads "are now much less valued because the hairstyles of negresses are also subject to the changing caprices of fashion".

The Arms Trade

Venice also exported arms, and especially the firearms of many types and sizes imported from the arsenals of northern Italy and the German states. These were shipped in large quantities to the Turkish Balkans, the Levant, to North Africa and, through Tripoli, to Sudanic Africa. Indeed, so well-established and important was this trade that the name for Venice in Arabic, *Al-Bunduqiyah*, was also the name for a rifle or a gun in Arabic and other languages of sub-Saharan Africa, where imported German and north Italian guns, all supposedly of Venetian make, were owned and used by rival and warring states. (Similarly, so-called "Moroccan" leather came mostly from Sudan.)

Successive regimes in Tripoli were usually reluctant to encourage the trans-Saharan trade in European arms. It was, of course, desirable that their own land and naval forces were equipped with modern European weapons, either bought legitimately or captured during corsair raids. Turkish and Karamanli rulers nevertheless usually tried to prevent such arms, and particularly firearms, reaching the unruly and often rebellious tribes of the interior. But the international arms trade was, as it still is, so profitable that it was nearly impossible to stop smuggled weapons reaching inner Africa. Weapons found their way from Tripoli to the semi-Islamized Sudanic states beyond the Sahara, where firearms were used in state-organized slave raids and in more extended warfare, their noise alone perhaps ensuring the swift, terrified submission of peoples as yet unused to them, or panic among any local cavalry. As *The Edinburgh Review* had expressed it in 1826, "A gun, in the heart of Africa, is an object of almost supernatural dread... Armed with firearms, the Pasha of Tripoli is considered in the interior of Africa as the most powerful prince existing."

From about 1870 European armies began to replace their traditional rifles and muskets (loaded from the muzzle with black powder and ball) with breech-loading, metal cartridge rifles. Early breech-loaders fired only one round at a time, but in the 1880s spring-loaded magazines, holding five or more rounds, were introduced, giving much quicker rates of fire. Large stocks of obsolete military muzzle-loaders thus became available for supply to Africa, the Middle East and elsewhere. In the space of a few years the Saharan tribes and the Sudanic states beyond the Sahara received through Tripoli quantities of discarded European military muzzle-loaders of far better quality than the cheap "trade guns" that were often more lethal to their users than to their targets. But the advantages of such firearms over the so-called "white arms"—swords, daggers, lances and spears—were still limited by slow rates of fire, and the inaccuracy and short range of weapons often mishandled and poorly maintained. In the heat of battle, or the hunt, time and care were needed to pour an approximately correct amount of powder down the barrel, followed by wadding and ball, then to tamp them home with the ram-rod, withdraw the rod, and to prime and cock the lock for firing.

Yet with the swift evolution of European firearms technology from about 1870 to the early twentieth century, even many breech-loading rifles that had quickly become obsolescent were also soon available for export to inner Africa. In the 1870s the Sultan of the semi-Islamized eastern Sudanic state of Wadai had an arsenal of about 4,000 good-quality, muzzle-loading European military muskets supplied mainly through Tripoli; but his successor thirty years later had 10,000 modern breech-loaders of British, American and French make, most of them similarly delivered by Tripoli dealers with their own means of evading local import and trading restrictions.

One difficulty with the variety of such guns was that they used different types and calibres of cartridge, and it was not easy to maintain steady and appropriate contraband supplies across the full width of the

Sahara. Indeed, some tribesmen of inner Tripolitania preferred to keep their traditional, long-barrelled, flint-lock, muzzle-loaders because they knew they could rely on a steady supply of smuggled gunpowder. Nevertheless, the traveller Karl Kumm reported seeing in Tripoli in 1905 "large quantities of cartridges and Winchester rifles which had been smuggled into the country by Italians [to be sold in Sudan]. Everybody in Tripoli seemed to know about these smuggling operations." And another contemporary traveller noted that "European guns of every pattern and origin can be found [in Tripoli] and will be supplied by unscrupulous agents of respectable firms so long as there is a profit." And if south of the Sahara guns were used to capture people for enslavement, slaves were used to acquire guns by providing the most ready exchange for these imported weapons coveted by every would-be warrior. In 1907 one slave from Wadai was the exchange for an 1874 breech-loading French rifle in good condition, with forty cartridges included.

Tripoli's merchants imported other trade goods in fairly regular shipments from both southern Europe and the Levant (mainly the Greek islands under Turkish rule as well as Constantinople, Smyrna and Alexandria). Some of these goods were for local use, others for re-export across the Sahara. According to Consul Fraser's trade report of 1767, Venice, besides its glass, was the source of sewing thread, needles and thimbles; "Damask with gold sprigs"; gold and silver thread; and fine wire. These materials were clearly ordered for the town's many Jewish tailors who specialized in making elaborate, colourful and richly-embroidered ceremonial clothes for the potentates and royal courts of inner, trans-Saharan Africa.

Also from Venice came reams of writing paper which on the far side of the Sahara could also be used as money: literally a paper currency. British goods (largely textiles at that time) were shipped from Livorno, while other European imports included coarse cloth from Naples; tobacco (Turkish as well as American); and scrap brass and tin (needed for minting coins in sub-Saharan Africa). From the Levant came coarse linens; plain and striped Smyrna cottons; drugs, carpets and slippers. Tunis supplied the typical red caps (*chechia*). Imports from the Levant were worth more than double the imports from Livorno and Venice. Once local demand in Tripoli had been met, the rest of this imported merchandise was re-exported into and across the Sahara.

Rather surprisingly, Consul Fraser's international trade report of 176? made no mention of the large volumes of alcohol that were regularly imported from southern Europe for local consumption: so much of it in fact that "empty barrels" were always a significant export item. Yet nearly a century earlier the English Consul had in July 1680 alone counted the delivery of 310 butts of wine (150,000 litres) from Naples, Greece and Sardinia. The few resident Christians were not the only ones drinking all this imported alcohol: the ruling *Dey* and his court certainly accounted for some of it, and if public wine houses (some run by Christian slaves) were a common feature of the town, so were its many drunks, as George Lyon found in 1818.

What is also shown by Consul Fraser's trade report is the poverty of other imports from the far side of the Sahara, apart from the all-important trade in slaves. Parcels of senna, natron (commonly added to snuff), dates, ostrich feathers, some gum Arabic and a little gold dust altogether represented only 15 per cent of the import trade by value. According to the same report, two-fifths of the exports to the Mediterranean world by value were the black slaves shipped off to the Levant. Exports to Europe (mainly Livorno, Venice and Malta) were mainly senna and feathers. But the report made no mention of a Mediterranean export trade in either civet musk for perfume making, or ivory.

As in previous centuries, trans-Saharan trade in the nineteenth was still basically an exchange of European, Levantine and a few North African products for the unprocessed raw materials of the African interior. As the century evolved, European industry increasingly came to dominate the south-bound caravan business with a widening range of cheap, shoddy goods. The British anti-slavery agent and traveller, James Richardson noted at a mid-Saharan market in the winter of 1845-46 that "it is for detestable rubbish of this sort that human beings were purchased". At the same time, Africa's exportable products had only a limited appeal on international markets. Similar raw products, perhaps cheaper and of better quality, became more easily available from newly-exploited tropical colonial possessions elsewhere.

Yet from the early nineteenth century the nearby Maltese archipelago had become a valuable trading partner. At the best of times, these small rocky islands, always short of water, were unable to feed all their own people. Despite the religious and ideological differences between this

The Trading City: Between Sahara and Mediterranean

"Christian bulwark" and the nearby coastlands of Muslim Barbary, for centuries Malta had contrived to import some of its food through Tripoli. In 1800 this historical relationship took on a new importance with the British occupation of the archipelago, with its immense value to Britain's central Mediterranean naval strategy against the Napoleonic dominance of continental Europe. By 1803 the British realized that if the Maltese were themselves short of food, substantial meat and grain rations had also be imported to feed the garrison defending the islands and, more importantly, to provision the large naval forces (eventually the full Mediterranean Fleet) securely based all the year round in Grand Harbour, Valletta. With continental Europe blockaded, Tripolitania was one of the nearest, and politically one of the most reliable, sources of supply. In due course the British Consul General in Tripoli was made responsible for the smooth flow of what soon became fairly regular shipments of locally-produced grain (barley in particular) and live cattle. These shipments in due course fell into the hands of the leading entrepreneurs of the Maltese expatriate community in Tripoli. Confident in its new British protection, this community grew quickly to about 1,500 at the end of the Napoleonic Wars (and to about 2,600 by the early twentieth century).

The city's role as a food exporter was always weakened by the constant threat of drought which, on average, devastated flocks, herds and crops for an average of two years out of every ten. During a long series of droughts in Tripolitania in the 1840s, Cyrenaica became a more important supplier of food to Malta, shipped through Benghazi. But in the later nineteenth century, cattle exports from Tripolitania never fell below 5,000 head a year, and in some years amounted to well over 10,000 head. Large quantities of barley, wheat and olive oil were also shipped. Much of this produce was re-exported from the islands, even to Britain itself. For the fact is that Malta, largely through its own enterprise and its close links with British worldwide maritime trade, became a prime Mediterranean trans-shipment hub. It also served, and in many ways promoted, the international trade of the port of Tripoli, whose own Maltese community contributed to this mutually advantageous enterprise.

With the decline of the Saharan caravan trade, the Turkish administration did make some effort to promote economic alternatives. From the 1860s Tripoli became an export market for esparto grass (*alf-*

alfa). The grass was gathered by hand, the harvester winding each handful round a stick and then ripping it away, thus tearing up the root as well and with it the chances of another harvest. The grass was dried and then carried in large, swaying nets on camels to town, where it was cleaned sorted and weighed. It was then sold at the regular Monday market outside the city walls, most of it shipped to Britain for making fine paper especially banknotes. The trade was said to have amounted to 30,000 tons, worth £50,000, in some good years, with the landowners taking the largest share of earnings divided also between the harvesters, the camel-drivers and the other workers.

In the 1870s a British traveller could insist that the port had become the centre of the caravan trade of northern Africa because Tunis and Algiers had by then "lost their footing in this lucrative business" Although Tripoli was indeed still the main trans-shipment entrepôt between the Mediterranean (Europe and the Levant) and the Sahara (Sudanic Africa) it was in the long run to fare no better than Tunis or Algiers. There were several reasons for this collapse. First, its core business of trans-Saharan and trans-Mediterranean slave trading was by the 1860s in terminal decline. As early as 1859 the British Consul General, wrote of "the almost total cessation of the caravan trade with the interior since the abolition of the slave trade". Despite the claim the abolitionists had been making for almost the past century (that abolition would open up the Sahara to a rich and morally-acceptable "legitimate" commerce), there was in practice no alternative business with anything like the same long-term profit-making potential as slaving.

Then the Saharan caravan system based on Tripoli—unimproved over the centuries in either its methods or its organization, inefficient, under capitalized, and reliant on a few well-tried routes and limited numbers of load-carrying camels—was unable to react swiftly to international market fluctuations. In the long run, Saharan traders could not compete with newer, easier sources of supply (South African ostrich farms, for instance or other means of transport on new, alternative routes such as European steamer services to west Africa and up the River Niger, or European colonial railways into the African interior. In the early twentieth century the railway reached the great trading hub of Kano in northern Nigeria linking it by train to Lagos, and so by steamer to Liverpool. A parcel of goods could then be sent from Liverpool to Kano more quickly and securely by sea and rail than a similar delivery across the Sahara from Tripoli, and at less than half the price.

Faced with the end of the slave trade, at least on the central desert roads from the 1860s, Tripoline merchants and their associates across the Mediterranean and the Sahara did make serious efforts to exploit alternative business in the other raw exports of inner Africa: ivory, ostrich feathers, hides and skins. During a series of successful years, these trades seemed to show that the abolitionists had indeed been right all along. There was no steady rise in such business, which made but slow progress up to 1872, followed by a strong surge in 1873-80. A sharp setback in the 1880s (perhaps partly reflecting the European recession of 1878-84) was followed by a slight recovery in the 1890s, and a swift, final decline after 1900.

Almost the final blow to Tripoli's historical domination of trade across the central Sahara was struck with the depredations of the Sudanese military-slaving adventurer, Rabih Fadlallah, between Wadai and Bornu in 1879-1900. Resident Tripoline merchants in the Bornu capital, Kukawa, west of Lake Chad, suffered huge financial losses when his forces took and pillaged the place in 1893, and the ancient trade route to the Mediterranean was closed for two years. The Jewish traveller Nahum Slouschz found that while at the beginning of the twentieth century there had been in Tripoli "about 100 families who made a living by cleaning and dyeing ostrich feathers, by 1907 I found nearly four hundred girls, who were in this trade, out of work". He also reported that "in 1906 there were only eight [business] houses doing a trade with the Sudan, and by 1909 there were even fewer". No wonder that even in the 1890s a British visitor had described the town, among its other shortcomings, as "nearly tradeless".

Colonial Economy

Such was Tripoli's commercial situation as the Italians found it on arrival in 1911. This was by then a trading town of only slight significance on the global economic map—"a port of the twentieth order", according to a contemporary French geographer. But to Italy, its prime value was anyway not as a commercial gateway to Africa, but as an imperial possession which, with the ports of Benghazi and Tobruk, would confirm Italian strategic domination of both sides of the central Mediterranean narrows. Then, according to Italian hopes, both it and Benghazi would soon be shipping to the Mother Country the abundant farming produce that Libya would yield with wise Italian management and the dedicated labour of Italian peasant settlers. Many foreign visitors over the past fifty years had agreed that under Italian rule Libya could be brought back to the agricultural prosperity of the Classical era. That Tripoli might also recover its place as a main Mediterranean outlet for the "wealth" of inner Africa and develop a reciprocal trade across the Sahara in the industrial products of Italy may have been another, lesser consideration; but it was in the long run as unrealistic as the other delusions about Libya and its potential that drove Italy to venture there in the first place.

The fact of the matter was that the trans-Saharan trade, which might have seemed a rich and exotic commerce by the meaner standards of past times, had collapsed under the weight of its own contradictions by the beginning of the twentieth century, and there were few realistic prospects for its revival. The British, at least, had realized by about 1860 that the Saharan approach to inner Africa was not worth pursuing, not only because of the physical difficulties of the desert crossing, but because of the inherent poverty of the Sudanese markets once they had lost the essential prop of the export slave trade. Yet the French deluded themselves until the end of the nineteenth century that a Saharan railway from Algiers to Timbuctu and the River Niger was a worthwhile commercial proposition, while the Italians still believed in 1911 that by taking Tripoli they would gain control of all the rich trade that would soon flow to and from Lake Chad. Yet by then any revived trans-Saharan trade with what had become French-dominated Sudanic Africa would have had its outlets in French North Africa, not Italian Libya. Under colonial rule, the territories of French West Africa (including what later became Niger, Mali and Burkina Faso) and French Equatorial Africa (including Chad) looked both commercially and politically towards the centres of French power in Atlantic Africa (Dakar, Abidjan, Brazzaville), rather than across the Sahara towards Tripoli. Under Italian colonial rule in Libya, and French rule in the western and central Sudan, political and ideological barriers, if not actual trade barriers, were erected across the formerly open Sahara where trading caravans had once passed freely. And those barriers remained even after the great wave of independence swept across Africa in 1960.

The Trading City: Between Sahara and Mediterranean

The overall effect of these changes was to make Tripoli after 1911 merely a *colonial* port. As such, it largely served the narrow interests of the Italian Mother Country in Libya, and no longer the diverse but interdependent markets of the Mediterranean world and trans-Saharan Africa, as it had done for centuries past. True, the Tripoli trader would continue to be a familiar figure in the market places of Chad and other parts of the Sudan, but by the mid-twentieth century he was more likely to be a solo freelance operator rather than one of several local representatives of a wide and continuing international trans-Saharan trading system, as he would have been a century earlier.

A calculated process of Italianizing the Tripoline economy started around 1905 with Rome's official policy of "peaceful penetration". The main agent of this policy was the Banco di Roma, which opened its first branch in Tripoli in 1907. In the face of increasing Turkish and local hostility, the bank managed to invest in various enterprises processing local produce, as well as an ice factory and a printing works. But the authorities constantly frustrated its attempts to buy cultivable land, as they rejected all Italian proposals for civic works and other improvements in and around the city. By 1911 it was clear that peaceful penetration had been an utter failure in the face of Turkish obstruction.

By the time the Italians arrived as conquerors in 1911, Tripoli had already lost its historic trading contacts with inner Africa and the Levant. Instead, and particularly under the Fascist regime from 1922 onwards, it became the main point of entry for the material necessities of an artificial, imported economy, primarily serving the needs of an immigrant Italian population and supported by the lavish direct and indirect subsidies of the Italian state. New industries, businesses and services came to the colonial capital to meet new demands generated firstly by the over-large military forces needed to conquer and "pacify" the interior of this unruly possession; then by the bloated colonial civil service; and later by ambitious, state-subsidized urban, infrastructural, agricultural, transport, social and tourist developments in and around the city. Of course this colonial capital in the 1920s and 1930s gave visitors an impression of burgeoning prosperity in an economy where all but the most basic demands, resources and necessities (and much of the labour) would be readily supplied by the Mother Country alone: even a large part of the raw building materials for the new Tripoli and the new Libya was shipped from Italy.

Italy became in turn almost the sole outlet through the port of Tripoli for limited agricultural and other colonial products, helpfully freed from the competition of international markets. All such activity naturally stimulated a range of local businesses, both old and new—Muslim Arab to some extent, and Italian, Maltese and Jewish in particular. In the late 1930s it might have been reasonably argued that this subsidized over-reliance on the Mother Country, and resultant large yearly trade imbalance, would be corrected once the colony's agriculture became fully productive within ten to fifteen years under the stimulus of thousands of Italian peasant farmers settled on wide arcs of land beyond Tripoli and Benghazi under the state's "demographic colonization" schemes of 1938 and 1939. But Italy's entry into the Second World War in June 1940, and Libya's close involvement in that war for the next thirty disruptive and destructive months, cut short the time, the resources and in due course even the opportunities for such ambitious economic and social experiments.

So, by the time the British Eighth Army finally rolled into Tripoli in January 1943, three months after the Battle of El Alamein, the city

Italian colonial architecture of the late 1930s: National Social Insurance building, opposite the cathedral.

and its port were a strategic and propaganda prize of prime importance to the Allied war effort; but they had precious little other value. On the contrary, they were an economic, as well as a political and social burden to the British Military Administration (BMA) that had to be quickly set up to look after them on a strict "care and maintenance" basis while the war lasted.

So long as Tripoli remained a vital supply port and forward base for the Allied campaign in Tunisia, and then the invasion of Sicily and southern Italy, it was still moderately prosperous. But as the fighting and the free-spending foreign armies moved away from North Africa in 1943-44, so the economy inevitably collapsed. Italian imports, funds and subsidies had all ceased, and the banks were closed. The BMA had neither the money nor the mandate to improve things and Tripolines—Muslims, Jews and Italians (all of whom were   competently administered, up to a point, and no longer in a war zone) —had patiently to survive thin times and meagre rations as best as they could until the end of the war.

The only food for the civilian population of greater Tripoli (about 170,000 people) was either grown locally (the largely undamaged state farming concessions of 1938 and 1939 were by 1943 becoming productive), or imported from Egypt with whatever transport could be spared from the war effort. Under its wartime rationing system, the local Italian administration had allocated more to its own people (and the German military) and less to the native Libyans, and particularly those living outside town. But the BMA soon made it clear that "no distinction of race is to be made in the issue of rations"—such as they were. Thus the daily bread ration in Tripoli in 1943 was 300 grams (one small loaf); the *monthly* allowances were half a kilo of flour for pasta-making (perhaps six adult helpings), 400 grams of sugar, 200 grams of cooking oil; and a little red tea for the Libyans. Many in wartime Europe were faring far worse.

Yet with three years of good harvests, food supplies (even allowing some exports) improved in 1944-46. In the meantime, demand for skilled and unskilled labour, with a related boost for the local economy, came from big new military projects nearby. These were notably the development for the RAF of the military airfield at Castel Benito (later Idris Airport) amid the dunes to the south of the city, and at Mellaha Field, on the coast near Tagiura. There from 1943 the USAF reportedly started to spend $100 million on greatly expanding the former Italian airfield, laying out immensely long runways for its biggest bombers (later to become nuclear bombers), and a complete American township for its personnel. Such spending was in addition to yearly grants-in-aid from the British government.

If Libya after the Second World War was considered one of the poorest countries in the world (with an average yearly income of $35 per head) and to have an uncertain future, its capital city also reflected this general poverty and uncertainty. In 1950, when it was still under temporary British administration, a British visitor argued that

> The Tripoli of the Italians, a great cosmopolitan seaport, had no logical reason for its existence and in its present form seemed doomed to extinction. Perhaps it will revive, perhaps some power will be found with the necessary millions to pour into it to bring back its former life; perhaps, some day, it will diminish to the size its hinterland can justify. But what in the meantime is to happen to the great buildings, the banks and shipping offices and the imposing boulevards, the cafes and restaurants and lavish hotels of the Italian era?[61]

Yet Tripoli survived and Libya, despite its poverty and apparent unreadiness for self-rule, in 1951 became an independent kingdom. Italy thus in effect wrote off all its work and lavish investment in its former colony since 1911, leaving a magnificent, modern built infrastructure, particularly in and around Tripoli. In its early years as joint capital (with Benghazi) of a federal monarchy uniting Tripolitania, Cyrenaica and Fezzan, the city and its port survived in small part by exporting low-grade agricultural output (chiefly peanuts). But like the kingdom as a whole, its real survival depended largely on foreign aid; on base-leasing agreements with Britain, the USA and France; and on the local spending and employment by some of the biggest of those military bases, which happened to be in or just beyond the Tripoli oasis.

Yet the advantages of its Saharan-Mediterranean setting, the geographical basis of its historical trading enterprise and prosperity, once again served Tripoli well in the twentieth and twenty-first centuries. From the 1950s it took on an entirely new role as joint capital, first of an oil-prospecting state, and then of an oil-producing state of the first order. That oil (and associated natural gas) came mostly from the Saharan hinterland, while the Mediterranean provided the open, unrestricted tanker access to the close, and booming, oil markets of southern Europe.

Thus even under the initial stimulus of mere prospecting for oil by the big international companies from the mid-1950s, Tripoli itself soon began to revive. It did so simply by being (with Benghazi) once again the obvious local entry point and base for dynamic foreign enterprise, a city and a port where the American and European oil industries and their many satellite businesses were hurrying to open operational and servicing subsidiaries. These incomers in turn stimulated expansion of many local service industries, including banking, transport, housing, shopping, entertainment and travel, and hence demand for local skilled and unskilled labour. After an anxious wait of only a few years since Italy had left and its subsidies had dried up, here was "the power with the necessary millions to pour into the city to bring back its former life", as the British traveller, quoted above, had doubtfully anticipated around 1950.

Once again, the city's extremely narrow range of economic choices had been suddenly widened by outside stimulus. Unlike the almost artificial economy Italy had promoted in this prestige possession, the moderate economic recovery stimulated by foreign oil prospectors in the 1950s, and then the economic boom brought by actual oil revenues in the 1960s, were at least grounded on real economic activity and the exploitation of a valued and eminently marketable natural resource. Yet this new-found prosperity, with all its implications for the city's economic and social growth and development, still seemed to be unreal and unearned. This was no longer a trading city, as it had been for centuries past, relying for much of its essential wellbeing on the intercontinental enterprise and risk-taking of its merchant and financial communities trading by land and sea. Now Libya's oil was shipped by foreigners from a series of specialized oil terminals, built and manned by foreigners on the Gulf of Sirte, or at Tobruk, and not from Tripoli, or even Benghazi. In the 1960s both these cities accordingly became largely *import* terminals. They exported little or nothing of value, but sucked in all the material goods (including food), as well as the services and human skills that the local economy and society could or would not provide, but which could instead be readily bought abroad with oil revenues.

Great harm was done to Tripoli's business community and its remaining entrepreneurial spirit during many of the 42 years of Muammar Gaddafi's bizarre and essentially juvenile political, economic and social experiments. This leader had a deep, personal objection to private enterprise; but after twenty years of his "revolution", some urgent economic reform from the late 1980s allowed the emergence of a new, younger generation of private entrepreneurs. These black market dealers would bring from nearby Malta all the latest consumer goods Tripolines and other Libyans had been denied for years, and do a brisk trade in reselling them at street and market stalls; or they would (despite the supposedly draconian punishments for doing do) deal profitably in foreign currency. Their early main centre of operation in Tripoli was Sciara Rashid, a run-down area near the city centre; they later migrated to, and created, more upmarket forums. Thus according to one political observer,

> By the end of 2004 Tripoli once more resembled a boomtown, reminiscent of the 1960s and 1970s... To anyone who had known the country during the austere years of its revolution, when virtually all private businesses had been abolished or withered away for lack of provisions, the city's streets had been transformed beyond recognition. Many of the revolutionary slogans... were giving way to commercial advertising signs. The once ubiquitous portraits of the Leader now vied for attention alongside commercial dioramas that touted an array of products Libyans once could only dream about... Small shops lined the main streets of the cities, selling imported food, appliances and furniture.[62]

Yet even after Gaddafi's overthrow in 2011 the fact remained that the capital's economic and social wellbeing still depended on a continuing inflow of oil and gas export revenues. For in all their years of power Gaddafi and his regime had done little or nothing to resolve the basic underlying dilemma of the Libyan oil era. Since the oil had started to flow fifty years earlier, there had been no coherent attempt, no long-term plan to prepare Tripoli and its people, or the country and its people as a whole, for a future without the temporary fortune of bounteous and unearned wealth from depleting reserves of hydrocarbons.

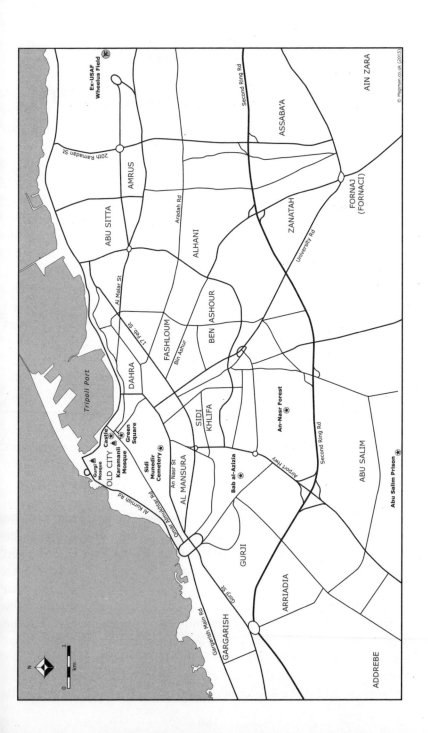

Chapter Nine
The Built Environment

The building, town-planning and sanitary activities of the Italians have been remarkable... The town of Tripoli has been transformed from a dusty, ramshackle Turkish village into a modern city. Alan Broderick

The Old City of Tripoli, sitting on its little peninsula, has the shape of an irregular pentagon. The longest side is on the harbour; another commands the rocky seashore to the north-west; three other sides face the land. Even in late Roman times, this five-sided space (1,000 by 700 metres at its longest and widest) was defined by a defensive wall dominating the landward approaches. But the sea front was left unprotected, a defensive defect that the invading Arabs exploited when they arrived overland from the east in 643 AD and began to besiege the town. Strangely, these city walls had only two gates: one the *Bab al-Menscia*, leading to the well-populated *Menscia* suburb of palm-groves and watered gardens to the south-east, and another newer one thus called the *Bab al-Jadid*, giving access to the more barren, western stretches of the Tripoli oasis. During the Spanish occupation of the early sixteenth century the walls were rebuilt and extended some way along the reef to protect the harbour; they ended at an advanced, sea-girt strongpoint, known for centuries as the Spanish Fort; in 1864 its huge powder magazine blew up, leaving it as an uncleared pile of rubble.

Here at Tripoli, as with London's so-called "Square Mile" and the cores of some other, still flourishing former Roman cities, the line of the Roman wall may still mark the limits of the original centre. And, as in many continuously-occupied cities, Tripoli's defensive walls have been damaged many times by enemy action, both by land and sea, and then renewed, rebuilt, reinforced and adapted to new forms of warfare. The introduction of heavy siege artillery and naval cannon at the end of the Middle Ages made conventional, towering fortifications obsolete: what was then needed were massive, low-built walls with battered stone bases (sloping from the vertical) and defensive ditches and other earthworks to absorb or deflect the impact of cannon balls. (The people had tried to reinforce their city walls with a moat as far back as the thirteenth century, but their excavations had been repeatedly filled in by wind-blown sand; only in the seventeenth century was a moat completed and filled with sea water.) As late as 1561 Nicola Maria Caracciolo, Bishop of Catania, who had spent some time in Tripoli as a prisoner (and later ransomed) was highly critical of the city's defences as he had seen them:

> The circuit of Tripoli is a good two miles round, not less than that of Catania. It needs much guarding because the walls are weak and they cannot be defended with long-handled weapons because the battlements are so narrow that neither pikes nor halberds can be wielded there. It lacks defensive ditches; there are no flanking walls; and the few bastions are so disposed that any one of them cannot defend any other.[63]

The bishop suggested that an invasion fleet of ships carrying 9,000 soldiers, together with artillery, and transports loaded with siege equipment and engineers, could "bring to a happy conclusion" the Christian re-conquest of an important strategic possession lost by the Knights of Malta to the Turks a decade earlier.

Over the centuries the city, its harbour and its defensive forts and walls came under other, if less destructive, assaults from the greater European naval powers, outraged by the continuing activities of the corsairs in the central and eastern Mediterranean. In the 34 years between 1638 and 1672 there were six such attacks: three by the French, two by the English and one by the Dutch. At the beginning of the nineteenth century the young American Republic mounted similar attacks in defence of what it regarded as its local rights, while Sardinia did so in 1825 and Naples as late as 1828. All such attacks damaged the town's buildings and more especially its built defences, to a greater or lesser degree.

But successive rulers did not always properly maintain such works, and the restored Turkish regime of 1835-1911 no doubt by the late nineteenth century considered the city walls to be useless against modern high explosives. The Italians in the early years of their rule after 1911 demolished two long sections of the walls in an over-enthusiastic desire to create an urban space with a new tree-lined avenue separating the Old City from the new—over-hasty vandalism that they later regretted.

The Romans have left other marks on the Old City. We have seen that when the Tunisian traveller Al-Tigiani was there in 1307-08, he found the streets remarkably clean, straight and meeting at right angles giving, he said, the appearance of a chessboard. This suggests that much of the original, regular Roman street layout was then still largely intact. But Al-Tigiani was describing the town some two centuries before Spanish forces captured it in 1510, destroying in the process much of the ancient street pattern, together with other surviving Roman work. Yet even today stretches of the Roman main layout can still be clearly traced along some of the main streets. It seems, for instance, that two Roman thoroughfares, a *decumanus* and a *cardo*, met at the Forum where the Old City's most striking Roman monument, the Arch of Marcus Aurelius, still stands. But irregularity and confusion take over in the frequent, narrow side-turnings off such main thoroughfares; for many of these alleys, far from linking up with others, are simply multiple dead ends. They are made even more claustrophobic by the blank, anonymous walls of the enclosing houses and other buildings that have most, if not all, of their windows facing into inner courtyards. The alleys of two former Jewish quarters on the north-west side of the Old City are by far the most confusing. The confined atmosphere of such places is deepened by the lack of unexpected little piazzas and other public open spaces relieving the oppression of the close-built environment.

Still the most striking standing monument of Roman Tripoli is the Arch of Marcus Aurelius, built in 163 AD. This venerable pile, topped by a shallow dome, is no great beauty: it stands four-square and solid, its huge stone blocks held in place, without any mortar, by the force of gravity; which is probably why it has survived for some 2,000 years. Very likely it dominated the Forum of Roman Oea. In the early fourteenth century Al-Tigiani was greatly impressed by this massive structure, while many European visitors of later centuries stressed the contrast between its venerable solidity and its run-down modern surroundings. According to Miss Tully in the late eighteenth century,

> It is thought by all good judges to be handsomer than any of the most celebrated in Italy... this arch is very high, but does not appear so, being from the great accumulation of sands carried by the winds, exactly as deep beneath the surface of the earth as it is

Half-buried by the accumulated rubbish of centuries, the Roman Arch of Marcus Aurelius as it appeared (top) in a sketch of the 1780s (Tully) and (below) in one of about 1820. (Lyon).

high above it. It is composed of stones so extremely large that it seems wonderful how they were conveyed hither...[64]

With its openings blocked up, the Arch was long used as a storehouse; but when the Italians arrived in Turkish Tripoli in 1911 it was serving as one of the town's two cinemas (although it can hardly have provided a spacious auditorium). These new rulers had no doubt about its significance: "historically the most precious monument of the city", the Italian guidebook called it. In effect the Arch represented Italy's title deeds to the city, just as the other abundant Roman remains of northern Tripolitania and Cyrenaica seemed to justify Italy's assertion that in returning to Libya she was merely reclaiming her Roman heritage (on which basis she might equally have claimed other provinces of the former Roman Empire, from Syria to Morocco and from Egypt to Britain).

Still unexcavated and unrestored, the same arch, apparently used as a shop, in an impression of the early twentieth century. Note the woman on the right, completely enveloped in her *barracan*, apart from one cautiously exposed eye.

Dismayed by the sorry, neglected state of this precious monument, nearly half-buried below the modern, higher ground level, and with its squalid setting, the newly-appointed director of the Tripoli Archaeological Bureau started a six-year programme of consolidation and restoration in March 1912, barely six months after the Italian occupation. The surrounding modern ground level (raised over the centuries by the locals' failure to remove their accumulated rubbish) was lowered to expose the Arch to its full height of nearly ten metres. Several encroaching *fonduks* (hostels with arcaded courtyards accommodating

The results of painstaking Italian excavation and restoration: the arch (now with a roof) in its neat little piazza, as it appeared in the 1920s. The slender, two-balconied minaret marks the Gurgi Mosque, one of the city's finest, dating from the 1830s.

travelling merchants and their goods) and other vernacular but historically important buildings were demolished. When these works were finished the Arch was left sitting, isolated and rather meaningless, in a genteel little piazza easily accessible to tourists deprived first of the surprise, and then the pleasure, of suddenly coming upon this unique monument in its previous unprepossessing but more "authentic" and crowded urban setting.

Probably also of Roman origin is the town's most prominent and important historical complex, the Castle. It stands, four-square and glum, on the harbour at the north-east corner of the Old City. It was largely rebuilt by the Spanish occupiers after their destructions of 1510, and many more bits and pieces were added by other rulers over the following centuries.

Historically, the Castle had much the same function as the Tower of London had in the Middle Ages. It was the ruler's residence; a seat of state and civic administration with secretariat and archives; a fortress; a barracks; a court of law; a prison; a place of execution; and, with its looming presence, a symbol of state oppression. With many additions and dilapidations, by the early nineteenth century it had become almost a little town in its own right: a complex of vaulted chambers; long, street-like passageways; open, arcaded courtyards; dark barracks and dungeons; "those gloomy passages which always seem as if they led to some dreadful abode for the purposes of entombing the living" (as Miss Tully put it); and more attractive living quarters for the ruling *Dey* or Pasha, his harem and family. These domestic sets were arranged around arcaded courts (many of the supporting columns were re-used Roman or Byzantine work) with coloured tile wall inlays and central marble fountains. The different levels were connected by steep, broken, unprotected and poorly lit stairways. But by the early nineteenth century the ruling Pasha himself was receiving his guests while enthroned in exotic, oriental splendour in a sumptuous new audience chamber that hardly reflected the increasingly desperate financial realities of his little city-state.

When Constantinople re-imposed its direct rule and overthrew the last Karamanli Pasha in 1835, the Castle became the seat of the new Turkish administration. When the British traveller James Richardson was in Tripoli in 1845, he was escorted to the Castle by the long-serving British Consul Hanmer Warrington for an official interview with the current Turkish Pasha:

On entering the place I was astonished at its ruinous and repulsive appearance. Nothing could better resemble a prison, and yet a prison on a most dilapidated condition. Walking through the dark, winding, damp, mildewy passages, shedding down upon us a pestiferous dungeon influence, Colonel Warrington suddenly stopped as if to breathe and repel the deadly miasma, and turning to me, said: "Well, Richardson, what do you think of this? Capital place for young ladies to dance in, so light and airy. Many a poor wretch has entered here, with promises of fortune and royal favour, and met his doom at the hand of the assassin. In the course of my long service, how many Kaeds and Sheikhs I have known, who have come in here and have never gone out..."[65]

When the Italians arrived in 1911, the Commander in Chief of the invading forces, General Caneva, set up his headquarters in the Castle. One of the Italians' first acts on entering it was to tip the archives of the Karamanli and Ottoman secretaries into the sea. They were rescued by an officer with some sense of history who found them floating in the harbour. He ordered them to be dumped in a small storeroom where over thirty years later they were found—"a disintegrating mass of mouldy papers, piled in disorder from floor to ceiling"—by the first British Eighth Army officers who entered the Castle after the fall of Tripoli in January 1943.

Tripoli and its oasis in 1912 had a civilian population of about 72,000, two-thirds living outside the walls, and especially in the new suburbs that had started to spread into the eastern oasis, the *Menscia*, in the last decades of Ottoman rule. In a series of plans and studies in 1912-14, the Italians decided that this prestigious capital (in name, if not yet in appearance) of their new North African possession was to be suitably modernized, with a new European city laid out alongside, but separate from, the old walled town. The historic centre was to be respectfully preserved, sympathetically restored and given modern civic services. Similar town planning policies were then being followed by the French in the great "imperial" cities of their new Moroccan Protectorate, by the British in New Delhi and Cairo, and by the Americans in colonial Manila.

But little of this planned work was carried out until after the First World War. Then in 1921 the Venetian industrialist and financier Giuseppe Volpi was appointed Governor of Tripolitania. His new and dynamic political, military and economic programmes for the province effectively anticipated later Fascist policy in a colony still in a state of chaotic rebellion against Italian rule. As Volpi's programme included Tripoli's transformation into a city reflecting Italian sovereign authority and dignity, one of his first projects was to make the Castle into a fitting centre of his administration.

The outsides of the bastions were first cleared of all the squalid sheds, stalls and mounds of rubbish that the Turks had allowed to pile up against them. Governor Volpi then decided that the walls and corner facing the harbour needed to be higher, more assertive, to impress new arrivals taking their first sight of the low, white town and its dominating Castle as they sailed into port. He called in the Roman architect Armando Brasini and in 1922 commissioned him to embellish and dignify the Castle on the outside and remodel it as a seat of modern administration on the inside. Brasini accordingly built an extra storey on the wing overlooking Piazza Castello, while he gave the important harbour-side corner and walls greater regularity and interest by heightening them with a great screen-wall pierced by a series of huge open arches—a meaningless but visually stimulating conceit.

Without unduly vandalizing this complex and venerable series of buildings, Brasini contrived a new, ramped street entrance from Piazza Castello and inserted a new suite of administrative offices and approach staircases intended to reflect the dignity and authority of a modern colonial administration. The journalist Mario Corsi described these additions soon after their completion:

> The suite of the Governor and the Secretary General at the highest point of the Castle has fine marble staircases and spacious, simple, airy reception rooms and offices. Where there was a mass of roofs, terraces and platforms there is now a superb hanging garden. The old Turkish and Venetian bronze cannon form a strikingly severe decorative motif, stationed at the embrasures that overlook the magnificent new Lungomare Volpi, and along the battlements.[66]

The works were finished off with a mole and landing place on the waterside, with two square obelisks, one supporting the Roman *Lupa* suckling Romulus and Remus, and the other a Venetian galley. Originally, this was the starting point for one of the most attractive new features of modern Tripoli: the balustraded, tree-lined, seafront Lungomare Conte Volpi which followed the fine curve of the harbour eastwards for nearly a kilometre. (The character of this pleasing and typically Italian layout was spoilt and lost most of its visual impact when new sea container quays were built alongside it in the revolutionary 1970s.) In the 1930s a magnificent archaeological museum to house treasures dug up at Leptis Magna, Sabratha and other sites in Tripolitania was contrived inside the Castle complex. The *lungomare* was at the same time extended under new arches through the Castle itself. On the far side it joined up with the old harbour road (Strada dei Bastioni) that had previously run awkwardly round the Castle before emerging through the defensive walls at Bab al-Menscia.

Under Fascism, the Castle, as the local seat of government, was the focus of a brief but daily public ceremony, as witnessed by the newly-arrived British Consul, Geoffrey Furlonge:

> On my first evening in Tripoli, in 1938, I was walking home along the Lungomare amongst a mainly Muslim throng. As the sun set, a gun was fired from the Castello, at that time the Governorate, and on the instant I found myself the only person in the street both moving and facing eastward, for everyone else had stopped in his tracks (those in cars or cabs leaping out of them), had turned west to face the Castello and was doing the Fascist salute. I was never again in the street at that hour.[67]

Islamic Tripoli

Even with its brief intervals of European occupation, Tripoli has been an overwhelmingly Islamic city for over half its probable existence of around 2,500 years. At the same time (up to 1970) it housed a considerable Jewish minority, for Jews arrived in what is now Libya at least 1,000 years before the first Muslim Arabs did. And there have nearly always been small Christian communities as well: residual communities of native Christians up to about 1000 AD, with foreign Christian traders, diplomats, travellers and slaves also usually present. But Tripoli is unusual among Islamic cities in having no recognized, separate quarters where the different faiths lived and worked apart, among their own people. There was not even an identifiable diplomatic quarter housing the consulates of the half dozen foreign powers that had opened relations with Tripoli in or after the seventeenth century. The only exceptions were the two defined Jewish quarters at the western, landward side of the walled city.

In the historic town centres of Christendom and Islam, the religious buildings are still at least as prominent as any other. This is certainly true of the Old City, which has for centuries displayed its Islamic character in its mosques with their prominent minarets, and in its *madrasas* (religious schools). Islamic prohibitions against portraying living creatures, human or animal, has meant that representative painting and sculpture (with such exceptions as Persian and other West Asian schools of miniature-painting) have largely been disregarded. Artists have tended instead to concentrate on elaborate, abstract pattern-making, based on geometry flower and vegetable forms, or on the expressive potential of calligraphy. Thus the Islamic visual arts usually find their most fertile output in both religious and secular architecture and its decoration, and also in other practical or applied arts, such as glassware, pottery, ceramics, textiles metalwork and jewellery.

The Old City has at least half a dozen notable historic mosques of different periods and styles—a respectable tally for a community that seems never to have had more than 20,000 members within its walls and not all of them Muslims. All these mosques have in common their simple purpose as a place for the faithful to gather in daily communal prayer and also to hear a weekly sermon on Fridays. Their main feature is thus a prayer hall, usually square in plan, with regular rows of columns supporting the roof which, in an environment lacking heavy building timber, may be composed of masonry or brick half-domes over each bay. A converted Christian church, such as Tripoli's former Roman Catholic Cattedrale del Sacro Cuore, rarely makes a satisfactory place of Islamic worship, whatever its age or style. This is because most churches (but not necessarily chapels) impose a strong sense of direction on their congregations, with the basic, usually processional ground plan culminating in the sanctuary with its sacrificial altar. Mosques as essentially prayer and preaching halls, by contrast usually prompt a more diffuse, almost static sense of space, and a less assertive orientation especially if they are divided by equal rows of columns into regular and equal aisles. Muslims at prayer face towards Mecca, its direction shown by no more than a decorated niche (*mihrab*) on the appropriate wall while the Friday sermon is delivered from an often elaborately raised and decorated pulpit (*minbar*) with similarly decorated access steps. The faithful are called to prayer by the *muezzin* (or now by publicly amplified recording) at the prescribed five daily times (dawn, midday, sunset, evening and night) from a balcony (or balconies) encircling the shaft of the mosque's minaret. The minarets of the Old City are of differing heights and styles; they are important landmarks, signposting the location of mosques perhaps otherwise hidden anonymously behind other blank-walled buildings. Mosques usually offer washing facilities for the faithful at the entrance; some may have public baths attached.

Most builders of the Old City mosques favoured semi-circular arches rather than pointed "Islamic" (or even "Gothic") ones. But those within the oldest mosque, the tiny *Jamaa al-Naga* (Mosque of the She-Camel) are pointed. According to various traditions, this mosque was founded by the first Muslim Arabs to reach Tripoli in the seventh century, or by the Shi'ite Fatimids in the tenth. It was destroyed with the rest of the town during the Spanish conquest of 1510 and was rebuilt a century later. The prayer hall is divided by squat, well-used columns (probably Roman) into 25 square bays with pointed arches, each bay roofed by a small dome. The minaret is low and square in plan (a typical North African feature) topped by swallow-tailed crenellations. At the adjacent *Jamaa Al-Kharruba* (Carob Tree Mosque) the *muezzin* is by tradition blind and thus unable to watch domestic life unfolding in the nearby, close-packed houses.

Dating from around 1580, the Darghut Mosque (the largest in the Old City) is named after the first ruler of Tripoli after its capture by the Turks in 1551 (and a main player in the great, and unsuccessful Turkish siege of Malta in 1565). He is buried in one of the series of tomb-chambers attached to the unusual, T-shaped prayer hall. This mosque seems to have been built on the site of an earlier church. The Mosque of Mohammed Pasha, built in 1698, has fine carved marble doorways with rosette decorations, and wooden doors with carved crescents, cypresses and rosettes.

Almost the finest and most impressive of all is the Karamanli Mosque, started in 1736 by Ahmed Karamanli, the first of the effectively independent dynasty named after him, and whose four generations of rulers are buried here. This architectural complex fills a more or less square site at the main entrance to the Old City, by the Bab al-Menscia, and opposite the Castle. The need to orientate the prayer hall towards Mecca means that it sits at an odd angle within its surrounding layout of tomb chambers, open courtyard, religious school, octagonal minaret with one balcony and an elegant entrance colonnade onto the street. The prayer hall is divided into five aisles in each direction by grey marble, Tuscan order columns topped by decorated entablatures upholding corner squinches which in turn carry 25 hemispherical domes—what might be considered a restrained "Islamic baroque". The interior walls are decorated with stucco carved into complex geometric and calligraphic shapes. The outside walls (still within the mosque complex) are wholly covered with panels of highly coloured blue, green and yellow glazed tiles displaying vase, flower and foliage forms organized on a strict geometric grid contained within assertive border panels. The overall effect is of rich, continuous decoration, making its artistic statement through the repetitive use and re-use of a narrow range of approved, stylized, natural shapes.

The Gurgi Mosque and its minaret (the city's tallest) seen from another angle.

The Built Environment

Yet perhaps the finest of the Old City mosques is the newest, started in 1833 at the very end of the Karamanli regime. It is named after its builder, Yusuf Gurgi whose family was from Georgia. Inside, carved stucco work, coloured tile panels and inlaid marble show even more elegant, elaborate and sumptuous designs than any others in the Old City. The prayer hall is divided by only nine tall columns into four aisles in each direction, with the resultant 16 bays roofed with domes. The octagonal minaret with two balconies and the typically Turkish green tapering finial (similar to the one atop the Karamanli minaret) is the highest in the Old City; it makes a strong architectural statement near the harbour front and just behind the Arch of Marcus Aurelius.

Other Islamic foundations, including the Madrasa (religious school) of Othman Pasha (1654) with its unusual ribbed domes, attest to the former wealth of a small city and port which, despite invasions, destructions, plagues and revolutions, traded profitably with the three Old World continents from the early Middle Ages to the mid-nineteenth century. Tripioli's historic commercial and domestic buildings repeat the same story.

Other small but noticeable features of the urban and suburban landscapes are *marabuts*—the low sanctuaries or tombs of revered holy men placed almost casually at the sides of streets and roads, or at more surprising public locations. They are mostly small, whitewashed, plastered domes, some but a few feet high, decked with coloured banners and glazed earthenware lamps.

The style of Tripoli's traditional Islamic building is not "Moorish", for that is the predominant Islamic style of Morocco and Moorish Spain. Rather, one of the two main influences on its architecture is an uncomplicated, purely functional and robust building style of northern Tripolitania, an interplay of unadorned white cubic shapes and simple round arches. Italian colonial architects in the early twentieth century were keen to classify this, alongside south Italian vernacular building, as "Mediterranean", a generalized term that would allow them to adapt its main features to their own schemes without any need to acknowledge its local origins. But then, in the richer, more sophisticated and cosmopolitan milieu of Tripoli itself, both Turkish and North African influences (Tunisian especially) predominated during the long rebuilding of the city after its almost complete destruction by the Spanish in 1510, and its Ottoman conquest in 1551. Thus some of the decorative material (and especially coloured glazed tiles) and finer workmanship of the later mosques and other religious and secular buildings of the eighteenth and nineteenth centuries were likely to have been brought in from other North African and eastern Mediterranean provinces of the widespread Ottoman Empire, most notably from Turkey itself.

Yet other faiths were also quietly represented within this predominantly Islamic milieu, since the Ottoman Empire and its semi-independent Barbary Regencies (and Tripoli especially) were more tolerant of their religious minorities than are many modern regimes. Christianity and its churches have nevertheless had a chequered history in Tripoli. The Christian city of later Roman and Vandal and Byzantine times became an increasingly Islamic one under its Muslim Arab conquerors and dynasties that followed. The Church was briefly revived under the Normans in the twelfth century and again under Spain and the Maltese Knights in the sixteenth. Then, with the Turkish conquest in 1551, Islam again predominated, as it still does. Yet in 1620 the Greeks were allowed to build a small Orthodox church, *Hagios Giorgios*, in the heart of the Old City; and in 1630, the Franciscan Order was able to open a small mission: its purpose was not even to attempt to convert Muslims, but to minister to Christian slaves and dissuade them from bettering their prospects by converting to Islam. (Muslim galley and other slaves in some Italian ports were allowed similar freedom of faith and worship.) In 1683 the Franciscans were allowed to build their own small church close to the existing Greek church. In the nineteenth century, and on the same site, work started on the new bigger Santa Maria degli Angeli in the Gothic style that Italians have never properly understood; this rather charmless church was finished in 1897 and from 1911-28 it served as the city's Roman Catholic Cathedral. The Jews had one main synagogue and half a dozen others scattered up and down the narrow alleys of the two Jewish Quarters (*Hara al-Kabira* and *Hara al-Saghira*) at the western end of the Old City.

Commercial and Domestic Architecture

Commercial and domestic historical buildings have their own distinctive characters. As in most "oriental" (Islamic) cities, each market (*suq*) was usually organized according to a particular trade or product. Each *suq* commonly consisted of a central passageway with small merchants' cells or booths on both sides. Some, like the great *suqs* or *bazaars* of the East (Aleppo and Damascus in Syria, or Isfahan and Tehran in Iran, for instance)) are covered. The Old City's *Suq al Rabaa* is roofed with notably fine ribbed vaults with brick infilling; others are open and may be covered with awnings and vines. Most of the markets are at the southern end of the walled city, or run parallel with the harbour front. Here are the *Suq al-Attara* (druggists, perfumers), *Suq al-Siaga* (goldsmiths), *Suq al-Mushir* (clothes) and the main *Suq al-Turk* which by the late nineteenth century had some smart, European-style shops with plate glass windows, some owned by Indians from the British *Raj*. Here also is the *Triq al-Halqa*, the Street of the Link (of a chain), where Miss Tully in the 1780s reported a thriving slave trade.

Another feature of the city's historical trading economy, and usually associated with one or another of the specialized markets, are the *fonduks*. In Italian the word *fondaco* (as in *Fondaco dei Tedeschi* and *Fondaco dei Turchi* in Venice) is commonly translated as "inn" or "hotel". But the real *fonduk* is much more than that. Although of different sizes, *fonduks* follow the same basic plan as the common courtyard houses of the city. They have a secure entrance leading through an arched hallway into an enclosed and spacious courtyard (some with a fountain) surrounded by two tiers of arcades. These give access to store rooms and stabling on the ground floor and, by a large central stair, to artisans' workshops, counting houses and living accommodation on the upper. They offer travelling merchants security for their animals, goods and valuables and an enclosed, private space to promote and conduct business. From the Middle Ages onwards, visiting Jewish and European Christian traders (neither group was allowed to accompany commercial caravans into the Sahara) would transact all their import and export business in such temporary accommodation during their periodic visits. Merchants from a particular foreign trading port with special, local commercial privileges (Venice, in particular) might have their own *fonduk*. Several such *fonduks* survive in the Old City. Sadly neglected and dilapidated, most now date from the early nineteenth century. With their two tiers of arches, they are still a striking and handsome reminder of times when the city's prosperity, over and above mere survival, largely depended on the initiative and enterprise of local and foreign merchants trading with three continents by land and sea through this place.

At the beginning of the nineteenth century Ali Bey al-Abbassi, a Spanish gentleman travelling across North Africa in the guise of a Turk, judged the city's domestic buildings to have been

> regular, well-built and almost all of a dazzling white; the architecture approaches more to the European than the Arabian style; the doorways are generally in the Tuscan style. The stone columns, and the arches of the courts, are of a round form, whereas those of Morocco are pointed. It is very common to see stone buildings; and even marble is employed for the construction of the courts, gates, stairs and mosques.[68]

Most domestic houses in the Old City, dating originally from its sixteenth-century reconstruction to the nineteenth, turn blank, anonymous, white or colour-washed walls towards the street. They give no suggestion of the splendid interiors (or the impoverished squalor) that may lie behind them. One sign of a patrician residence may be a street entrance door of fine stonework carved in shallow relief. These are of a squat, basically classical design, within a rectangular frame with entablature encompassing an arched doorway with pilasters and lintels. Some doorways have simple carving with rosettes and other circular motifs; others are highly elaborate, with carving covering the whole of the available surfaces (including jambs, arch, lintels and panel above) with flower, foliage and abstract motifs.

With its obligatory seclusion of women within the enclosed environment of the dwelling, Muslim domestic life (and Jewish life within an Islamic milieu) results in houses, both rich and poor, turned in on themselves. The only entrance is usually through a narrow, unwelcoming passage-hallway known as the *skiffer*, apparently designed more for security than hospitality. It leads to the internal courtyard, the main focus of family life and female activity, as the fireplace may be in other cultures and climates. The court may have a basin to collect rainwater on the same principle as the Roman *impluvium*. Larger houses may have a second court to allow separate male and female quarters. As the ground floor rooms are not usually interconnected, each is reached through the courtyard, from which it takes light and air. Those on the first floor are served by galleries supported on wooden uprights in the poorer houses, or on fine stone or marble arcades in the richer ones. These inward facing, largely sunless rooms are moderately cool in summer, and relatively warm in winter. As one room usually occupies a whole side of the central court, its length is much greater than its width. According to Ali Bey al-Abbasi, the visiting Spaniard disguised as a Turk, there was at each end of the room

> a sort of stage of planks, about four feet high with narrow stairs. These alcoves are furnished with rails and wooden ornaments, and there is a door under each of them. On enquiry I found that they are made to contain the complete household furniture of a woman, as upon one of the alcoves a bed is placed; upon the other the wearing apparel and that of the children; under the one are the table utensils and victuals; under the other, the remainder of the wearing apparel, &c. In consequence of this arrangement the middle of the apartment is in no ways encumbered, and affords plenty of room to receive the company, and a man may keep in a house of three or four rooms, three or four women, with all possible convenience, and without their being in the way of each other.[69]

The open, flat roofs of houses were also important domestic spaces: first for collecting winter rains for long-term storage in underground cisterns; as airy evening space for women and their work; and as surfaces for sun-drying fruit and vegetables.

Some of the larger houses of the Old City are as elaborately decorated with carved wood, stucco and coloured tile-work, as are the nearby mosques; indeed, not only the same materials, but the same techniques, the same styles and the same skilled artisans were very probably employed on both types of building at much the same time.

An American visitor of the early twentieth century, a guest at the British Consulate in the Old City, used to peer down from its high roof terrace into "many a little court yard where children and mothers, dogs and cats, had slept and eaten, rolled, tumbled and lived a daylight programme".

> Here and there such a home spot was almost roofed by passion-flower vines in full blossom. Strange tinkling music ascended, and a happy if restricted life filled them with a certain sort of pleasantness all day—deserted at evening for the clear [roof terrace] space above.[70]

There had never been any urban planning in the Old City since Roman times. Domestic residences, *fonduks* and markets grew and spread organically, each individual family or trade staking its claim to its own piece of urban space, so that the private houses of rich and poor were jumbled up against each other. The irregular, narrow back alleys seemed less like public thoroughfares dividing these houses than semi-private passageways linking them: this sense of enclosure was reinforced by the many semi-circular arches spanning the passageway from one house to another. These arches, a striking feature of the Old City, are intended to buttress otherwise unstable walls; to break and filter the strong sunlight; and perhaps to dissuade riders of horses or camels (hostile or otherwise) from penetrating this essentially domestic domain.

Large public bath houses were another feature of daily life. These were usually prominent, domed buildings where the hot, steamy atmosphere prepared sweating bathers to be rubbed clean by attendants with a hair glove. This was followed by a hot rinse. Wrapped in towels, bathers were then led to an outer room to be offered coffee, water-pipes to smoke, and

The *barracan* is much in evidence in this view (apparently from the 1920s) of a characteristic, partly arched and narrow street in the Old City.

incense to perfume the beard. Men bathed in the morning, women in the afternoon.

When the Ottoman Turks returned to Tripoli as direct rulers in 1835, ending more than a century of effective independence under the Karamanli Pashas, there was little apparent change in the domestic and commercial life of the city. Of the two activities that helped make the difference between some local prosperity and unrelieved poverty, corsairing in the Mediterranean had by then been effectively ended by the overwhelming naval pressure of the European powers. Only the second activity of trans-Saharan slave trading continued, and was indeed actively encouraged by the new regime as perhaps the surest (and maybe the only) means of raising revenues from an otherwise largely destitute imperial province. Although Tripoli itself had submitted passively to direct rule from Constantinople, the tribes of inner Tripolitania continued to resist Turkish rule for over twenty years. This drain on revenues, and the natural poverty of the local environment, left the authorities with little to spend on the city and its infrastructure. But in 1869 they managed to express some modern municipal pride in erecting a new landmark: an elegant, three-storey clock tower by the harbour front and markets (whether many locals were at that time actually able, or needed, to *read* a clock face was another matter). The Tripoli Arts and Crafts School was opened in 1897 in a handsome, two-storey arcaded building outside the walls. A lighthouse was also built on the prominent knoll at the north-west end of the Old City, but little was done to improve or develop the port itself. Paul Melon, a French visitor of the 1880s, lamented that the Turkish administration, "careless and fatalistic as ever, has no idea how to invest the modest sums of money that would make this a magnificent and well-protected port".

Yet as foreign visitors to Turkish North Africa noted, after overcoming local resistance in Tripolitania and Fezzan, the Ottoman Empire kept its subjects in submission with remarkably few troops, either Turkish or local levees, particularly compared with the large forces the French had to deploy in contemporary Algeria. In and around Tripoli itself in the late nineteenth century there were perhaps 4,000 troops between infantry, cavalry, gunners and other corps. Some of these troops seem to have been accommodated in more or less permanent tented camps outside the city, but by the early twentieth century they were better housed in a large infantry and cavalry barracks at Sidi Mesri, to the south-east of the town, and there was a military hospital alongside.

Since any would-be attacker of this last Turkish possession in North Africa was reasonably expected to approach from the sea, the city was defended by a series of earthwork fortresses with heavy, if obsolete, guns sited for defence against naval assault. There were three such forts to the west of the city walls; two batteries on the reefs protecting the harbour; a fort at Sidi Mesri; and the Hamedia Battery (formerly known as the "English Fort") on a bluff of land overlooking the harbour from the east, and covering its narrow entrance.

By the end of the nineteenth century Tripoli's economy had all but collapsed, largely because its most profitable business, the trans-Saharan slave trade had been gradually abolished from the 1850s onwards. The city nevertheless continued to expand, and particularly to the east, towards the suburban groves and gardens of the *Menscia*. This process had perhaps been unwittingly started by the long-serving British Consul General, Colonel Hanmer Warrington. Defying the established expatriate prejudice that it was unsafe to live outside the city walls, in 1820 he sought escape from the prying eyes, noise, squalor and general unhealthiness of life in the Old City by building himself a modest English Regency-style country house for his large and growing family. This so-called "English Garden" was a small seaside estate of some six acres about a mile east of the Pasha's Castle. Warrington himself described the site as "delightful... the house itself commands an extensive view of the sea, and the salubrious air which always prevails renders it most healthy." When it was seen that the Warrington family was able to live in perfect comfort and safety amidst sea breezes and country greenery, other expatriates moved out to the *Menscia* as well, building themselves modest suburban homes by the seashore or along the sandy, sunken lanes of the oasis. (By the early twentieth century the original Warrington house seems to have become the official summer residence of the Turkish Pasha and to have been destroyed during the Italian invasion in October 1911.)

In the meantime, the city was slowly overflowing into the new suburbs. A daily bread market had grown up along the seashore beyond the Pasha's Castle, and other commercial activities followed. The new export trade in esparto grass (to supply European fine paper makers) was based further along the harbourside, with its own shipping quay (*Molo dello Sparto*).

The Built Environment

New commercial streets began to radiate in a fan pattern from the Bab al-Menscia. Although this may have been a sign of renewed economic activity and population growth, this apparently random, unplanned orientation from the one focal point had a fundamental flaw: it imposed on the new, twentieth-century city a street layout which, prolonged in due course eastwards and south-eastwards through the oasis, failed to take account or advantage of the local, Mediterranean coastal landscape. This probably fortuitous layout pointed the new thoroughfares away from the city's predominant natural feature of the sea: they thus effectively ignored the existence of the fine, sweeping curve of the Mediterranean shore rising gently inland. Modern Tripoli became a city where the nearby sea of multiple midday blues was only to be casually glimpsed at brief, occasional intervals down side streets, and where the benefits of daily onshore sea breezes were baffled by intervening buildings. This was the basic, ill-contrived main street pattern outside the Old City walls that the Italians inherited from the Turks in 1911, for by then the new suburbs were too widely spread for the main layout to be changed. True, the newcomers were to make one partial remedy in the 1920s with the fine harbourside sweep of the *Lungomare Volpi*; but central Tripoli was (and still is) a Mediterranean city where the Mediterranean has to be sought, rather than being constantly in sight.

By the time France declared a protectorate over Tunisia in 1881 and Britain occupied Egypt in 1882, Libya's main value to the declining Ottoman Empire was as "a buffer state of sand" between the North African possessions of these two powers. It might have (but never did) again become a main trade artery to central Africa (where Turkey still had wide, fanciful and unenforceable territorial claims). As capital of this last remaining Turkish possession in North Africa, neglected and impoverished Tripoli did not even have the cachet of being regarded as a *colonial* town. Its Turkish rulers seemed not to care—not even for the sake of imperial prestige—whether or not it made any physical or visual impressions on its foreign visitors, or inspired its people with any hopes for the future. Preserving "all its medieval originality", the city at least up to 1911 remained a curiosity, a picturesque religious, political, economic and social survivor from earlier times. It has even been suggested that the Turks deliberately neglected the place to make it seem less attractive to other would-be colonizers.

The Italian Imprint

Enter at this stage the Italians—a race of master-builders, if ever there was one, since at least the time of the pre-Roman Etruscans. Whatever ancestral political, martial and other qualities Italians may have retained by the early twentieth century, they had surely kept their native genius as architects, builders, town planners and civil engineers. Such was apparent in their own incomparable cities, large and small, in their roads, railways and other civil works, justifying the public claim of the Italians of America that "We found it. We named it. We *built* it." Libya in the early twentieth century, with its wide open spaces, meagre population, two small port-cities (Tripoli and Benghazi) and few other settlements, seemed almost an open frontier, a blank canvas for Italian architects, builders and civil engineers to work on. Clearly there was much to be done, since even in Tripoli the previous Turkish rulers, with their beggarly revenues and small sense of colonial advancement, had restored or built little, planned less and had not even left any coherent maps, charts or town plans.

While the Italians were in control from 1911 to 1943, Tripoli was treated as a *colonial* city (but not an *imperial* one, as Addis Ababa in Italian Ethiopia was intended to become). In this sense it was an overseas possession treasured and promoted to proclaim and symbolize the colonizer's national character, power and prestige. More than any other colonial power, Italy in 1911 yearned for these national attributes as it tried to establish its place and recognition as one of the Great Powers. True, the kingdom already had the colonies of Eritrea on the Red Sea and Somalia on the Horn of Africa, but they were hardly desirable possessions; and they were geographically, historically, commercially and culturally remote from the Mother Country. (Nevertheless, Eritrean Asmara did become a remarkable Art Deco city, while Mogadishu was made a charming Italo-tropical pastiche—until the locals all but destroyed it in their uncivil wars of the 1990s.)

As the possession of Tripoli seemed at last to endorse modern Italy's wider Mediterranean and Roman credentials, history and cultural legacy, so this poor, neglected and not especially distinguished little port was expected to uphold and celebrate Italy's swelling colonial pretensions and aspirations, just as more prestigious possessions did for other colonial and imperial powers. (New Delhi, for instance, in 1911 became the new capital f British India and the setting for the Great Durbar that reconfirmed the British imperial role when the all the sub-continent's native rulers made their formal obeisance to the newly-crowned King-Emperor, George V.)

By early 1912, three months after their landings in North Africa, the Italians had understood that they would not easily conquer their new possession. But they still needed to make two basic points. One was to show the other Great Powers that, with an efficient colonial administration, Italy's historical claims to Libya were fully justified; and the other was to make it known that its benign intentions as a "civilizing nation" were being ungratefully rejected by the Libyans' unexpected, rebellious hostility. The quickest and most effective way of proving these points seemed to be the rapid improvement of the infrastructure, built environment, public services and sanitary conditions in Tripoli (where cholera had already broken out).

The first master plan for the city was published in March 1912, although handicapped by lack of any detailed Turkish maps or town plans. Drawn up by Rome's Chief Civil Engineering Inspector, Luigi Luiggi, it was concerned mainly with urgent works on the port (vital for continuing military supply) and water, sewage and power supplies, especially in the Old City. Discussing the future of this new colonial capital, the plan looked also to modern town planning in Europe and America, and at recent colonial work by the French in Tunis and Rabat, the British in Cairo, Khartoum and Port Sudan, and the Americans in Manila in their new Philippines possession.

The 1912 plan made it quite clear that the fabric and character of the Old City were to be respected; it was to be given much-needed modern services; but there were to be no large-scale demolitions and clearances, such as the French had carried out in historic Algiers. The new "European" city, already taking shape to the east of the defensive walls in the last decades of Turkish rule, was to be developed alongside, but separate from, the old, with proper respect for the local terrain. Palm and olive groves were to be preserved, as were the many little white mosques with their gardens, to provide "picturesque background" to the new urban layout. A new industrial zone (with power station, tobacco factory, railway station, goods yards and workshops) was to be sited on barren open ground to the south-west of the Old City (where the world's first military airfield in an active war zone was already operational). There were also plans for the development of the historical settlement of Tagiura at the eastern end o the *Menscia*; at Gargaresh and Zanzur to the west (perhaps as fashionabl winter resorts, as Algiers and Egypt then were); and at Ain Zara on th pre-desert fringes to the south.

But there were no grandiose visions of long-term growth, n overbearing prestige projects. The plan was largely concerned with quick low-cost solutions to pressing problems. In the event, moreover, there wa little money for such schemes, and the press at home was already beginning to question lavish colonial investment when so much needed to be spen in Italy itself, and particularly on "internal colonialism" in the economically and socially undeveloped southern and island regions. Nevertheless, many objectives of the 1912 plan had been completed by 1921.

By then it was time to start building the new city alongside but a a respectful distance from the old. Here was the chance to make larg and long-term physical and visual impressions on this colonial capital, a buildings may reasonably be expected to last for several generations, a least. But there was no established or uniform building style. The Fascis regime came to power in October 1922, but not for some years did i become a lavish patron of public art and architecture. And even when i did, particularly in the 1930s, it rarely imposed its own strict rules of styl and expression on its favoured artists and architects, as did the Communis regime in the contemporary Soviet empire and the National Socialis authorities in Germany. In Fascist Italy these professions were still lef largely free to decide for themselves how, if at all, the ambiguous ideology and ideals of Fascism were best to be expressed in city planning, building and public art (sculpture especially); which is probably why the genera artistic and architectural standards in Fascist Italy and its colonies are markedly higher than those of other contemporary totalitarian regimes.

One of the first monuments of the new, Italian, city was Armand Brasini's *Monumento ai Caduti e alla Vittoria* (Monument to the Fallen and to Victory, 1923-25). It was sited prominently on the high ground dominating the rocky shoreline on the north-west flank of the Old City Built to satisfy the Italian obsession with cemeteries, ossuaries and the contribution of the fallen to perceived military successes, the monumen was a fine, circular, neoclassical structure under a shallow dome with eigh massive (if largely unnecessary) buttresses, each topped by a couchan lioness. Commemorative medallions filled the spaces between the buttresses. The whole scheme had more than a suggestion of contemporary British India; and until the Second World War it was an essential stop on any round-city charabanc tour. After the war the British Military Administration (concerned about typhoid) took advantage of the elevated site to replace the monument with a large khaki-coloured water-tower which, whatever its practical and sanitary value, made what seemed to be an outsize gasometer a new, dominant feature of the city skyline.

All was aesthetic confusion in the Tripoli of the early 1920s. A series of grandiose, mostly dazzling white public buildings went up by the seafront, eastwards from the Castle: the *Teatro Miramare,* the *Municipio* (Town Hall), the *Banca d'Italia* and the *Grand Hotel.* There were also a new town centre mosque (Sidi Hamouda). Brasini later contributed *La Cassa di Risparmio della Tripolitania* (The Savings Bank of Tripolitania, later the Bank of Libya) on the sea-front to the west of the Castle. This is a heavy, squat design with an arcaded entrance, two domed wings, and a dark brown stone exterior which contributes to an unwelcoming, sullen effect.

On higher ground inland was the Governor's Residence (1924-28), a Sicilian Moorish hybrid with domes and some jarringly disproportionate features: contrived architectural *kitsch* at its best. That sensitive aesthete, Sacheverell Sitwell, who saw it in 1939, dismissed it as "a peculiarly ugly modern building in Oriental style, like a cigarette factory". In 1923 work started on the domed Cattedrale del Sacro Cuore di Gesù completed in 1928 with a detached *campanile.* It was in "Romanesque Tuscan-Lombard" style which, both internally and externally, would never have been particularly pleasing, not even in its imaginary medieval original.

In 1926, less than four years after coming to power, Mussolini visited Tripolitania to promote faster development of this colonial province where Libyan rebellion had recently been curbed but not yet wholly overcome. One outcome of the *Duce's* visit was his personal patronage of the Tripoli Samples Fair, with its first session opening in February 1927. The theme of the main, overbearing entrance pavilion was the City of Rome and its return to a province where it had supposedly left such a profound historical impression. This proposition was clearly stated by the Roman entrance arch with its sculptures, including a Roman eagle and the *Lupa* (she-wolf) suckling Romulus and Remus.

Other public buildings of the time offered a series of modern European interpretations of a fictional "Moorish" style that may have made its best intended impression on new arrivals by sea. It was a style somehow reassuringly familiar to Italians because, despite its exotic flavour, it was more or less what they would then have expected to find in such a destination as Tripoli—or in Rimini, Riccione and other fashionable Adriatic watering places.

In retrospect, much of this new work added up to a disappointing architectural portfolio that hardly represented Italian visual genius at its best. In the words of one recent critic, these buildings were "haphazard uncoordinated grand architectural investments that were completely indifferent to the non-Italian-ness of their environment... uninventive to the point of parody". No wonder some younger architects began to complain that Tripoli was beginning to look more like a European fairground than a North African city.

One of them was Carlo Enrico Rava, the architect son of Maurizio Rava, Secretary General of Tripolitania, who had his own distinct views on the development of the city and its oasis where, he believed, there had already been too much uncontrolled suburban spread. In 1929 the young Rava wrote an influential article in which he attacked both the "imaginary Moorish style" which, although in wide use locally, had no roots in Libya, and also the translation of unmodified European building types into North Africa. He instead drew attention to local "Arab" building, arguing that it was characterized by a simple interplay of white, geometrical and largely windowless cubes, enclosing a private court or patio with arches and arcades helping to create contrasts of light and shade evolving during the course of the day. Such local building seemed, he suggested, to have much in common with southern Italian vernacular; both were undeniably "Mediterranean". They both seemed also to echo the then evolving, uncompromisingly "modern" white reinforced concrete, steel and glass structures of new European and American architecture. Here, then, was an adaptable, contemporary and functional style free from historical references. It took time for these and similar arguments to filter through the Italian architectural profession. There seems to have been a particular reluctance to accept that examples of native, vernacular building might have had any use or relevance as a contribution to "fine" academic architecture intended to suggest the cultural and technical superiority of the colonizer over the colonized.

At the end of the 1920s, three main town-centre squares were still incomplete: Piazza Cattedrale; and the two nodal points of Piazza Castello to the west of the Castle, and the adjoining Piazza Italia. Piazza Castello had been completed with an access ramp to the Castle's new official entrance and two waterside columns supporting a Venetian galley and the Roman *Lupa*. In Piazza Italia the all-important, prestigious corner site where a main street, Corso Sicilia, led off to the west, was reserved for a new local headquarters of the Banco di Roma. The project was awarded to Alessandro Limongelli who before his early death in 1932 devised a building arcaded on the street front, its mildly exotic, rhythmic and simplified classicism dominating this central site. Completed with some variations by a trio of Limongelli's Milanese colleagues, this handsome building, a prototype for Tripoli's new Fascist-colonial style, still makes a forceful statement when seen across the greatly enlarged open urban space, the *Maidan al-Akhdar* (Green Square), created by the Gaddafi regime in the 1970s.

In the second half of the 1930s Tripoli became an impressive setting for contemporary Italian colonial building, and an open stage for Fascist public celebration and spectacle within the political context of the New Roman Empire (proclaimed in 1936). In 1932 Florestano Di Fausto arrived in Tripoli as artistic consultant to the Municipality. In the 1920s he had worked on big renovation, development and building schemes in the Italian Dodecanese Islands (especially on Rhodes and Cos) and in the Albanian capital, Tirana. Then in 1934 the pioneer aviator and former Air Minister, Marshal Italo Balbo, was appointed Governor General of the combined colony of Libya (See Chapter Five). This dynamic organizer and administrator at once set about transforming the city into a fitting capital of a colony where air displays, motor races and tourism were already promoting a high public profile. Balbo named Di Fausto head of a new commission to oversee the city's aesthetic development and to implement the new (1934) town plan, intended in particular to take account of a population growth from 63,000 in 1928 to nearly 90,000 in 1933.

Supported and encouraged by Balbo, Di Fausto was responsible for many important new projects. These included the further widening of the open spaces around the Arch of Marcus Aurelius; the new road continuing the *Lungomare Volpi* through the Castle; the sensitive insertion of the important new Archaeological Museum inside the Castle complex; the Church of San Francesco (with frescoes by Achille Funi); the Uaddan and Del Mehari hotels; and new government buildings. Di Fausto's work reflected a certain eclectic neo-imperial style, also including suitable local and vernacular references if the siting and purpose of a particular building allowed it. Thus the Uaddan Hotel included architectural borrowings from traditional Tripoline domed bath-houses (although Fascist officialdom insisted that these advertised "Turkish" baths were renamed "Roman") while the diffuse layout and ambiguous room plans at the *Del Mehari* (with a pair of rooms having common access to one bathroom) gave it a certain (no doubt undeserved) reputation for impropriety. Di Fausto's most striking work was the 1938 building of the Istituto Nazionale Fascista di Previdenza Sociale (Fascist National Social Insurance Institute) that closed off the seaward side of Piazza Cattedrale, while still allowing sight of the Mediterranean through the mighty triple arcade piercing the central block. The whole scheme was dominated by twin towers, square on plan and rectangular in elevation, relieved by balconies, blank arches and cylindrical cap features and splayed outwards from the central arcade in parallel with the axes of the two streets meeting on that side of the piazza. Here was fine "modern" architecture, its minimalist Fascist adjectives dramatic and convincing, of much greater strength and original interest than the weak, derivative Cathedral façade and *campanile* on the opposite side of the square, completed some ten years earlier.

At the same time the architect Umberto Di Segni was designing villas and corporate housing in the "Garden City" suburbs, using curves and arches to relieve his basic, rectangular plans and elevations. With its dazzling white, sun-deflecting exteriors, this housing was designed to provide visual satisfaction, as well as tolerable living conditions in such a climate, before the widespread use of that mixed blessing, air conditioning. Italian builders, in the colonies as at home, always took special care to provide windows with solid shutters (*imposte*), louvred shutters (*persiane*) or roller shutters (*tapparelle*) to exclude an otherwise overwhelming sun—a practical necessity often skimped or ignored by other nations.

The travelling Danish Muslim, Knud Holmboe, was in Tripoli in 1930 and found that "the modern quarter has the appearance of a theatre town, built up hastily; but it must be admitted that it is splendid". But he added, "everything smells so new and is so exaggeratedly splendid that one is inclined to doubt whether it can be real".

All this activity, these great urban layouts and public buildings, the fine hotels and the smart shops, seemed to beg the question: *for whom* were they being built, *who* were they intended to impress—other Italians (residents or visitors); foreigners (at least those with some visual appreciation); or the Libyans? The contemporary published evidence suggests that those most inclined to comment (and favourably) were foreign visitors, and not least the British military who entered undefended Tripoli in January 1943 and, if critical of the local Italian record as colonizers, were suitably impressed by the Italian built environment they found. And this same architecture (including the remarkable colonial agricultural villages the Fascist regime established in Tripolitania and Cyrenaica in the late 1930s) is now rightly becoming the subject of serious study by architectural historians.

More than one British visitor to this new colonial capital was deeply impressed by what he saw. The journalist George Steer recalled his arrival by sea in 1939:

> We sighted Tripoli at about nine next morning, a line of white marble steps on the horizon that grew into superb towers and domes and blocks signifying hotels for tourists. The place was the antithesis of Tunis; it glittered along a shore of royal blue that threw handfuls of foam at the bordering balustrade; it glittered with newness and functional good taste. Tripoli was a jewel personally carved by Italo Balbo, Governor since 1934.[71]

So Tripoli presented itself on the eve of the Second World War. This was the climax of its new-found (or newly-imposed) role as the premier colonial possession and showcase of the New Roman Empire. (Addis Ababa, conquered in 1936, would eventually have taken its place as the jewel in the Italian Imperial Crown had it not been restored to Ethiopian rule by British force of arms in 1941.) When Italy declared war on Britain and France on 10 June 1940, Italian Libya became the setting for a three-year struggle for the mastery of Egypt and the central Mediterranean. Most material destruction and human losses were caused in Cyrenaica (Benghazi alone had over 1,000 air raids) while Tripolitania in general and Tripoli in particular were less harmed by the fighting. Indeed, the people of Tripoli seemed rather surprised when civilian refugees started arriving from Benghazi after its first fall to British forces in February 1941. One of them, the young Paola Hoffman, found that:

> Tripoli presented itself as a bigger copy of my own city, but finer, more imposing, more obviously a seat of government; everywhere one was struck by the profound Italian imprint. And despite the war, it had kept its taste for life's enjoyments.[72]

But the city and its port were then briefly within range of the RAF based on airfields in Cyrenaica, and in early 1941, as the main supply centre for Italo-German forces in North Africa, it suffered 240 air raids, with 460 civilians killed and much property damage. But there were fewer raids over the following two years as the war raged back and forth in Cyrenaica and western Egypt. When the British finally marched into Tripoli on 23 January 1943, the port was badly damaged, while the city as a whole, although shabby and scarred, was basically intact, for the retreating Axis forces had not tried to defend it.

The British Military Administrations set up in occupied Cyrenaica in 1942 and in Tripolitania in January 1943 were supposed to be temporary arrangements. But they remained effectively in power until Libya's post-war future was finally settled with an early independence in December 1951. During their eight years in Tripoli, the British had neither the mandate nor the funds to make much lasting visual impression on the wartime and post-war city, where there were few materials for repair and maintenance.

A British visitor in 1949 found that "the gilt on Tripoli's spectacular facade" of ten years earlier had "worn off and the facade has been broken off in many places..." Two years later this rather drab and impoverished city became joint capital, with heavily-blitzed Benghazi, of the independent Libyan kingdom. As then one of the poorest countries in the world, Libya in 1951 had little money to spend on construction, and the main building activity was at the British and American bases in and around the town. But then some economic salvation came in the mid-1950s with prospecting by the international oil companies and their many subsidiary service providers. Expatriate staff and families needed housing and services, and they were largely found in the low-built garden suburbs of Gargaresh and Giorgimpopoli on the western seaside approaches to the city. But there were few large, prominent or architecturally notable developments to compete with the pre-war Italian townscape in and around the centre. Most new hotels, housing and business buildings of the 1960s were the unremarkable, anonymous and visually sterile "international modern" blocks of the post-war era in which the excess heat admitted through unnecessarily large and unshaded windows usually needed to be tempered by air-conditioning.

The revolutionary city of the 42-year Gaddafi era began to present a new face to the world. This man of the desert, brought up in the tented encampment of his semi-nomadic family, seems himself to have had no urban vision, no master plan, for a city that was always essentially alien to his background, experience and prejudices. He did not even want it to remain as national capital, preferring, but never moving it to, a more central location in the Sirtica. But Tripoli grew and developed regardless of what Brother Leader might have intended. The Galleria de Bono, an attractive, ornamental Fascist-era shopping arcade with an octagonal courtyard between the two main shopping streets and named

The Italian Cathedral of Sacro Cuore, unconvincingly transformed into a mosque, the former campanile now a minaret.

Dubai on the Mediterranean? Tripoli's twenty-first-century builders aim high.

after an Italian Governor of the 1920s, General Emilio de Bono, was sympathetically restored, surprisingly so in view of the regime's inherent hostility to any reminder of Libya's Italian past.

By contrast, the Romanesque former Cathedral, which in its style, plan and orientation had never made a convincing or convenient place for Muslim worship, was selectively "Islamized" by being partly rebuilt and, among other things, provided with a new façade. This incorporated an elaborate, meandering arcade with a small half dome over the main entrance, vaguely "Tunisian" in character, while the Romanesque and very Italian *campanile* was remodelled as a seemingly more slender and more acceptable minaret.

Meanwhile, this capital city of Gaddafi's "State of the Masses" grew sideways, out into its oasis, the new suburbs interconnected with the gyrations of overpasses, ring roads and super highways. Its population, and its extent, had grown perhaps a hundredfold in one hundred years. And it also grew upwards, into the tower blocks and other high-built fantasies now considered the essential metaphors of a modern, progressive metropolis. While pleasing or intriguing some viewers, to others these buildings may seem monumental displays of architectural bad manners. Such are the Al-Imad Towers, a cluster of multi-storey blocks raised precariously on stilts from a two-storey base, angled away from each other with the appearance of the outsize microphones of some monstrous Ministry of Truth (or perhaps upturned whisky bottles). Another is the Burj Tarablus (Tripoli Tower)—twin towers linked by a high "Islamic" arch with the inevitable revolving restaurant perched over it. This tower stands next to the yet higher and less coherent Boulayla Tower, while even taller constructed conceits have taken shape nearby.

These are presumably the high-rise developments which may yet help Tripoli attain the title of "Dubai on the Mediterranean". Yet this presupposes that the security and the political and social conditions of the city may one day be right for such a transformation into a fantasy vacation stopover for international travellers looking for a new and untried destination. For all its trials and tribulations, Tripoli still remains a city with many more real and varied historical, cultural and visual rewards than may be found in any small Persian Gulf sheikhdom.

Chapter Ten

Infrastructure and Expansion

With a good port, the town of Tripoli could become the first city of North Africa.
Dutch Consul Testa, 1856

The remark of a French visitor in 1911 that Tripoli was "the only Mediterranean port that has preserved all its medieval originality" implied that, apart from anything else, it then had little modern infrastructure. Probably no city claiming the title in any age or climate can survive without *some* public infrastructure; otherwise, it is probably, in reality, little more than a dangerous, disease-ridden slum, a *bidonville* or a Brazilian-style *favela*, or quickly becoming one. Disregarding its perhaps once necessary defensive works (walls, towers, gates, forts and castles) as well as its religious, political, administrative, commercial and domestic built environment, a viable city has various other basic needs if it is to survive, prosper and grow as a healthy, attractive, creative and intellectual human environment. Such needs include means of access and circulation: roads, streets and open spaces; a secure port if on the sea, lake or river; markets and means of wholesale and retail distribution; ample clean water and easy disposal of waste water, sewage and rubbish; cemeteries; places of relaxation, recreation and entertainment; and by the nineteenth century, or the twentieth at the latest, hospitals, schools, a university perhaps, libraries and museums; public transport systems; public power and telecommunications services; and, if large enough, an airport.

Combined with such natural, unimproved features as the harbour, the oasis with its underlying water table, and the ancient caravan trails along the coast and into the interior, Tripoli's infrastructure and public amenities as the new Italian rulers found them in 1911 had been barely adequate to support the city's role as a minor Turkish port, garrison and provincial capital. And they were clearly inadequate to sustain the city's new intended public role as a Mediterranean and African showplace of

192

the Italian "civilizing mission". Indeed, public health had very quickly broken down with an outbreak of typhoid and cholera under the extra population pressures of Italian occupation forces.

According to the French, with their wide experience in North, West and Equatorial Africa, effective colonization was first and foremost conditional on transport: *coloniser, c'est transporter*. Turkish Tripoli, and indeed all Libya, had an extensive transport system stretching deep into the African continent, but it was based purely on pack animals (camels and donkeys) and not on the wheel. After the Classical era the wheeled vehicle had disappeared from the Sahara and from other parts of northern Africa where it had once been used; it was only reintroduced by European colonialism in the nineteenth century. Wheels ideally need built-up, demarcated roads, preferably smooth and paved; pack animals do not: camels, in particular, travel better on soft sand than on hard surfaces. Thus the streets, lanes and alleys of Tripoli and its oasis were mostly unmade and sandy until the early twentieth century, even if they were chokingly dusty in dry weather, or were churned into mud in the wet. Late Turkish Tripoli had few wheeled vehicles—the only public "cabs" were little two-wheeled, one-horse traps (*araba*). As an American visitor in those years found it:

> The two-wheeled *araba* was a very gay little cart with bright awnings and blue paint, decorated with fancy designs as well as red curtains against the blinding sun. But it had no springs and the axle lay uncovered on the floor, inconveniences scarcely compensated on unpaved thoroughfares by a string of merrily jingling bells around the horse's neck.[73]

Elegant, European-style four-wheel open carriages ("Victorias") riding on springs, as well as a few motor cars, were introduced shortly before the Italians arrived. But the alleys of the Old City were too narrow for these modern vehicles. And outside the city, the well-used country lanes, sunken between sandy banks planted with Indian figs—"of immemorial age, quite as bad as when first trodden"—provided a rough ride for carriage passengers, and also for motorists who had the further and constant horror of coming to an ignominious and impotent halt as the still-spinning rear wheels sank into a patch of soft sand.

The Italians brought many hundreds of military automobiles to Tripoli in 1911, the first time motor transport had been used anywhere on active service. They were mostly Fiat light trucks with double rear wheels which ideally ran best on paved roads. So the Municipality and the military built them, paving existing streets and roads in and around the modern city and its oasis, and then out to the elaborately entrenched front lines on the fringes of the desert. The streets, at least those outside the city walls, accordingly became *Italian* streets, in form, layout and (some of them) in name. They were drained, lit at night, and pavements were built to the same standard width and height as those at home. They were signposted, and ornamental or useful trees were planted at regular intervals along these thoroughfares—mainly oleanders in town and eucalyptus along the main access and arterial roads. (Eucalyptus, quickly growing to provide tall avenues of shade, was a happy Australian import, well suited to local conditions and climate.)

A significant feature of the Tripoli oasis in the early twentieth century was the elaborate defensive wall that for years protected this besieged bridgehead from the assaults of the "rebels" from the interior. It was in effect a concrete symbol of Italy's continuing inability to bring Tripolitania under its effective control, confirming the siege mentality of

An Italian cityscape: Emhemmed Elmgharief Street in central Tripoli.

a military machine that never fully understood the need to dominate an essentially desert environment by movement, not static defences. Starting at the western edge of the town early in 1912, military engineers replaced the elaborate system of defensive trenches with a stout wall, four metres high, built of local stone, concrete blocks and, in places, compressed earth and lime. When completed in April 1915 (just before Italy's entry into the First World War), the wall extended for about seven miles in a semi-circle around the landward side of the oasis. In places it had raised and loop-holed firing positions; undefended sections were topped with broken glass. There were several artillery positions, watch towers, guard posts and barracks for the defenders, while the fifteen road and railway entrances were secured with massive iron gates. Although the wall was particularly effective in defending Tripoli and its oasis from the rebel insurgents in the confused politico-military crisis after the First World War, it later fell into disuse, became a recommended tourist curiosity in the 1930s, and had largely disappeared or been demolished by the 1960s.

As Tripolitania was conquered and "brought to colonial order" in the 1920s, so the network of hard-top roads and marked motor tracks spread out from Tripoli—along the coast in both directions, and into the pre-desert and Saharan hinterland. But Cyrenaica and Tripolitania, the two wings of the Libyan colony, were still separated by the dangerous and nearly impassable barrier of the Sirtica: until the late 1930s the only safe and regular means of travel between Tripoli and Benghazi were either by air or by sea. Only in March 1937 did Mussolini go to Libya formally to open one of the greater infrastructural works of Fascism, the newly-completed coast road, the *Litoranea* or *Via Balbia*, running for over 1,000 miles across the full width of the colony and linking most of its main population centres. Tripoli thereafter sat astride a highway of international political, strategic and commercial importance. Although the road was claimed to be a tourist route, few tourists ever used it; rather, it offered Italy potential military access to French Tunisia to the west and British-dominated Egypt to the east. But, as the events of the Second World War were to show, it also provided the British military with reciprocal access from Egypt into Italian Libya and, eventually in 1943, all the way to Tripoli itself.

When the Italians arrived in Tripoli in 1911, railways, rather than roads, were then still considered the main and most effective means of opening up any country, but especially colonies, to military and political control, and to economic and social advancement. Apart from Europe and the Americas, over the past half century railways had been laid with great success and benefit to serve the large populations of British India and Egypt, and also across French North Africa and through south, east and west Africa—all places where population densities and/or economic prospects seemed to justify their building.

But Libya was different, and Tripoli always seemed an unpromising hub for a colonial rail system. The Italian journalist Domenico Tumiati may in 1911 have had an over-excited vision of a future "network of electric railways branching out from Tripoli to the great plantations of Mesellata, to the mines of Yefren and Fassato, one line extending from there to Ghadames and another to Murzuk". Yet the reality was that the port, the town, the oasis and the immediate hinterland had neither the actual or potential economy, nor the population, to justify anything more than perhaps the building of a light tramway. (Even the French ambition of a trans-Saharan railway to link Algiers with the River Niger foundered on similar, if vaster, economic and demographic realities.) But in Tripoli the static military situation around the oasis in 1911-12, and the need to supply large, entrenched forces defending a perimeter extending in a semi-circle beyond the city and its suburbs, did at least encourage military engineers to build lines from the port out to the combat zones at the edge of the oasis. The track from the waterfront was laid round the north-western flank of the Old City and then branched out westwards towards Gargaresh, south eastwards to Ain Zara and eastwards to Tagiura. Once the zone of conquest advanced inland, the western line was extended along the coast, through Zawia, past the site of ancient Sabratha, and as far as Zuara (73 miles), where it might have been, but never was, linked to the Tunisian rail system. Beyond Gargaresh, a branch line was pushed southwards to Azizia and eventually to the foot of the steep *gebel* escarpment, about fifty miles from Tripoli. But as not even Italian engineers could get a railway up that precipitous natural barrier, the last four miles up to Garian were covered by a finely-engineered, typically Italian, mountain road. All these railway works were a purely state enterprise; no private company was prepared to take the risk of building a line very far beyond Tripoli, since it seemed unlikely to attract enough passenger or goods traffic to generate a worthwhile return.

Infrastructure and Expansion

Italian colonial railways were built on a very narrow gauge—950 mm. rather than the slightly more generous one metre, itself only two thirds of the standard 4' 8" gauge. (It is said that the 950 mm gauge arose from a misunderstanding of gauge measurements, which are taken from the inside edges of the parallel rails and not from their centres.) The rail system based on Tripoli had only seven small steam locomotives (German and Italian makes) dating from the 1890s. All the 240 goods wagons dated from 1912 and most of the first and second class passenger coaches from 1920. A modern touch was added by one diesel rail car, built in 1939. The passenger and goods rolling stock operated through and from Tripoli was drab, narrow and ugly; the fussy, graceless little locos performed indifferently on the imported coal. By 1960 all this obsolete equipment was worn out, and there was little prospect of improving an extraordinarily slow, infrequent and inherently loss-making service. So the separate rail systems based on Tripoli and Benghazi were abandoned in 1962 on the recommendation of the International Bank for Reconstruction and Development, which had commented in its 1960 report on the Libyan economy that "it is creditable that the railways administrations have managed to keep the railways running at all".

Mussolini has long been popularly credited with "making the trains run on time". What he (or his Fascist regime) actually did was to make them run *faster* (for instance, halving the journey time from Milan to the Sicilian capital, Palermo, from 48 hours to 24.) But by 1929 Fascist concern for train speeds had still had little apparent effect on the service between Tripoli and Zuara: the *official* time for the 73-mile journey was three hours 45 minutes by the "accelerated" train and just under six hours by the "mixed" (goods and passenger) train. Assuming the trains ran to time, this gave the fast train an average speed of around twenty mph; the slower train averaged barely twelve mph. (The line from Tripoli to Tagiura was even more leisurely, with the official timetable allowing well over an hour for trains to cover the eleven miles of track.)

The contemporary colonial Guide Book of the Italian Touring Club seemed more inclined to discourage than to reassure would-be rail tourists. Passengers on the Tripoli-Zuara line were warned that "not all trains have First Class, and not all have Third Class, which is anyway only taken by native passengers" (since it lacked seats). The implication of course was that with no First Class service, Italian and other European passengers might have found themselves obliged to travel in close company with native Libyans when both races had to share compartments in Second Class. Passengers were also warned that, although the line followed the coast, there was "little view of the sea, which is almost entirely hidden behind coastal dunes". Then they were advised that as the duration of the journey depended on the day of the week, they should be sure to "study timetable carefully to choose the most suitable day" if they hoped to make a one-day round trip to the Roman ruins at Sabratha. But at least there was the compensation that the Guide Book extolled Tripoli's Stazione Centrale at the south-western approaches to the city as "an elegant building in oriental style".

In 1935 a party of British visitors took the westbound early train from Tripoli to visit Roman Sabratha, some forty miles away:

> We were up at the crack of dawn to catch the early train from *Tripoli Centrale*. This was an express in miniature, the fussy, teakettle loco seemingly barely capable of hauling its little fairground train. This was made up of First and Second Class carriages, no wider than a tramcar, and at the end some open trucks where the Third Class 'native' passengers squatted on the floor. We made uncomfortable, swaying progress, 20 mph at best, through the sand dunes, the palm groves and the new Italian agricultural concessions along the coastal strip. We halted for prolonged waits at a dozen miniature stations until, some three hours from Tripoli, we puffed into our stop, *Sabratha Vulpia* (named after the first Fascist-era governor of Tripolitania, Count Giuseppe Volpi.) This left us a full six hours in the heat of the day to visit the sublime Roman ruins before the return express was due to depart for Tripoli at half past four. It actually departed only half an hour late.[74]

The New Port

Tripoli's fine natural harbour on an almost tideless sea had for centuries helped to give the city its essential political, strategic and commercial importance, helping also to ensure its survival when its two early rivals, Sabratha to the west and Leptis Magna to the east, fell into disuse and were more or less abandoned at the end of the Classical era. The Romans had made some efforts to develop the port with a mole and quays, but little was done by successive regimes to improve this natural haven. The Turkish administration did eventually allow a French company to build and operate a lighthouse in the nineteenth century as an aid to navigation; but there was no attempt to mark or enlarge the difficult, narrow channel between low, half-submerged reefs at the port entrance; or to chart the reefs and dredge the shoals inside the harbour; or to give shipping some protection from the dangerous north-easterly weather. Thus a French visitor in 1884 lamented that the initial enchantment of sailing into the port was short-lived:

> The sight of a long line of boats washed up on the beach, turned keel upwards to the sun like so many huge stranded whales, makes a poor impression. For in the roadstead where one has just dropped anchor there are some fearful winter storms. Yet the Turkish administration, careless and fatalistic as ever, has no idea how to invest the modest sums of money that would make this a magnificent and better-protected port.[75]

For centuries the harbour was barely surveyed, and charts and other practical information were lacking. The American frigate USS *Philadelphia* ran aground on the Kaliusha reef in 1804 because it lacked charts of these unfamiliar waters. The first professional hydrographic survey of Tripoli harbour and its nearby coastlands was made by Commander W. H. Smyth, RN, some fifteen years after the *Philadelphia* incident. For many years from the 1820s the main navigational aid to ships making port was the large black disc painted on the high, white garden wall of the British Consul General's prominent harbourside villa, the so-called English Garden. Helmsmen had only to align their bows with this disc and the middle window of the Consul's first-floor bedroom to lie on a safe course along the narrow entrance channel between the low, half-submerged reefs.

Italy was a Mediterranean power; Tripoli was a Mediterranean city, and as such its port was for its new rulers in 1911 its most valuable feature. The port in effect offered the sole means of access to this new and as yet unpacified possession. The initial invasion of Turkish Tripolitania and Cyrenaica had been the task of the fairly formidable Italian navy, and for months afterwards the great guns (and searchlights) of the warships still patrolling the Tripoli coastline provided the ultimate defence of this besieged bridgehead against counter-attack by regular Turkish and irregular

Libyan forces from the interior. The improvement and development of the port was thus an urgent military priority, particularly with the approach of winter, since it was the sole means of supplying the large naval, land and even air forces that Italy had deployed offshore, and in and around the city and its oasis. Even the first contingents of troops who went ashore in the natural harbour had been surprised to land on the beach "because there is no port", as one of them complained in a letter home.

The first works started early in 1912. Two great protecting breakwaters were planned, to be built with massive blocks of stone, some weighing up to five tons, from the quarries at Gargaresh at the west end of the oasis. The main mole was planned to extend north-eastwards from the ruins of the so-called Spanish Fort, for a mile along the low reef, finally tending south-eastwards for a further 500 yards. A secondary mole was planned to extend north-westwards for half a mile on the Kaliusha reef. The port entrance was a channel about 500 yards wide between the ends of the two moles. A long commercial and passenger quay was to be built on the harbour side of the main mole, linked by rail to the tracks south of the city. Although started in 1912, these works were interrupted by the First World War (1915-18) and were not finalized until the mid-1930s.

By then the port that revealed itself to incoming ships was a splendid sight. The area enclosed by the two great breakwaters, protecting it from the winter north-easterlies, was 1,800 by 2,500 yards, or nearly double the size of the Port of Genoa. The picturesque Old City, with its minarets and high Castle, dominated its own historic corner, while the curving sweep of the *Lungomare Volpi*, with its lines of palm trees and the white architectural masses and domes of the new town behind them, completed the landward panorama. But under the new revolutionary regime of the 1970s, this natural and contrived composition of the Tripoli sea front was ruined by the building of a container port alongside the *lungomare*. This was no doubt a commercial necessity, but it was also a gross intrusion that disfigured the city's finest civic feature, and thereby sadly degraded its visual values and meaning.

Between the world wars imperial powers expressed their modern, technical competence by linking their distant colonial possessions to the mother country by air, even if nearly all travellers still went by sea because airliners' passenger capacity was small and the price of tickets, the risks and discomforts of air travel were high. Tripoli had the Pietro Manzini

Infrastructure and Expansion

Airport at Mellaha, near Tagiura (the future Wheelus Field), and a flying boat terminal at the eastern edge of the harbour. By 1929 there was a weekly flying boat service to Rome, via Syracuse. Boats took off from the sea at Ostia at six in the morning on Thursdays, landing on Tripoli harbour at five in the afternoon after a stop at Syracuse. The return flight was on Saturday. A single ticket cost 1650 lire (Libyan labourers earned less in a year) plus an extra 14 lire for each kilo of luggage, and passengers were warned that the flight offered "nothing out of the ordinary" in the way of views. By the 1930s there were regular Ala Littoria air services from Tripoli to Italian East Africa, including Addis Ababa after Ethiopia's conquest in 1936. The first regular commercial flights between Tripoli and Benghazi started in 1931 with Caproni tri-motors. The flights, with a refuelling stop at Sirte, took six hours. Eight passengers were carried in first class and two in second, "to avoid metropolitan and native passengers of low social standing travelling together in close proximity", it was explained. Extraordinary though it may seem, the regular Ala Littoria civil flying boat service from Tripoli to Ostia apparently still operated even in wartime; a young Italian evacuee from Benghazi, Paola Hoffman, recalled that she and her mother were able to take (and survive) such a flight from Tripoli as late as May 1941.

Much of the urban infrastructure installed in Tripoli from 1911 onwards was more modern, and often more lavish, than in many early twentieth-century provincial cities in Italy itself. Residents, both native and foreign, were provided with services that many depressed peasant agricultural communities, especially in the Veneto, the south and the islands, would then have been amazed to encounter, let alone be encouraged to use.

Fresh water supplies were always difficult in a city and an oasis with no rivers, streams or even permanent ponds. Ahmed Pasha Karamanli is said to have built an aqueduct raised on a long series of arches (some sources mention 156, others 300) in the 1720s to carry fresh water about a mile from the Menscia to the Castle and the city bath houses. The source was near the so-called English Fort (later the Turkish Fort Hamidie) overlooking the eastward end of the harbour; ships filled their water butts at the same source. The aqueduct seems to have been utterly destroyed without trace at the end of the eighteenth century. When large Italian forces arrived in October 1911 the city was largely supplied from wells at

Bu Meliana, on the southern fringes of the oasis. There was not enough water to meet their extra demand from 20,000 troops, and sea water had to be desalinated as an expensive emergency supply. But military engineers soon rediscovered the old source by the new ruins of Fort Hamidie, laid filter beds and pipes, installed pumps and so brought the water into town. Other sources were developed in the Menscia, providing the city with just about enough fresh water until the late twentieth century, when the hundred-fold increase in population, a considerably greater increase in per capita demand since 1911 and resultant sea water salination of the aquifers called for the drastic remedy of the Gaddafi regime's Great Man-Made River, hailed on its first-stage completion in 1991 as "The Eighth Wonder of the World" (see below).

Early in their occupation, the Italians renewed and enlarged the existing sewerage system, and organized regular street-cleaning and rubbish collection. An American visitor had found a few years earlier that "for considerations of cleanliness, walks were generally taken in the morning". As she explained:

> Small boys went about at sunrise, sweeping with the bushy part of the date palm and, collecting accumulated rubbish in baskets, took it to the beach for burning. During the day however housekeepers gradually threw out into the street augmenting piles of everything discarded—decaying vegetables, fruit, bones, eggshells, fish, all imaginable refuse—so that toward sunset walking, at all times precarious, was but divided pleasure.[76]

The Italians brought in more electricity from a new power station in the new industrial zone to the south-west of the Old City (it burned 2,000 tons per month of imported coal); installed street lighting; began work on a new city hospital; started public health campaigns against the near-universal eye complaint, trachoma, and the common practice of branding the affected body part with a red-hot iron as a cure for physical and mental ailments. Also in the industrial zone, a state tobacco factory, processing local output as well as imports, became the colony's largest industrial enterprise; and many other small manufacturing and processing businesses, including a brewery and a distillery, were opened.

Even under the full weight of Fascist ideology, in the late 1930s, this remained a remarkably open and cosmopolitan city. There was probably less segregation of races, religions and classes than in most other colonial cities at the time. Even the Old City was not really "Arab" because, in addition to its Muslim Tripolines, it also housed many Jews, Greeks, Italians, Maltese and others whose local roots went back for generations (or millennia in the case of Jews). Many Italian town planners wanted to end such promiscuity and to direct different races, religions and communities into their own defined and separate quarters, with the new colonial town outside the walls clearly reserved for Italians and other Europeans (as was supposed to happen in the new "imperial" Addis Ababa and elsewhere). But such ideals of a Fascist Apartheid soon ran into practical difficulties, not the least being the existence of long-established Arab, Jewish and black African settlements within the new suburban layout (especially at Dahra) or beyond its latest boundaries. It was also a fact that any existing settlement or quarter (with the notable exception of the two Jewish *Haras* in the Old City) was itself a mixed, cosmopolitan agglomeration and not an exclusive ethnic enclave. But the planners did quickly displace one community—the so-called "Negro Village" in the Menscia ("a perfect village from the heart of central Africa", according to a British visitor of 1877). This collection of round straw and palm-frond huts housed a community of freed former black slaves and their families. Supposedly Muslims, their persistent practice of imported African animist rituals (although tolerated by the Islamic authorities) meant that they largely remained social outcasts. The Italian authorities very soon demolished their homes on public health grounds, and the Africans were housed elsewhere.

By 1964 traffic conditions and car parking in the "new oil capital of North Africa" were such that the Municipality decided to introduce traffic meters into the busiest central business and shopping streets. Traffic and parking became denser and more difficult thereafter. In the 1960s there were already, in effect, two bypasses linking the eastern and western suburbs: one was Sharia Mohammed ben Ali al-Sanussi (named after the founder of the Sanussi Order and thus, indirectly, of the post-1951 Libyan Sanussi monarchy) while the outer one swept cross-country from the Bu Setta race course in the east to the Wadi Megenin in the west. In the Gaddafi era, when the built-up city encroached on and eventually absorbed these outer bypasses, more had to be built, even further from the city's core and historic centre.

The challenge of providing a *seaside* city with a full ring road wa
eventually met by in effect by moving the sea further off. This create
the necessary space for dual sea-front carriageways, slip roads an
roundabouts. They allowed an unimpeded stream of traffic to speed alon
the harbourside, circle the Old City and its promontory on the *seawar*
side and, still hugging the coast, flow out to the eastern and wester
suburbs. Such arrangements may have done wonders for traffic acces
and circulation, but the visual and cultural costs were high. In the lat
nineteenth century modern Tripoli outside the walls was first laid ou
and so developed, parallel to the fine sweep of this Mediterranean have
(see Chapter Nine). Thus, instead of the new streets and vistas openin
onto the sea, they seemed almost to shun it, allowing only rare glimpse
of the water, and few hints of the cooling onshore breezes. The seafron
traffic routes of the Gaddafi era, together with an enormous expansion c
the port's quays, now reinforce this sense of the city's isolation from i
predominant natural feature. They create an artificial barrier of concret
highways, speeding traffic, container terminals and cranes between lan
and sea, diluting any feeling for the city's historic place as a port on th
central Mediterranean. The Castle, the robust prime symbol of the city an
its past, no longer broods above the wide extent of the harbour. Instea
it is now safely confined, tamed as a mere tourist curiosity, behind a lo
balustrade and the wavelets of what seems to be a suburban boating lak
(but without any boats), cut off from the living waters of the port and th
open sea.

Until the twentieth century successive regimes had managed to suppl
the city and its oasis with just about enough water for their year-roun
needs. So long as numbers were more or less stable, there was usuall
enough for the human and animal population, and the irrigated garden
and palm groves of the oasis. Households, after all, did not expect, c
use, much water—the main urban consumers were probably the publ
bath houses. But as the Italian colonial city grew and spread in the earl
twentieth century, more water was supplied from new sources within th
oasis; these were still adequate to meet local needs until the 1970s. B
with the huge increases in its population and extent during the Gadda
era, the capital faced a two-fold crisis of short supply and increasir
salinity of what was available. For decades, water for local agricultur
and domestic use had been pumped up at least six times faster than

was replenished. As a result, sea water was infiltrating the domestic water supply (for up to four miles inland in some places in the 1980s) and reducing the range of crops that could be raised on the dwindling areas of irrigated land that had not yet been built over and swallowed up by uncontrolled urban spread.

A crisis was avoided—for the time being—by what Muammar Gaddafi described (for once without overmuch exaggeration) as "The Eighth Wonder of the World". Large reserves of pure fossil water (laid down perhaps 20,000 years ago) had been found at the remote Kufra oases in the 1960s, and later also in Fezzan. Attempts to turn Kufra into an irrigated agricultural zone had failed by the early 1980s. It was then decided to pump the water to where it was really needed—for irrigation, industrial and domestic use on the coast. The Great Man Made River was planned to carry five million tons of water a day at an estimated cost that had tripled to $30 billion by the time the water was actually flowing through some 2,500 miles of concrete pipes twelve feet in diameter. By 2010 the GMMR was providing three-quarters of the country's irrigation water, as well as increasing volumes for household use. The first stage of the GMMR, bringing water to Benghazi from Kufra, was completed in 1991. Tripoli received its first GMMR water from a separate pipeline system fed by fossil aquifers in western Fezzan in 1997. Such was the

Moammar Gaddafi as the mastermind of the 'Eighth Wonder of the World', the Great Man Made River, supplying Saharan fossil water to coastal cities and farms.

pressure behind this new, clean flow that the city's old mains, originally installed seventy or eighty years before by the Italian colonial regime, were unable to cope. As the valves were opened, spectacular, spontaneous fountains burst up from fractured pipes under the streets, flooding homes and businesses whose occupants mopped up with cheerful appreciation of this fresh, free-flowing bounty.

This was perhaps the main practical and beneficial achievement of the Gaddafi regime. But Tripoli was now even more reliant on another finite source of economic and personal wellbeing. Like the national reserves of oil and natural gas, the pure fossil waters delivered by the various branches of the GMMR could not last for ever. Although enormous, the full extent of the Saharan aquifers is uncertain: what is known is that they contain undisturbed prehistoric water reserves that are not being recharged. According to some pessimistic assessments, this supply is expected to last (at present drawdown rates) for only forty or fifty years; optimists suggest continuing flows of up to five centuries.

Yet perhaps a greater constraint on the continued flow of the GMMR into the domestic baths, showers, sinks and washing machines of Tripoli is the supply of cheap and abundant fuel for the pumps lifting the water from at least 1,000 separate and distant wells, some of them well over a mile deep. Water levels are already falling, the pipelines are growing longer and demand from a growing native and immigrant population (expected to double again by 2025) increases daily. In 2008 it was estimated that every barrel of oil used for water pumping cost the country at least $100 as a lost export.

If finite resources of oil, natural gas and fossil water all start to run short at about the same time (perhaps late in the twenty-first century) the outlook will be bleak indeed in the poor natural environment of Libya as a whole, and in its great coastal conurbations of Tripoli, Benghazi and Misurata (where more than two-thirds of electric power supply is generated by oil). But fuel and power are so heavily subsidized that households (the main consumers) have little incentive to economize. The summertime air conditioning and winter heating essential in Tripoli's newer buildings consume prodigious amounts of power, with resultant black-outs when the generating stations can no longer meet demand. Meanwhile, Tripoli's motorists fill up their cars with fuel priced at barely half the average in other Mediterranean capitals.

Infrastructure and Expansion

There is no saying for how much longer this city will enjoy such temporary bounty, based as it is on the easy exploitation of finite natural resources discovered, developed and delivered by foreign enterprise. But Saharan solar power could offer a long-term energy alternative when the hydrocarbons run out, and solar-powered desalination, or importing fresh water in huge plastic containers by sea from Turkey, might be realistic solutions to the water deficit. But it is harder to predict what will be the role and purpose of this historic city (perhaps a future megalopolis between Sahara and Mediterranean) without the temporary fortune of oil and gas revenues that have underwritten its people's growth and prosperity since the 1960s. So far, after more than fifty years of the oil era, no plans or preparations have been made for such a bleak future.

Chapter Eleven
Arts, Customs and Society

A knowledge of letters... is by no means necessary to constitute a great man or to advance him to any post of trust. George Lyon (1821)

A cosmopolitan capital city and trading port on the central Mediterranean may hardly be considered remote; nor can it be overlooked or ignored. Even in past centuries, Tripoli has always had a certain distinctive role in the interplay of Mediterranean history, societies, civilizations and cultures. While this has usually been a supporting rather than a leading role, taking its cue from other players, it has often contributed a certain character to the complexities of the human and historical dramas of the Mediterranean and the Sahara.

This city is not, and never has been, a great fountainhead of learning of the arts and sciences, nor a place noted for its saints and martyrs, its philosophers, original thinkers, or men of wisdom who may have inspired and influenced others (no matter what "Brother Leader" Muammar Gaddafi may have imagined). Rather (and despite also the pretensions of its many other rulers), it has historically been too small and too poor to be other than a practical, workaday, yet still intriguing, forum where people have been preoccupied with making a living from this favoured centre of human amenity in an otherwise largely impoverished natural environment on the fringes of the central Sahara. Almost until the twentieth century the city lacked many cultural and intellectual resources such as the museum, publishing houses, public libraries and learned societies originally founded under late Turkish or Italian colonial patronage, or the university and other places of study, higher learning and research set up with the help of the international agencies and the oil-rich independent state.

Yet the people of Tripoli always had, and enjoyed, their own domestic and social culture, expressing their artistry in architecture and its ornament (discussed in Chapter Nine); in their clothing and

A view from the 1960s of a typical arched street in the Old City. The walking man shows how the all-enveloping woollen *barracan* may be worn.

jewellery; in music, song and the poetry of the Arabic language; and in their food and drink.

A Western visitor in Tripoli may be surprised to hear Arabs from other countries confiding (perhaps by way of excuse), "We don't understand these people either". It is not merely a question of language, pronunciation or dialect (although Maltese visitors can usually understand a fair part of Tripoline Arabic), but also of mode, manner and culture. If Tripoli is clearly not a Middle Eastern capital, it is not really a Maghrebi one either: if it has little in common with Cairo, it seems almost equally set apart from Tunis, let alone more distant Algiers or Moroccan Rabat. This has always been a unique place, out on its own, alien (but not unfriendly) even to visitors familiar with other Arab cities. And it is unique among Arab capitals in having fallen under the rule and influence of Italy, rather than Britain, or of the French Republic that has had such a profound imprint on other parts of the Maghreb (Algeria in particular). Tripoli still tends to eat pasta as a daily food, and for preference will shop and holiday in Rome and Milan.

The people of Libya and Tripoli were in the past always distinguished in appearance from their North African Arab, Berber and other neighbours by their most visible and remarkable piece of outer clothing, the *barracan*, worn by both men and women. A British visitor of the 1890s described this universal garment:

> It consists of a single white robe wound dexterously round the body, leaving the right arm free, and so arranged that the end can be adjusted over the head as a hood, as, indeed, it is generally seen... Graceful and eminently artistic as it is, nothing could, however, be less practical as an everyday garment for all classes... There are, of course, many varieties of the baraccan. That of the poorest people is of coarse, browny-white texture, or sometimes of a dark brown. The sort worn by ordinary people is, however, of white wool; while the dandies and well-to-do wear them of beautiful striped silk. Although the garment never changes, the fashion in stripes does from year to year.[77]

Like most outer and visible clothing, the *barracan's* elegance (or lack of it) may depend as much on the wearer as on the garment itself. Worn with poise and self-assurance, a *baraccan* may make a strikingly gracious, almost patrician, impression; bundled on without care for appearance, comfort or style, it seems nothing more than the long, dirty, old woollen blanket it may actually be. Women outside the home in the past wore the *barracan* drawn over the head and covering all of the face except, perhaps, for one eye, to allow the wearer some slight idea of where she was going. But such practice is now rarer in town: both sexes (and particularly the urban young) are now more likely to wear the Euro-American clothing of their globalized contemporaries, even if women and girls might still wear a *barraccan* over their house clothes while out of doors.

Tripoli women used to wear heavy silver jewellery, and sometimes gold, in traditional patterns, both as a display and as a store of wealth.

Most of the gold- and silver-smiths in the jewellery market of the Old City were Jews: they supplied urban society, the country districts and a small export trade to Tunis, Cyrenaica and Egypt. The demand for Tripoli silver jewellery tended to fluctuate with the size of the harvest "because the nomads, even the poorer ones, always liked to make gifts of silver ornaments to their women, especially in the years of better crops"—at least in the nineteenth century. High grade gold (18-22 carat) and silver (900/1000) trinkets formed the main part of nuptial dowries, providing brides with a capital reserve that could

This print from the early nineteenth century portrays an upper class Tripoline lady at home. She is loaded with "a considerable weight of silver ornament" (and perhaps some gold) produced mainly in Tripoli's Jewish workshops. (Lyon)

always be pawned for cash. Fine jewellers' work included silver clasps, rings, head ornaments, necklaces and bracelets; gold and silver earrings mounted with small pearls. Muslim and Jewish women of Tripoli also favoured broad silver belts and ankle bands. Even in the later twentieth century many women in the country districts outside the capital often carried

> a considerable weight of silver ornaments about their person... They... have about them a number of amulets, those most often worn being a little hand, the Hand of Fatima, for good luck, and a fish-shaped charm. Amber beads are also worn as amulets.[78]

Up to the twentieth century the main manufacturing industry of Tripoli was weaving on horizontal wooden hand looms with shuttles worked by hands and feet. In 1911 the city had over 2000 such looms, most of them weaving cotton, but also wool and silk for the local market and for North African and trans-Saharan export. This work was largely done by Muslims. Tailors, by contrast, were mostly Jews. Some Tripoline tailors traditionally made a speciality of heavily-embroidered clothes (enriched with elaborate patterns stitched with imported gold and silver thread) to be worn locally for special occasions or ceremonies, or to be exported across the Sahara to adorn Sudanic potentates and their court favourites. But particularly after the Italian occupation of 1911, many tailors abandoned the traditional dress of the city and began instead to supply their customers (both men and women) with the evolving contemporary styles of Italian fashion.

Tea in Tripoli

Like all Libyans, Triplines are great tea-drinkers: national consumption per head is among the highest in the world. There is no slopping about with tea-bags, tepid water and milk or lemons: this is serious tea, thoroughly boiled and re-boiled to extract all its stimulants and flavours. It is taken in three scalding consecutive rounds in small glasses: the first bitter and frothy, the second with ample sugar, the flavour of the third perhaps amplified with mint or peanuts. To prepare tea, ample leaves are spooned into a small enamel (usually dark blue) tea-pot to about one-quarter of its capacity; it is then filled to the brim with water and boiled. As the pot bubbles, the tea-maker deftly raises it high above the necessary glasses and pours his brew into them in one continuous, cascading motion to induce a froth (or he may pour into a second pot). The tea is then returned to the pot, which is boiled again, the glasses refilled with another cascade and emptied, and so (after the tea-maker has loudly tasted his brew) for the third time. By now the tea is a dark brown, frothy and bitter infusion, ready to be served out and sipped slowly, the drinkers sucking loudly and appreciatively. The tea-maker, meanwhile, pours a handful of sugar over the well-stewed leaves in his pot, sets it to boil again and then refills the glasses with his luscious brew. As this second round is being sucked down, the tea-maker adds more sugar to his pot and stuffs it with dry sprigs of mint, or perhaps puts some peanuts into the glasses as they are emptied. The third round follows the same routine as the other two. Only when the glasses have been emptied for the third time may discussion of the business in hand begin.

In past centuries, Muslims, Jews and Christians alike imported, and drank, considerable quantities of wines, spirits and alcoholic cordials from southern Europe. The English Consul Thomas Baker noted in his journal that in the seven weeks between late July and early September 1680, incoming ships landed 240 butts of wine from Naples, Sardinia, and Provence amounting in total to 130,000 litres, an average of nearly 20,000 litres every week, or about one litre a week for every head of population.

Another beverage that has long surprised and intrigued foreign visitors is the juice of the palm-tree known as *laqbi*. The celebrated nineteenth-century German explorer of Africa, Gustav Nachtigal, explained how this juice was tapped:

> In order to get *laqbi*, an incision is made in the *jummar*, the green wood of the date palm, and a small drainage tube inserted which, sloping sharply downwards, carries the copious flow of sap to the vessel fastened below... Good bearing trees are not used to produce *laqbi* since the harvest of the year would then be lost, and similarly trees which are too old, since there is only a sparse flow of sap from them.

As everybody knows, a Muslim is forbidden to take intoxicating liquor, and respectable believers therefore drink *laqbi* only in its fresh state, before it has gone through the processes of fermentation which produce alcohol. The sap which has been freshly drained off (the outcome, for instance, of one night) is whitish blue colour, and is revoltingly sweet. The sugar of the palm, however, disintegrates very quickly, and already on the second day one has a highly alcoholic drink... Zealous followers of the Prophet luckily find it difficult to check the rapid transition from one stage to another, and under the pretence of drinking date juice, many a strict believer excites and narcoticises his brain with highly alcoholic *laqbi*.[79]

Besides dates and *laqbi*, another delicacy from the date-palm was the heart. Miss Tully described in 1784 how it was obtained, to be served at the great feasts of the richest nobles, for extracting it naturally killed the tree:

The heart lays at the top of the tree between the branches of its fruit, and weighs when cut out from ten to twenty pounds: it is not fit to be taken out before the tree has arrived at the height of its perfection. When brought to table its taste is delicious, and its appearance singular and beautiful. Its colour is composed of every shade, from the deepest orange and bright green to the purest white... The flavour is that of the banana and pine except the white part, which resembles more a green almond in consistence, but combines a variety of exquisite flavours that cannot be described.[80]

Visitors in past centuries commended the seasonal fruits and vegetables. According to a popular British geography book of the 1840s, "the fruit of Tripoli generally possesses an exquisite flavour", while the dates were judged to be "of a quality superior to any other to be found in Barbary". Miss Tully in the 1780s commended in particular the local sweet oranges ("finer than those of China both in flavour and beauty"); water melons ("as if ordered by Providence, are particularly excellent and plentiful"); she also mentioned "several sorts of fine plums and some very high flavoured sweet grapes", while the local olive oil was "as clear as spring water, and very rich... when a year old it often surpasses the finest Florence oil".

The basic Tripoline dish, the local equivalent of the British fish and chips, must be couscous. This is a dish common across the Maghreb and, in the opinion of the journalist Giorgio Assan, writing in the 1950s, it is one of the oldest in the world. The whole point of couscous is that its prime ingredient of semolina is not cooked in the same container with the others, but is suspended *over* them in a colander. The granules thus cook by slowly absorbing the vapours and flavours given off by the mess of meat (kid, lamb or young camel), vegetables to choice, unshelled eggs, and spices and flavourings simmering together in the main stew pot below.

An American visitor of the early twentieth century reported that a "strange, hypnotic quality characterized the native music of Tripoli". Various crude instruments were used, goatskins in the hands of Sudanese, as well as flageolets, cymbals and stringed instruments. These and the street singing, storytelling and weird chants performed by black women at Arab weddings "all had some peculiar effect very hard to analyze". The death dirge rising from a nearby courtyard throughout a whole night "carried a wail of despair from which no escape seemed possible". As for the Turkish military band, she found that it "discoursed the most amazing music, always ending with a blessing on the Sultan in unison". Early morning sleep in the city was sometimes broken by "strange men from the desert" who would invade the narrow streets "making uncanny music". Among them was a tall black man "playing melodies in a minor mode unknown in the West" on an instrument like a Scottish bagpipe and accompanied by a companion with a small tom-tom.

> Hardly less insistent was an old women who played upon a *gimbei*, like an undeveloped banjo, and sang in a high and cracked but tireless voice words apparently fraught with disastrous meaning... she chanted for hours, surrounded by a fascinated audience...[81]

The human voice still dominates the music of the town, perhaps because it is the first means of communication. Other musical instruments may support, extend, amplify, contradict or out-perform it. Such is the case when the singer is interpreting the "folk" music of Tripoli and the Maghreb; or the regional, so-called "Andalusian" music with its origins in Muslim Spain; or the musical traditions of Fezzan and the Sahara; or modern, local pop songs and reggae; or the repertoire of professional *zamzamat* female singers. *Zamzamat* singing women (who charge dearly to chant songs in praise of the bridal families at the segregated female gathering at weddings) are supported by performers on two different types of hand-drum, sometimes backed up also by an accordion. Performers of *Maluf* music are male singers who memorize and perfect a large repertoire of traditional poetic texts and melodies. These are performed as a long suite of songs led by a *sheikh* backed up by a chorus and a group of instruments.

Besides drums of various types and sizes (including traditional ones made of clay), common instruments include the bagpipe (often played by a black Sudanese piper), flute, *shawm* (oboe) and the stringed zither and the gently plucked lute (the European word derived directly from its name in Arabic, *Al-Oud*.)

Wind bands playing Western brass instruments sometimes parade through the streets of Tripoli, particularly on days or anniversaries of political or military significance, continuing a tradition going back to the periods of Ottoman Turkish and Italian rule. The music performed by these bands represents a curious amalgam of Arabic musical material, arranged as military marches; modern military marches from Egypt; or marching tunes of purely Western origin.

Postscript: Dubai or Mogadishu?

What is to become of Tripoli? In 2011, for the third time in exactly one hundred years, foreign forces intervened to help save this city and its people from the perceived "tyranny" of its current rulers. This was the mission the Italians had proclaimed when in October 1911 they ousted the Ottoman Turks; the British implied a similar purpose when their Eighth Army marched into the undefended capital and ended Fascist Italian rule in January 1943; and regime change in Gaddafi's Tripoli, as in "his" Libya as a whole, was one of several objectives of the NATO and other interventions in 2011. Thus the death of Muammar Gaddafi, the collapse of the State of the Masses he had created, sustained and personified, and the deaths, detention or dispersal of his children, all offered the third and probably the best opportunity since Libyan independence sixty years before for a renewed country and a renewed capital city to emerge from the disasters of the recent past.

So is Tripoli, as some have suggested, ready to become "another Dubai on the Mediterranean"? For a city that in 1911 was rightly termed a "noble possession", for this ancient, historically distinct Mediterranean port and Saharan caravanserai, a stronghold of piracy and aggressive naval warfare, for this much-contested, strategic and imperial prize and possession, this would be a sorry fate. This distinguished city and its people surely deserve better than to become a Mediterranean money box, a meaningless, artificial, multi-storey stopover of spectacular frivolities and multi-star hotel accommodation, where bored weekenders are sent to shop for unnecessary goods while disregarding or misunderstanding the accumulated historical evidence all around them of past histories, civilizations and tragedies.

Or is the alternative to become something even worse, the "Mogadishu on the Mediterranean" that some see as the city's other possible fate? The post-Gaddafi chaos, the dangers and insecurities of a capital where (at the time of writing) rival militias confront each other on the streets, where fundamentalist threats are seemingly growing, and where even a Prime Minister is not safe from temporary kidnap, suggest to some observers parallels with the Somali capital. That was once a charming Italian tropical pastiche, created out of an ancient port of the Indian Ocean monsoon trading tradition, since terrorized and devastated by decades of Somalia's uncivil wars.

Surely Tripoli should have greater expectations than these. It has the necessary human and geological resources. Libya as a whole, and especially Cyrenaica, can still contribute wealth from rapidly-depleting reserves of oil, gas, even fossil water, that in the twenty-first century may still serve to transform a deprived natural environment into one able to sustain a young and fast-growing population in working, creative and lasting prosperity. The first fifty years of the long holiday of Libyan oil prosperity have not inspired great confidence in the ability of either the former monarchy or its revolutionary successor to make the best political, economic or social use of such temporary fortune, or to make proper provision for an oil-less future when that fortune runs out as, inevitably, it must. But, if they can resolve their own internal differences and work together, Libyans in general and Tripolines in particular could again make their capital the "Jewel of the Mediterranean", the "Gateway to the Sahara" or the "Bel Suol d'Amore" it was once reputed to be. Such were the titles conferred by earlier admirers of this ancient, and noble city, continuously-inhabited for the past 2,500 years, with its own very special and celebrated position between the open Mediterranean and the wide Sahara, close to that ambiguous place where Africa, Europe and Asia come together. Perhaps such titles may yet be earned again.

Further Reading

As national capital and the most prominent city, Tripoli is the main subject of any general guide book to contemporary Libya. When security conditions allow, most visitors arrive there (if not at Benghazi) and spend most of their time there, using it as a base to visit the sites of north-west Tripolitania, and perhaps Fezzan as well. And over the centuries the city has always had its fair share of notice in North African or specifically Libyan travel books.

Two women who in the past were deeply fascinated by Tripoli and its society have left very personal and perceptive accounts of the city, its people and their customs, the first written in the late eighteenth century and the other in the early twentieth. Miss Tully, sister of the British Consul Richard Tully, sent a series of letters from the city to an unknown correspondent over a period of ten years (July 1783-August 1793). They were published in a handsome volume with coloured plates in London in 1817 (*Narrative of a Ten Years' Residence at Tripoli in Africa*). A new edition, limited to 1,000 copies and without illustrations, map or index, was edited by Seton Dearden and published in London in 1957. The second lady writer, also with a sharp and revealing perspective on Tripoline life and society, was the American Mabel Loomis Todd, whose *Tripoli the Mysterious* was published in Boston, Mass., in 1912, illustrated with numerous photographs. There are modern reproduction editions of both these books.

Among past writers on the city and its surroundings who had more to record and describe than mere commonplaces were the former Spanish Muslim, Leo Africanus, who travelled widely in northern and inner west Africa in the early sixteenth century. He probably never visited Tripoli itself, compiling his brief account as an "armchair traveller". Leo's survey of Libya and Tripoli itself appears in the *La descrizione dell'Africa di Giovanni Lioni Africano* published in Venice in 1550, a book which gave Europe a new understanding of the political, economic and social geography of then largely unknown Africa. Translations into many other European languages followed, the first English edition appearing in London in 1600 under the title *A Geographical Historie of Africa* (republished in a new, three-volume edition by Hakluyt in 1896).

Other visitors, travellers and residents from the past who have left worthwhile accounts of their experiences of historical Tripoli include the seventeenth-century English Consul Thomas Baker: (Pennell, C. R. (ed.), *Piracy and Diplomacy in Seventeenth Century North Africa. The Journal of Thomas Baker, English Consul in Tripoli, 1677-1686*, London 1989); the Spanish traveller D. Badia y Leblich who, disguised as a Turk under the name of Ali Bey Abassi, visited Tripoli in 1804 and included a long account of the place in his book *Travels of Ali Bey in Morocco, Tripoli, Cyprus, Egypt, Arabia, Syria and Turkey, etc.*, (English edition London, 1816); and the British Traveller George Lyon, who wrote amusingly of the city and its people as he found them in 1818-19 in his *Narrative of Travels in Northern Africa*, (London, 1821). Then the German historical painter Wilhelm Heine included four chapters on his productive stay in Tripoli in the summer of 1859 in his book (now rare) published in Berlin the following year, *Eine Sommerreise nach Tripolis*. Other worthwhile accounts from the later nineteenth and early twentieth centuries include H. S. Cowper, *The Hill of the Graces* (London, 1897); C. W. Furlong, *The Gateway to the Sahara: Observations and Experiences in Tripoli* (New York, 1909); and Nahum Slouschz, *Travels in North Africa* (Philadelphia, 1927). Many passages on Tripoli from these and other books are published in John Wright's *Travellers in Turkish Libya, 1550-1911* (London, 2011).

Italian Tripoli is described at length by A. Piccioli, *The Magic Gate of the Sahara* (London, 1935), while Henry Serrano Villard (*Libya. the New Arab Kingdom of North Africa,* Ithaca, 1956) and Agnes Newton Keith (*Children of Allah*, London, 1966) offer American perspectives on the city as joint capital of the independent Libyan kingdom. Philip Ward contributes a brief but useful *Tripoli, Portrait of a City* (Stoughton, Wis, 1969), while aspects of the city's face under the Gaddafi regime are lightly sketched by Justin Marozzi in his *South from Barbary: Along the Slave Routes of the Libyan Sahara* (London, 2001).

Basic books on the history of Tripoli, rather than the personal experiences of travellers, include

Bergna, P. C., *Tripoli dal 1510 al 1850,* (Tripoli, 1925)
Rossi, Ettore, *Storia di Tripoli e della Tripolitania dalls conquista araba al 1911,* (Rome, 1968)

Further Reading

Dearden Seton, *A Nest of Corsairs. The Fighting Karamanlis of the Barbary Coast,* (London, 1976)

Nora Lafi, *Une ville du Maghreb entre ancien régime at réformes ottomanes: Genèse des institutions municipales à Tripoli de Barbarie* (1795-1911), (Paris, 2002).

Notes

CHAPTER TWO:

1. R. Dozy and M. J. De Goeje (eds.), *Description de l'Afrique et de l'Espagn par Edrisi*, Amsterdam, 1969, pp.142-3.

2. Don Pedro's despatch to the Viceroy of Sicily, 29 July 1510. Quoted in C. Manfroni, *Tripoli nella storia marinara d'Italia*, Padua, 1912, pp.3. *et passim.*

3. Quoted in J. Wright (ed.), *Travellers in Turkish Libya, 1550-1911* London, 2011, p.21.

4. S. Lane-Poole, *The Barbary Corsairs*, London, 1890, pp.137-8.

CHAPTER THREE

5. Quoted in Wright, *Travellers*, p.25.

6. Quoted in Wright, *Travellers*, p.32.

7. Quoted in P. C. Bergna, *Tripoli dal 1510 al 1850*, Tripoli, 1925. p.201

8. Quoted in R. Micacchi, *La Tripolitania sotto il dominio dei Caramanl* Intra, 1936, p.102.

9. [Tully], *Narrative of Ten Years' Residence at Tripoli in Africa.* London 1817 (henceforth Tully), pp.1-2.

10. Anthony Knecht, quoted in C. R. Pennell (ed.) *Piracy and Diplomac in Seventeenth Century North Africa.* London, 1989, p.37.

11. Tully, pp.2-3.

12. Tully, p.8.

13. Tully, p.6.

14. Tully, p.168.

15. Tully, p.91.

16. Quoted in Wright, *Travellers*, p.69.

CHAPTER FOUR

17. W. H. Smyth, *The Mediterranean: A Memoir Physical, Historical and Nautical* London, 1854, p.487.

18. Quoted in Wright, *Travellers*, p.64.

19. G. F. Lyon, *A Narrative of Travels in Northern Africa*. London, 1821, p.16.

20. Lyon, p.9.

21. Lyon, p.12.

22. Lyon, pp.12-13.

23. Lyon, p.13.

24. Lyon, pp.14-15.

25. Quoted in Wright, *Travellers*, pp.150-1.

26. H. S. Cowper, *The Hill of the Graces* (London 1897) p.36.

27, 28, 29: All quoted in Wright, *Travellers*, pp.151-2.

30. P. Gladstone, *Travels of Alexine*. London, 1970, p.198.

31. G. Nachtigal, *Sahara and Sudan*. 4 Vols, London, 1971-84, Vol.I, p.10.

32. Quoted in Wright, *Travellers*, p.213.

33 Cowper, *The Hill of the Graces*, pp.35-6.

34. M. L.Todd, *Tripoli the Mysterious*. Boston, Mass., 1912, p.149.

35. Todd, *Tripoli*, pp.7, 203.

CHAPTER FIVE

36. Wright, *Travellers*, p.224.

37. Wright, *Travellers*, pp.225-6.

38. G. Mattioli, *L'aviazione fascista in A.S.* Rome, 1937, p.61.

39. *I primi voli di guerra nel mondo, Libia MCMXI*, Rome, 1961, p.69

40. H. C. Seppings Wright, *Two Years under the Crescent*. London, 1913, pp.107-9.

41. L. V. Bertarelli (ed.), *Guida d'Italia del TCI: Possedimenti e Colonie*, Milan, 1929, p.172.

42. Quoted in G. B. Guerri, *Italo Balbo*. Milan, 1984, p.310.

CHAPTER SIX

43. A. Moorehead, *African Trilogy*, London, 1944, pp.485-6.

44. A. Clifford, *Three against Rommel*, London, 1943, p.355.

45. *Tripolitania under British Rule*. Tripoli, ND, p.12.

46. British Military Administration, Tripolitania, *Annual Report, 23 January 1943-31 December 1943*, Tripoli, 1944, p.15.

47. H. S. Villard, *Libya, The New Arab Kingdom of North Africa*. Ithaca, NY, 1956, pp.75-6.

48. P. W. Copeland, *The Land and People of Libya*, Philadelphia, 1967, p.76.

49. IBRD Report, *The Economic Development of Libya*, Washington DC., 1960, p.55.

50. A. N. Keith, *Children of Allah: Between the Sea and Sahara*. London, 1966, p.437.

51. Keith, *Children of Allah*, p.26.

CHAPTER SEVEN

52. K. Adie, *The Kindness of Strangers: The Autobiography*. London, 2002, p.331.

53. N. Lewis, *A Suitable Case for Corruption*. London, 1984, pp.30-1.

54. B. Valli, *La Repubblica*, 7 September 1989.

55. Adie, *The Kindness of Strangers*, p.352.

56. G. Tremlett, *Gadaffi, The Desert Mystic*. New York, 1993, p.289.

57. J. Wright, *A History of Libya*. London, 2012, p.218.

58. J. Marozzi, *South from Barbary: Along the Slave Routes of the Libyan Sahara*. London, 2001, pp.30-1.

59. D. Vandewalle, *A History of Modern Libya*. Cambridge, 2006, pp.196-7.

CHAPTER EIGHT

60. National Archives, Kew, London: Foreign Office Papers: FO76/2, Consul The Hon. Archibald Fraser to Principal Secretary of State the Earl of Shelbourne, 24 August 1767, enclosed *Some Account of the Trade carried on by the Tripoline Moors to the Inland Parts of Africa*.

Notes

1. W. MacArthur, *Auto Nomad in Barbary*. London, 1950, p.233.
2. D. Vandewalle, *A History of Modern Libya*, pp.196-7.

CHAPTER NINE

3. Quoted in Wright, *Travellers*, p.24.
4. Tully, pp.8-9.
5. J. Richardson, *Travels in the Great Desert of Sahara in the Years 1845 and 1846*. 2 Vols. London, 1848, Vol. 1, p.18.
6. M. Corsi, *Terre dell'Islam*. Milan, 1927, pp.10-11.
7. G. Furlonge, *The Lands of Barbary*. London, 1966, p.43.
8. Quoted in Wright, *Travellers*, p.62.
9. Quoted in Wright, *Travellers*, pp.62-3.
70. M. L. Todd, *Tripoli the Mysterious*. Boston, Mass., 1912, p.87.
71. G. L. Steer, *A Date in the Desert*. London, 1939, p.131.
72. P. Hoffman, *La mia Libia*. Genoa, 1990, p.257.

CHAPTER TEN

73 Todd, *Tripoli*, p.23.
74. P. Weatherden, manuscript letter, 30 April 1935.
75. Quoted in Wright, *Travellers*, p.179.
76. Todd, *Tripoli*, pp.22-3.

CHAPTER ELEVEN

77. Cowper, *The Hill of the Graces*, pp.18-19.
78. M. Murabet, *Some Facts about Libya*. Tripoli, 1961, p.84
79. Quoted in Wright, *Travellers*, p.173.
80. Tully, p.52.
81. Todd, *Tripoli*, pp.141-5.

Index

Index

Index

Index